The Darker Side of Slash Fan Fiction

The Darker Side of Slash Fan Fiction

Essays on Power, Consent and the Body

Edited by Ashton Spacey

McFarland & Company, Inc., Publishers
Jefferson, North Carolina

ISBN (print) 978-1-4766-7121-5
ISBN (ebook) 978-1-4766-3174-5

Library of Congress Cataloguing data are available

British Library cataloguing data are available

Front cover: Dr. Watson (Martin Freeman) and Sherlock Holmes (Benedict Cumberbatch) in a 2014 episode of *Sherlock* (PBS/Photofest)

Printed in the United States of America

McFarland & Company, Inc., Publishers
Box 611, Jefferson, North Carolina 28640
www.mcfarlandpub.com

Table of Contents

Section III—Power, Desire and the Erotics of Consent

Preface

Writing and reading fan fiction is a massively accessible and powerful cultural dialogue. It's the ongoing result of hundreds of conversations, discourses and interpretive frameworks being tested and negotiated, both within and external to fan communities. Thanks to the dedication and labor of generations of fans—particularly metacommentators and those who elected to pursue their fannish interests as part of their academic activities—community discussion and scholarship in the field of fan studies continues to develop.

There has been a significant and arguably disproportionate degree of interest in slash fiction, particularly in the transformative potential of the genre. While still considered a fairly taboo undertaking in and of itself, the reading and writing of slash fiction is becoming increasingly celebrated as an active feminist resistance to harmful patriarchal ideologies and power structures. However, it is not a fully utopian genre. Within slash fiction and the interpretive communities around it, there has always been conflict, contradiction and confusion. Where fans have been exploring the deeper elements of slash fiction for years, fan studies as a discipline—which is still evolving and developing—is still only really looking at the surface.

Like most people writing about the genre, my engagement with slash fiction predates my academic interest in it. In fact, I had no idea that fan studies was a research field when I was an undergraduate. My 12-year love affair with slash fiction was something I kept to myself and a handful of friends, both those I'd met offline and those I'd met through a *Kingdom Hearts* roleplay forum. My understanding of slash fiction was limited; confined to what I had encountered within the very small interpretive communities and fandoms I was involved with. Discussion and conflict about problematic content was just as rife there as it is in almost all fan spaces. It was only after I had the opportunity to take a fan studies elective unit that I was formally introduced to the history of slash fiction and the critical dialogues around it. During this time, I began to understand how much more complex this phenomenal genre is, and was surprised to find that academic discussion about this complexity was comparatively limited. Ultimately, slash fiction (like other fan works) is a powerful form of cultural expression, which does not require legitimizing to wider academic institutions to be understood as such. However, fan studies has yet to engage with the darker side of slash fiction with the same critical rigor with which it has embraced other aspects of the genre.

Fan authors, community moderators and metacampaigners have worked for years to make fandom more intersectional, inclusive and kink-friendly. Their work has been instrumental in developing and moderating the safe interpretive spaces which fan communities aim to provide. However, fandom is comprised of members with vastly different cultural assumptions and individual reading positions, all co-existing within shared communities. Dissent, conflict, discussion and mediation are always ongoing, ensuring that an involvement with slash fiction and fandom in general has always been a learning process; one which results in constantly evolving discourses about the nature of slash and some of its more problematic elements. In organizing this book and learning about elements of slash fiction which I'd never even considered before, I've had my limited perspectives broadened. I have been introduced to debates about the ideological and interpretive conflicts within fan communities, and about the ways in which discrimination and power operate within and shape fandom's safe spaces. With this collection, we hope to be able to contribute to ongoing conversations about slash fiction and supplement them with some new discussions about some of its less celebrated elements.

In fan studies, there is a call from leading researchers to pursue new lines of inquiry and to develop new forms of study; ones where fan studies academics accept the research bias inherent in their dual positions as fans and scholars, and respect and prioritize the privacy and boundaries of fan communities. The intention is for this field to develop organically and ethically, ensuring that fan studies researchers are not exploiting the labor of fellow fans, but instead working cohesively to provide another intersectional platform of discussion—something that is itself a problematic undertaking. Where my knowledge has been lacking, I have very often deferred to the experiences of those who have been involved in this process firsthand, quite often for years—and so I would like to thank the following people who have guided me and supported this project.

First, I would like to thank each of the contributors, whose academic and personal insights and experiences have taught me so many invaluable lessons. Thank you to those of you who, along with the wonderful members of the Fan Studies Network, helped me to establish an ethical framework for this book and for sharing your insights on how to proceed when problems and disagreements arose. Additional thanks to those of you who took time out of your hectic schedules to look over my own essay. I am beyond honored to be part of this collection with you all and to have benefited from your advice, guidance and friendship. I couldn't have done it without you!

Special thanks must go to Kristina Busse for your support and for taking the time to help me become a better editor and researcher. Your work continues to inspire people and has formed the cornerstone of most of my studying to date. I look forward to reading the new book!

Particular thanks must go to Dr. Lincoln Geraghty and Dr. Rachel O'Connell for offering their time and support, which encouraged me to even contemplate pursuing my engagement with slash fiction at a higher education level. I would like to take this opportunity to also thank Dr. Laura Campillo Arnaiz for tracking me down in April 2015 to ask me about my research; without you, I doubt I ever would have had the confidence to start on this project. Your enthusiasm, optimism and tenacity in the face of unbelievable stress is inspirational and your students are lucky to have you!

I would also like to acknowledge a multitude of friends and roleplay partners across various fandoms, who have offered insightful feedback and suggestions during the development of this collection. Not only have you assessed and contested my ideas, brought me in line and made rethink my stances on so many occasions, you also continue to voraciously create and critique new stories. I promise that I will get around to the backdated replies that I owe you.

Most importantly, I want to thank my family and friends for their encouragement and belief when mine was faltering, and for being my support network. You have always accepted my passions and research interests, albeit sometimes with a raised eyebrow. I am more grateful than you will ever know, but I will do my best to show you my appreciation every day. Where possible, I intend to use any proceeds from this book to send you to gigs, festivals and conventions.—Ashton Spacey

Introduction

Ashton Spacey

In early 2012, Dr. Lincoln Geraghty led an elective unit on fan fiction as part of an undergraduate creative writing program. One of the classes was dedicated to slash fiction, introducing students to the cultural and academic history of slash as a form of popular literature and exploring the genre's queer potentiality. Some of the tropes discussed included alternate universe (AU), genderswap and crossovers—with which many of the students were fairly familiar. Discussion naturally followed to some of slash fiction's more controversial themes, such as mpreg, non-con and incest.

"Wincest!" blurted out a girl a few seats down the row from me. Up until this point in the course, she hadn't really said much—so this enthusiastic exclamation was doubly surprising. Not only did she know insider terminology specific to both the *Supernatural* fandom and the trope itself, she had declared her knowledge with excitement and a seemingly uncharacteristic zeal. There was a moment or two of stunned silence before Dr. Geraghty (in his affable and engaging way) acknowledged her contribution, and spoke with enthusiasm about how these more contentious themes form part of slash fiction's wider interpretive landscape. The awkwardness disappeared as quickly as it had occurred, and the conversation moved on. In those few seconds, however, my classmate's reaction changed. Her initial passionate pleasure degenerated rapidly into embarrassment, and finally transitioned into a subdued silence that lasted the rest of the lecture.

While I cannot claim to know how she was feeling, I suspect this had little to do with the actual reaction of the class. It was more likely a result of inadvertently outing a deeply personal part of herself to a community she did not fully know and could not fully trust. Although by this point in the degree program most of us knew each other fairly well, for the most part our individual fannish interests were something we shared only with those who shared them in return—either as part of a dedicated group like GameSoc,

Quidditch Club, or the Anime Society, or informally in our friendship groups. In other words, within safe spaces. While the context of her celebratory exclamation (i.e., a seminar where we were discussing slash fiction and its more controversial themes in generally positive terms) permitted and encouraged free expression of views, the short moments of pause that followed her admission caused my classmate's perception of our shared interpretive space fundamentally to change from *safe* to *unsafe*. She responded accordingly to a judgment she believed was being passed on her as a result and silenced her views to avoid further damage.

In cultural studies, there is a tendency to default to the question of whether or not something is politically motivated; in particular, to determine whether a cultural artifact is progressive or reactionary. Consequently, it has often been implied that slash fiction operates as a displaced form of idealized sexual fantasy; a feminist subversion of non-normative gender, power and desire paradigms which should be metaphorically understood as a desire for an egalitarian form of romance (Hellekson and Busse, 2006; Driscoll, 2006; Woledge, 2006). Heather Meggers notes that women in particular are "socialized to view sex in terms of relational intimacy, romanticism, commitment, and above all, privacy" (in Zubernis and Larsen, 2012, p. 66). If my classmate had happily admitted to liking a more traditional and acceptably feminine trope like hurt/comfort—where even explicitly violent and/or sexual scenes form part of a sequence of escalating intimacy, which can be mapped onto the authorized structures of romance fiction (Driscoll, 2006)—perhaps she might not have felt so embarrassed. After all, a definition of slash fiction which valorizes it as a genre depicting a love between equals, free from the restrictions of hierarchical gender roles, is an ideal defense against potential external judgment and feelings of shame.

Following the publication of Hellekson and Busse's ground-breaking collection *Fan Fiction and Fan Communities in the Age of the Internet* (2006), academic interest in slash fiction has continued to document the evolution and development of the genre as a whole. Slash scholarship has explored at length the ways in which the genre is primarily produced by and for marginalized communities, particularly women. It is now generally accepted that slash fiction enjoys a simultaneous intertextual function: it is partly a subversive cultural dialogue, and partly an unapologetically playful approach to traditional literary conventions. This function is ultimately more complex and nuanced than the traditional incorporation/resistance paradigm would suggest. However, there are many other kinds of slash fiction which do not adhere neatly to this idealized egalitarian romance theory and are underexplored, even though they are just as popular and emotionally resonant as their more salubrious and well-researched counterparts.

When critical research into the darker side of slash fiction and the controversial discussions around it is limited, it becomes necessary in collections such as this to take a scholarly but slightly more flexible approach in order to examine these complexities. In their books, for example, Zubernis and Larsen (2012) attempted to negotiate their dual fannish and academic perspectives in order to present hybrid texts; ones which united their emotional investment and their academic analytical stance—something they did not feel they were ultimately fully able to achieve. This collection must also attempt to negotiate this dual positionality and at times, it has been very difficult to make clear transitions between we-as-fans and we-as-scholars, or not to sound defensive from either position. However, this is not just about exploring these issues in a non-pathologizing way. This collection has attempted to provide an intersectional investigation into these works by actively embracing the confusing, contradictory and ever-evolving nature of fan studies scholarship. It has attempted to build on scholarly frameworks from an embedded, embodied fannish position, in order to present critical but engaged and nuanced insights into these underrepresented elements of slash fiction.

Meggers (2012) notes that more and more women are reporting interest in fantasies about erotic force, exhibitionism, voyeurism and other taboos—such as age difference, size difference, non-consensual sex and male pregnancy. Cynthia Jenkins (2006) notes that slash works which explore these themes are usually less tolerated; where they occur in slash fiction, these themes are often construed as "bad sex" (i.e., typified by mainstream pornography) as opposed to "good sex" themes (acceptably feminine, relationship-oriented, based in mutual love). She argues that this false dichotomy ignores how "bad sex" themes still occur within slash fiction's wider focus on interpersonal relationships and mutual emotional vulnerability. Jenkins also notes how this perspective suggests that all fantasy and representation is somehow ultimately leading towards actualization of the ideas and images featured in fantasies. This concern is predicated on the assumption that an enjoyment of problematic fantasies is indicative of an actual predisposition towards similar activities in real life. As she notes, "The assumption seems to be that our fantasies control us, not that we control our fantasies" (pp. 83–84). However, there is much more to the debate than just this.

In *Fandom at the Crossroads: Celebration, Shame and Fan/Producer Relationships* (2012), Zubernis and Larsen discuss the language used by fan communities and wider society to describe the "wrong" kind of desire. They highlight how it continues to act as a powerful agent in "dismissing aspects of feminine sexuality that are threatening, and is an integral part of the cultural containment of female desire in general" (2012, p. 60). When some slash fiction is labeled as acceptable and some as unacceptable, explorations of contentious themes are therefore doubly policed; externally by wider patriarchal society and internally within fan communities. This limits dialogue before the conversation about what role this exploration may play in our cultural activities even begins. Beyond that, when moral or ideological positions are assigned to either side of this line and reputations are challenged, the conversation can become even more complicated.

Zubernis and Larsen highlight how our identities, which are under constant surveillance by the self and by others, are often forced into a disconnect between a socially acceptable public self and a personal inner self. The public self therefore becomes a shield to guard against vulnerability. Any action or reaction that might expose or harm that inner self is experienced as a serious threat. If the inner self is threatened—particularly when accompanied by the possibility of social sanctions—we experience a sense of shame and personal inadequacy. Because shame is profoundly disempowering, we as fans often seek communities where our inner selves and our identities, passions and vulnerabilities can be articulated and explored—and furthermore, where they can also be shared with others, reframed and understood; something that fan communities are able to provide. Wanting to preserve these sites of safety and enjoyment, as fans present in these spaces we therefore meticulously protect the boundaries of our communities and strive to make them as safe, inclusive and utopian as we possibly can.

Given that consuming media texts is not a purely passive process, internalization of social attitudes is reflected in what we consume and create. Engagement with fandom is an interpretive process whereby we explore cultural events and attitudes and the resonances they have with us and with others. Participating within fan communities—and the generation and consumption of fan fiction—remains one of our most prolific forms of active cultural expression. There is a desire, therefore, for a step towards self-improvement in fannish activities; a drive to actively shape and produce more liberated communities and works that are freely available, accessible to all and socially inclusive. When our interests conflict with that desire, we may begin to experience a negative psychological disconnect—particularly in cases when such conflicts occur in the form of public disagreements.

As part of fandom's fundamentally democratic ethos, we are able to share our concerns within the community and critique content that we do not agree with, but we are also able to defend creative freedoms to explore complex and difficult themes. When we encounter fan-made content or discussions which profoundly offend, upset, provoke or challenge our identities and value systems, this may be perceived as a threat to the inner self and our ability to protect and articulate this within fan communities. For example, discussions and fan works which feature contentious themes can easily be offensive if presented in a way which appears flippant or discriminatory. Survivors of violence, illness and sexual assault have reported that they can be deeply triggered by this, particularly in the case of works which eroticize these themes. When their concerns go unheard, are rejected, or are mocked and/or deliberately dismissed within fan communities, this can cause real, lasting damage.

Additionally, fans who find themselves suddenly on the end of criticism and personal attack may become defensive—particularly when this appears unjustified, excessive, or aimed against the existence of a trope in general rather than at their specific treatment of it. Those who have personally experienced the themes they explore in their work may also find themselves being personally criticized for the ways in which they choose to engage with the genre. For example, some critics argue that certain fan works and their authors, regardless of their experience with these themes in real life, knowingly or unknowingly normalize sexual violence and promote rape culture. There is significant complexity around issues like this and around most problematic themes within slash fiction. Given that we are immersed in social paradigms in which sexual violence and rape culture are so deeply ingrained, harmful reproductions of these themes and power structures are indeed commonplace in both source texts and fan works.

As a result of this immersion, creating fan works and discussions which do not automatically and uncritically reproduce harmful ideologies and structures takes conscious effort. Furthermore, it requires an awareness of and an engagement with wider intersectional conversations around these elements. Degrees of familiarity with these discussions will often differ wildly, as will understandings and engagements with the associated discourses. While many communities do moderate discussions to allow free debate, there is always an underlying anxiety within fan spaces when discussion is underpinned by aggression, ignorance and a refusal to listen on either side. When conflicts erupt in the community, these can escalate from open disagreements and fair criticism to dismissiveness, mockery, personal attack or even the threat or actual act of doxxing—the malicious publishing of private or identifying information. The inner self is thus threatened again, communication breaks down and the space becomes toxic. A phobic reaction is clearly a very real possibility when a space we once perceived as safe becomes suddenly unsafe.

In order to avoid such situations, most fan communities have developed systems to help members navigate the vast network of conflicting cultural assumptions and reading positions co-existing within fandoms. As a general standard of conscientiousness and etiquette, across most fanwork platforms and communities creators are advised to warn potential readers of problematic elements in their work by using the infrastructures of established content tagging systems or by writing detailed author's notes. In this way, fans are better able to curate their experiences and avoid content which may be disagreeable or even triggering to them, but they are also able to uphold fan fiction's primary ethos of permitting the safe, creative exploration of any number of real or imagined scenarios, tropes, identity configurations and behavioral paradigms.

However, this is not a perfect system, given that marginalized groups in fandom continue to be ignored and their voices often go unheard. For all that fandom is considered a safe space to articulate our inner selves and identities, it is not always as safe and supportive as we would like to believe. People of color regularly face hypersexualization, desexualization or total exclusion from fan works, communities and discussions. People on the asexual and aromantic sprectrum, non-monosexual people, and people of non-binary genders are still routinely sidelined. Disabled people regularly face infantilization, Othering and damaging depictions of their identities as fetish objects, or as identities which require "fixing" in order to be complete. It is also difficult (if not impossible) for the "don't like, don't read" maxim to be adhered to when issues such as ableism, racism, misogyny and the erasure of asexuality and bisexuality regularly go untagged—often because someone may not consciously realize that such elements are being reproduced in their work or their arguments. Additionally, both slash and femslash are certainly not exempt from the wider criticism that these genres, no matter how politically engaged, subversive, and/or acceptably feminine they may be, ultimately still fundamentally sexualize and fetishize gay relationships, often through a heteronormative lens.

In reality, there is no such thing as a "darker side" to slash fiction; merely *another* side to this complex, multifaceted genre. Talking about this allegedly darker side, though, means talking about more than just the function and effect of raunchy stories. It means following metacritics in investigating the incredibly complex interplay between eroticism, representation, visibility and the structures of power. It means addressing how the erotic imaginary is constrained, how voices are silenced and how safe spaces can be shattered—and how shame and fear are weaponized to repeat restrictions and control on social and sexual expression. It means exploring how slash fiction is capable of both addressing and dismissing both real and fictional identities, sexualities and cultural behaviors. It's about trying to understand how human needs are being gratified or unmet by engagements with fan texts, source texts, and the discussions happening within fan communities. More than anything, it is contributing to ongoing conversations which acknowledge that slash fiction as a wider genre has both progressive *and* regressive elements. All of these elements contribute to the incredible impact slash has, both as a form of popular literature and on our perceptions of fan communities as safe spaces to articulate our desires and our identities.

This collection of essays ultimately aims to supplement existing dialogues around slash fiction. Drawing from a wide selection of TV, movie, book and real-life fandoms (such as sports fandoms and band fandoms), these essays explore the darker side of slash fiction through a combination of literary analysis, ethnography and metacritical investigation. They offer new insights into another set of elements within the genre; elements which are explicitly concerned with the negotiation of inequality rather than the advancement of egalitarian structures. Each text can be read as a standalone essay, or in conjunction as a set based around a common theme. Firstly: the marginalization of real, "fringe" bodies and identities as objects of desire, and the suppression of these subject positions and experiences within slash fiction and fan communities. Secondly: the inscription of sexuality onto—and as a result of—alternative sexual physiologies, and the methods through which bodily boundaries are transgressed or reiterated in slash fiction. Then thirdly: the power dynamics of consent and the ways in which slash fiction allows exploration of ideas and concerns about personal agency and autonomy. A breakdown of each essay in the collection can be found below.

Overview of the Collection

Section I—Abberant Realities: Fringe Bodies and Marginalized Identities

Slash fiction is defined by more than just its content. It is also defined by its context—its placement within wider discussions of identity politics and normative paradigms, and its treatment and representations of marginalized groups both within fan works and within fan communities. Part of acknowledging and exploring the more secretive and controversial aspects of slash fiction is discussing the ways that the genre represents and explores real identities and behaviors (both normative and non-normative) and the ways in which such themes are received and interpreted. It is important for us as fans and as scholars to explore how this seemingly utopian genre can be just as capable of perpetuating harmful ideologies and fetishizing real marginalized identities, casting them as aberrant, Other and/or purely as set pieces, or erasing them altogether.

Although slash is often lauded as being a more egalitarian genre of popular literature, it is still fully capable of being as misogynistic, queerphobic and racist as the source texts with which it engages. In some cases, fan works and discussions openly erase the agency of characters (and even the presence of characters themselves) or fundamentally disregard the concerns, needs and lived experiences of groups who do not fit the established fannish identity profiles. In addition to this, explorations into the darker side of slash fiction must also take into account the ways in which real-life problematic tropes and elements continue to resonate—including depictions of real-life traumas and behaviors such as sexual violence, drug use, phobic attitudes, illness, suicide, and bullying—and the ways in which these themes are depicted, received and interpreted.

Lýsa Westberg Gabriel's "Slashing the Invisible: Bodily Autonomy in Asexual Fan Fiction" explores the exponential growth of asexuality-themed slash fiction in a genre which mostly preoccupies itself with sex—even if only implicitly. Westberg Gabriel investigates the themes of bodily autonomy and interpersonal relationships in a society that regards sex as performance, and where a male body that experiences a lack of sexual attraction creates a problem by not fitting into a sexualized discourse. She explores how asexuality in slash fiction follows similar trends to the Omegaverse in foregrounding discussions about equality, the right to the body, the right to decline sex, and the ideas that nature and desire take precedence over informed decisions. Westberg Gabriel concludes that asexuality-themed slash fiction may prove to be the site where masculinity can be questioned and redefined and where asexuality-themed slash fiction's authors and readers can actively enter into an argument with the normative to navigate and engage with the complexities of identity politics—both their own and others'."

Ágnes Zsila and Zsolt Demetrovics' "Icons of Self-Destruction: The Portrayal of Aggression and Abusive Behaviors in Band Slash Fiction" presents an explorative psychological review of destructive and abusive behaviors within real-person band slash fiction through examinations of selected band slash texts and ethnographic research. Discussing the general portrayal of physical and verbal aggression, social deprivation, threats and sexual assault in band slash, Zsila and Demetrovics work closely with several active authors in the genre to present a new investigation of authorial engagement with complex and (at times) emotionally distressing themes. Additionally, Zsila and Demetrovics challenge existing theoretical frameworks of slash scholarship by exploring audience responses to problematic themes in fan works, and examine how the unique dialogic relationship shared between respondents and their audiences functions as a means of fostering and maintaining localized interpretive communities and support networks.

Divya Garg's "(Un)Sanctioned Bodies: The State-Sexuality-Disability Nexus in *Captain America* Slash Fan Fiction" urges slash scholarship to go beyond an interest in how the genre continues to subversively queer the mainstream in order to explore the politics behind queer forms of representation. Garg's essay investigates how historical *Captain America* slash fiction documents and explores marginal histories and expressions of sexuality and identity. Basing her critique in the theoretical frameworks of homonationalism and ablenationalism, she examines the representation of non-normative bodies and desires within slash fan fiction with particular respect to the State's regulation of these bodies and desires. Garg argues that in articulating experiences of body dysphoria, ableism and trauma in light of the *Captain America* storyline, slash fiction provides a script through which to read into the fissures between the dominant narratives of the homogeneous State and its production of normative bodies in accordance with its own national agenda.

Cait Coker and Rukmini Pande close this section with "Not So Star-Spangled: Examining Race, Privilege and Problems in MCU's *Captain America* Fandom"—a discussion of how fandom and scholarship continue to ignore the ways that race and privilege work within slash communities. Focusing on the character of Sam Wilson, Coker and Pande use examples drawn from fan fiction, metadiscussions, and fan author interviews to explore how Sam Wilson's race is treated in slash fandom along the spectrum of point-blank erasure, problematic depictions, and successful interracial romance. The essay also discusses the practical and theoretical gap in slash scholarship regarding race and fandom, and considers how the field of fan studies continues to reinforce the notion of fandom norms as a white and only nominally queer space—effectively Othering both fans of color and the objects of their fannish affections.

The essays in Section I highlight some of the more insidious problems within slash fiction. While not as sexually contentious as other problematic themes and tropes in the darker side of slash fiction, these issues are equally as prominent and perhaps some of its most troubling elements. However, these essays also highlight the ways in which fan works and fan communities are actively using the genre in order to foreground their concerns. They explore how fan communities continue to generate counternarratives to challenge the forms of hegemonic discourse which traditionally invisibilize and silence them. These essays call for more investigations into how the repetition of hegemonic power structures can both reinforce dangerous ideologies, yet simultaneously provide a means through which these can be articulated, reframed and explored within fan communities. The essays in Section I also highlight the need for further discussion about the ways in which slash deals with marginalized identities and behaviors—both within real life and within the context of fiction.

Section II—Sexual Inscription and Bodily Boundaries

The essays that comprise Section II explore the ways in which the physical boundaries of both real and imagined bodies are manipulated, reclaimed and repurposed in slash fiction. In the fan works under investigation in this section, the supposedly inflexible nature of bodily boundaries is transgressed. This allows an opportunity for the unstable and politicized interpretive frameworks surrounding gender, identity and sexuality to be reframed—providing a subversive challenge to some of society's most deeply ingrained ideologies. However, while these works may allow us to negotiate gender and power dynamics they can just as often reinforce heteronormative ideals where childbirth and domesticity are presented as the ultimate routes to a happy ending.

The slash works which these essays explore can also describe the difficult realities of transgender and intersex experiences with the language of body horror, or position them as temporary barriers to an otherwise conventional romantic fulfillment scenario. At best, this is an unflattering disservice—and at worst, it can be a deeply painful and damaging reading experience. The essays in Section II highlight how these narratives ultimately offer a space to facilitate a powerful reimagining of complex cultural understandings of selfhood and identity politics. They provide a vital critical lens through which to unpack and critique the definitions of what is socially constructed as "normal" and "natural."

Laura Campillo Arnaiz's "When the Omega Empath Met the Alpha Doctor: An Analysis of the Alpha/Beta/Omega Dynamics in the *Hannibal* Fandom" builds on existing scholarship around the themes of the Omegaverse in slash fiction. Arnaiz critiques the rhetoric of biological determinism which underpins this trope and performs a close reading of two popular *Hannibal* works which deliberately depict this dynamic as violent, sexually aggressive, emotionally manipulative and inescapably unequal. She discusses how dark Omegaverse narratives permit a space where inherently human feelings of powerlessness, unlovability and humiliation can be actively invited and subsequently explored, eroticized, and controlled. Additionally, Arnaiz also examines how dark Omegaverse plot events are received and interpreted by audiences and how the "happy ending" can be read in even the bleakest of narratives—even if this goes against the grain of an author's active decision to end a work in a dissatisfying way. She concludes that while the genre may not adhere neatly to slash fiction's more egalitarian romantic conventions, dark Omegaverse and negative themes continue to resonate deeply with the erotic imagination, despite an audience's full awareness of how inherently undesirable such realities would be.

Jesse Ashman's "Pregnancy as Bondage: Impregnating the Cisgender Man in Works of *Sherlock* and *Merlin* Slash Fiction" leads on in this section to investigate how in its darker forms, mpreg (a trope where cisgender men are able to become pregnant) draws away from the traditional themes of family and domesticity with which it is associated. Ashman explores how mpreg can operate within a taboo and explicitly pornographic framework which toys with elements of BDSM. He proposes that this presents a form of fetish which takes its erotic potential from the deconstruction of the cisgenderness of canon characters and the actors who portray them, culminating in a highly intertextual interpretive exchange which can only be present in fan works.

He concludes that what on the surface appears to be a taboo sex act primarily concerned with the operation of control is in fact a collaborative and counterpublic transformative act, which provides power to fan communities and creates a liminal space in which immovable, untouchable bodies become malleable and accessible.

Samantha Close and Cynthia Wang conclude this section by proposing that the ideological structures of feminism and queerness are being ruptured in slash fiction through the reinforcement of traditional structures of power and pleasure. In "Erotic Imaginaries of Power in Fan Fiction Tropes," Close and Wang focus on the futanari trope—where bodies sexed as female also have penises—and highlight how even though futanari switches the traditional focus of slash to female bodies, sex continues to be defined by the presence of the penis-phallus. Using examples of popular fan works, Close and Wang argue that while bodies in futanari slash fiction are being queered, sexuality and social power dynamics largely are not. They highlight how an academic focus on what is different in slash fiction often obscures what is staying the same and which power structures are being reiterated. They conclude that future scholarship must recognize the operation of *additional* non-normative counternarratives within fan fiction's now-familiar transgressive, queer frameworks, in order to understand how participation with social norms impacts on and restricts our erotic imaginations.

Slash fiction is far from a perfect model of transformative literature, wherein the complexities of identity politics can be reworked without invoking the same reactionary discourses that govern these issues in reality. Slash fiction does provide an interpretive space to explore complex and difficult questions about the articulation of our identity in relation to social constructs of what is considered "normal" and "natural" in terms of gender, sexual identity and sexual orientation. However, these essays also demonstrate how slash is equally as capable of perpetuating harmful discourses and brushing over difficult political realities for the sake of generating eroticism rather than challenging or deconstructing them. The essays in Section II therefore ask for continued investigation of the ever-evolving ways in which slash fiction as a genre both resists and reiterates the cultural models of selfhood, identity, sexuality and the complex interplay between these elements.

Section III—Power, Desire and the Erotics of Consent

Discussions around sexual agency, bodily autonomy and the ways in which we articulate and exercise these facets of our selfhood have gained increasing prominence, particularly with the emergence of new social awareness movements and fourth-wave feminism. Activist groups, legislators and researchers (in addition to many other support organizations, crisis and refugee centers and outreach programs) have consistently fought to raise the visibility of these issues through progressive, intersectional feminist discourse and through support and awareness campaigns. The essays in Section III explore how slash fiction—as a genre of literature which is primarily written for and by marginalized communities—preoccupies itself with exploring the unequal nature of our relationships to power and the ways that we articulate, moderate or suppress our desire in response.

Of all the problematic elements within slash fiction, it often appears that works that explicitly challenge understandings of agency and consent draw the most controversy and create the deepest divisions between fan communities. In order to address this controversy, a necessary degree of critical detachment is required in order to examine why and how this division occurs, while also exploring and acknowledging its significant effects and impacts from an embedded fannish position. Consuming and producing narratives which feature these elements can call individual subject positions into question, provoking passionate and visceral reactions either in defense or advancement of personal ideologies, which may be challenged by the content someone encounters. This may generate a desire to criticize works which appear ideologically harmful, or provoke an experience of confusion and embarrassment when an enjoyment of exploring contentious themes violently contradicts conscious understandings of who we are, our value systems and our lived experiences. However, such disconnect between social and erotic selves can also offer invaluable opportunities to investigate some of the most prominent and resonant cultural issues. The essays in Section III explore the ways in which the darker side of slash fiction can provide a means to reframe our exposure to these issues and acrtively articulate our concerns.

Charity A. Fowler argues that the transformative possibilities of fan fiction do not automatically make it political or progressive. "A Bad Bromance: Betrayal, Violence and Dark Delight in Subverting the Romance Narrative" celebrates the nuance and subversion inherent within fan works that deliberately avoid repairing problematic source texts. Fowler examines how these works instead elect to complicate and extend these issues, but offer both a critical resistance and a reiteration of heteronormativity. Analyzing a selection of fan works from three popular bad bromance pairings, Fowler explores how canonical antagonism, violence and manipulation are handled by fan authors and their readerships—and how disagreements on how to interpret and depict such elements can fracture fandom spaces, leading to instances of aggressive policing, bullying and calls for censorship. Fowler argues that existing frameworks of interpretation trend towards shaming and silencing women's expression of unruly or impure desire, and calls for a more open critical discourse. She concludes that in order for slash scholarship to evolve, we must permit a critical but balanced examination of the complex process through which women may find themselves being rendered complicit in their own subjugation, and how fannish sexual agency is policed by fans—even within allegedly dialogically open and progressive fannish communities.

My own essay, "Dubious Consent: The Revival of Ravishment," explores the evolution of the dub-con trope and suggests that dub-con is a revival of medieval ravishment scenarios. However, where classical texts have often presented enforced submission and sexual violence as an inevitable (and even desirable) product of heteronormativity, dub-con openly concerns itself with the representation of inequality. I propose that dub-con should not be understood as a rape fantasy, but instead as a submission fantasy—where one is in control of the scenario at all times and able to pleasurably navigate the complex (and often frightening) relationship between power, desire and personal agency. Additionally, I suggest that dub-con is a self-identifying and political genre; even the act of tagging or searching for a fan work which involves "dubious consent" makes us acknowledge that the depicted scenario is not an ideal that we should valorize or unquestioningly accept. I conclude by suggesting that dub-con is a trope which can *only* exist within the controllable confines of a fantasy scenario—and that consent obtained dubiously in reality is no consent at all. I propose further investigation into how dub-con as a wider genre allows the fantasy of a pleasurable sublimation of control, but how its nuances ask us to question the ways in which we perceive and articulate our identities and assert our bodily autonomy and sexual agency.

Milena Popova's "'Happy Consensual Gangbangs': Deconstructions of Sports Cultures and Hegemonic Masculinity in Football RPF" closes the collection, employing a close reading of two stories within the gangbang/team sex subgenre of Football Real Person Fiction. Popova explores how these stories deal with the themes of safety, vulnerability and issues of sexual consent—topics which are particularly controversial within sports culture contexts. They investigate how sports fans who are marginalized by sports culture's hegemonic masculinity structures can use slash fiction to explore hierarchal masculinity, and the behaviors and practices inherent within these hierarchies. Popova concludes that by comparing their knowledge and experience of marginalization within sports culture with the fictional representations they create, fan authors and fan communities are able to both navigate, and issue a challenge to, the structures and systems of oppression they encounter.

Summary

Ending with Popova's exploration of structural oppression and consent discourses reminds us how deeply the issues of selfhood, autonomy and power resonate within slash fiction's interpretive communities. Explorations of these themes allows deeper and more inclusive understanding of their complexity and asks questions about how slash fiction operates—although it is important to acknowledge that slash fiction in particular has received a disproportionate amount of academic interest as opposed to other forms of fan activity. We have celebrated slash's capacity to create a utopian, egalitarian genre written by and for the marginalized, which allows both reconciliation and resistance to forms of oppression. We have not invested as much energy into exploring its darker side.

If we take for granted the concept that there can be no event or activity which is totally separated from discourse and free from ideology, then it becomes evident that the incredibly popular cultural undertaking of writing and reading slash should be understood as more of a practice than a product. We exist within a society where objectification of and violence against marginalized communities is both systemic and omnipresent—it is so much a part of our lives that it insidiously guides us to oppress ourselves and one another on its behalf. Slash fiction operates as both a resistance to *and* a reinforcement of the same structures of power and inequalities it is trying to resist and under which it is continuously evolving. It is unsurprising that we find in slash the same conflicts, debates and regulation of modes of expression as we find in modern society—particularly in the case of contentious topics which provoke or challenge our subject positions.

Judith Fathallah (2016a) notes that contributions are needed to a less-discussed aspect of fan fiction: "fan fic and its kinks and tropes as self-discovery, self-empowerment, and a working through of trauma rather than as an explicitly political agent of change in the media industries" (Section 6, lines 3–6). While the essays in this collection demonstrate how the darker side of slash fiction provides opportunities for the former, I would argue that any engagement with slash fiction—particularly slash fiction which features contentious themes and problematic elements—is itself an inherently political activity. It makes us engage with the issues that these works depict and explore, and invites us to reframe and reassess our subjectivities, lived experiences and perceptions of wider cultural concerns. It is part of what makes slash fiction so unique. It exposes us to ideas, identities and erotic potentialities that we may never have even considered and offers learning opportunities.

There is an inherent risk that when we encounter such literature, we may find our sensibilities provoked and our boundaries violated, which then involves us in the discursive process of meaning-making from which slash fiction originates in the first place. However, part of showing conscientiousness and upholding slash fiction's unique accessibility is acknowledging that people can and do experience phobic reactions and can be traumatically triggered by content—particularly violent content. We must also acknowledge that within slash fiction and within fan communities we are fully capable of knowingly or unknowingly reproducing damaging power structures and behavioral paradigms, and perpetuating the systems of inequality which silence and invisibilize the desires, needs and identities of marginalized communities both within and outside of fandom.

Busse and Lothian (2009) highlight how the dual fannish desires to revel in comforting tropes and to address real world concerns can provide sites of contention within fan communities and generate a sense of dissatisfaction when a story fails to fulfill both (p. 18). Within fan communities and within fan scholarship there is a simultaneous desire to permit and promote freedom of sexual expression, and a desire to protect fandom as a utopian interpretive space. This underpins both the appeal and the problem of slash fiction—and there are subsequently increasingly difficult questions to face which yield no obvious answers. How do we raise criticisms of problematic texts in a way that encourages honest discussion, rather than hostility, defensiveness or dismissal of our concerns? How can we compassionately address the fear that reading and writing problematic slash fiction perpetuates the same issues it depicts? How can we uphold a fannish ethos of creative freedom and respect the democratic right to explore contentious content (some of which may be upsetting) but also acknowledge the real harms that some incarnations of such content can cause? Can we still contest elements of frameworks and discourses we do not agree with without disregarding opposing views or invoking the rhetoric of morality? If we thoroughly and unapologetically enjoy consuming and producing problematic content, can we call ourselves feminists?

Let me be the first to apologize for not actually providing any sufficient answers to these questions. However, I would like to propose that the essays in this collection can supplement ongoing conversations about slash fiction with some new insights into some of this well-studied genre's less celebrated elements. This book is an attempt to demonstrate how engagement with the darker side of slash fiction provides opportunities to explore modes of being and test our reading positions against new and often challenging or disagreeable interpretive frameworks. Ultimately, it is crucial to acknowledge how slash fiction, like any other form of massively popular literature, has both progressive *and* regressive aspects—and how privilege, power and repression work within slash fiction and its interpretive communities and make fandom's "safe space" only safe for some and not for others.

As these essays show, the darker side of slash fiction is thriving. If we can renew the discussion with ethical research and critical rigor, perhaps we can help to ensure that marginalized voices are being heard, concerns are being raised, acknowledged and addressed, and that enthusiastic admissions like my classmate's do not automatically result in embarrassment, silence and a reluctance to engage. While dismissiveness continues to compromise understanding, and while shame, fear, guilt and repression constrain open dialogue in fan communities, the transformative potentiality of these works will never be fully understood—and we will continue to do a disservice to this incredible literary phenomenon.

Ethical Considerations

With any investigation of fan works and fan communities, it is imperative that as fans and researchers we respect and acknowledge the very real underlying concerns about such research—particularly the risk of exposure and/or consequence that investigations may cause. This is particularly important when exploring controversial or problematic elements in source texts, fan texts and discussions. Given that many of the themes explored within this collection are considered sensitive, a commitment to respectful research practice and the protection of fan works, fan authors and audiences has underpinned this project.

The complex debate about the degree to which fan spaces are private, public or semipublic—and the extent to which fan privacy should be protected in light of this—is ongoing. Bethan Jones (2016) argues that fan works should be understood as a "private act in a public space," similar to a "woman talking about an abortion with a friend in a café" or "[a] parent dealing with a toddler having a meltdown at the grocery store" (para 10, lines 1–2). She proposes that though we may feel that we have the right to record or intrude on these private conversations as they are in a public space, in reality we understand that doing so would be unethical or at the very least, rude. We also understand that by recording or intruding on these private conversations, we could potentially bring harm to others, such as embarrassment or damage to their reputations. In *Identity, Ethics and Fan Privacy* (2012), Hellekson and Busse promote the importance of similarly respecting the context in which fan works are generated and shared—and acknowledging that many fans are not in favor of fandom and academia intersecting. As a benchmark, this means respecting the norms, values and expectations of privacy within fan communities and understanding anxieties about real-life harms which remain an inherent danger involved in the production, consumption and sharing of fan works.

Many writers in this field are actively involved with fandom in one way or another (an involvement which often predates their academic work by many years) and must reconcile their fannish and academic identities and subject positions in order to conduct research in an ethical way. Following on from the foundational hybrid approaches of Joanna Russ' *Pornography by Women, for Women, with Love* (1985) and Henry Jenkins' *Textual Poachers*

(1992), it is ultimately considered best practice to write about fan communities as part of the community to uphold the values of honesty, integrity and a respect for the cultural norms of fan spaces, but to try to avoid privileging either one's fannish or scholarly position. Some academics in fan studies are immersed in fan activities and openly known to their communities as researchers. Others remain more on the periphery of fandom with a smaller degree of active participation, but maintain a solid familiarity with the norms of fan communities—although the degree to which they are openly known as researchers varies from individual to individual. However, this is not to suggest that any research position is without problems or research biases, such as debates about how to access and treat information gained through personal involvement in one's fan community rather than through research.

Given that fan studies is a constantly evolving field there is no unified best practice framework underpinning fan studies scholarship. However, cohesive working models can be established through communication with both our fannish and scholarly communities. During the development of the collection I consulted other fans, practicing fan-academics with significant experience in fan studies research ethics, and the contributors themselves for guidance on how to be an effective editor in this diverse and developing field. It was determined that as best practice for this collection I would ask all contributors to adhere to an agreed ethical baseline when quoting from fan works, discussions or other materials (i.e., seeking permissions to quote, anonymizing data, no direct links to fan works). As such, as a minimum standard this book adheres to the ethical guidelines proposed by the *Journal of Transformative Works and Cultures* (Hellekson & Busse, 2009). Many of the contributors in this collection also strive towards adhering to the more stringent recommendations presented in the *Journal of Fandom Studies* (Volume 4, Issue 3)—notably those proposed by Nielsen (2016), Jensen (2016) and Fathallah (2016)—in addition to the proposals presented by Kelley (2016) and Hellekson & Busse (2012).

However, it was also agreed that as an editor I should not limit what contributors could and could not address in their research, and that I should also not mandate how researchers conducted their investigations. Although the degree of participant involvement in each contributor's essay varies, both fans and fan scholars pointed out that while they are absolutely in favor of following ethical best practices when quoting fan works, an editorial mandate which makes it compulsory to ask for permission to even *discuss* a piece of work makes talking about the problematics of fandom almost impossible—for example, when a work or community discussion is (either knowingly or unknowingly) deeply racist.

An inability for researchers to address problematic elements within both historical and contemporary fan communities and fan works would create a bias in fan studies as a whole, something which is itself an ethical dilemma which must be taken into account. While minimization of harm is a fundamental principle of research in this field, toxic fan works, discussions and instances of silencing and bullying in the community do cause harm to marginalized groups within fandom. If researchers cannot address these issues under the mandate of protecting fan spaces, or can only analyze these issues through policed perspectives, this could lead to research privileging only certain fan spaces and protecting some fans over others. This then raises questions about which power structures this reproduces—and which voices it is silencing in the process.

Some contributors (particularly from the fields of literature and the humanities) have conducted textual analyses of fan works. They employ frameworks of literary criticism to explore these narratives as objects of study in their own right and not simply as byproducts of a subculture or subgenre. Others have worked directly with respondents to formulate new collaborative conclusions about the nature of engaging with fan writing practices as part of the wider participatory cultures of individual fan communities. Many involve elements of both of these approaches. Regardless of the format of each essay in this project, ethical considerations and best practice protocols have remained at the forefront of this project's aims. All of the contributors who have submitted to this collection have therefore made an individual choice about how to balance their ethical responsibilities to protect fannish spaces and identities with their right to authorial autonomy, with their subject positions within fandom and the power dynamics inherent within researcher/researched relationships, and with their personal research methodologies.

Kelley (2016) proposes that where expert/subject hierarchies are abandoned in favor of ensuring that researcher and participant are able to share information and learn from one another, we begin to move towards what is, effectively, a transformative model of good ethical practice (2016, 4.11). If academia as an institution wields power over representation, privacy and ownership, the onus falls on fannish scholars to develop new research methods in order to accommodate both our research interests and the needs of the humans on the other side of the screen. Here more than ever, protecting the privacy of fan spaces and building respectful, reciprocal relationships is crucial if we are aiming to understand how incredibly nuanced slash fiction really is.

Definition of Terms

The essays in this collection use common terminology familiar to most readers with an awareness of slash fiction and wider media fandom—but given that such terminology is ultimately dependent on the evolution of fandom itself (and thus is prone to change and redefinition), for the purposes of this collection some clarifications are required. Where other or specific terms appear in the collection, these are defined by individual authors within their essays.

Academic publishing trends towards the use of the two-word term **fan fiction**, so this has been adhered to in this collection. In contrast, the most commonly used terms within fan communities and outside of publishing contexts are **fanfiction** and the abbreviated **fanfic** or just **fic**. For a more detailed debate regarding the differences in the spelling, definition and semantic use of these terms, please see Flourish Klink's *Fan Fiction vs. Fanfiction* (2017a) and *Towards a Definition of "Fanfiction"* (2017b).

The terms **fan author** and **fan writer** are used as descriptors rather than **fan fiction writer**. This phrasing foregrounds both the fannish identities of the individual and their status as a producer of cultural artifacts—a position which rightfully challenges wider cultural snobbery that fan fiction is a derivative (and thus somehow lesser) genre of popular literature. This attitude has been repeatedly challenged through discussions of how fan fiction operates within Bordieu's (1984) model of cultural capital; John Fiske (1992) and Abigail Derecho (2006) have notably investigated the nature of fannish investment in the cultural economy of fandom. Derecho in particular demonstrates how fan fiction operates as a critically engaged social practice rather than just a curious behavior located within smaller communities, and defines fan fiction as "archontic literature" to emphasize the highly engaged and intertextual nature of fan writing.

Where the phrase **fan communities** is used in lieu of the wider collective terms of **fandom** or **fandoms** this is often an intentional use of the term by individual contributors. As Nielsen (2016) proposes, this distinction "explicitly emphasize[s] the multiplicity and diversity of these groups while calling attention to their internal frameworks and mores" (p. 2).

References

Bourdieu, P. (1984). *Distinction: A Social Critique of the Judgment of Taste*. Cambridge: Harvard University Press.

Busse, K., and Hellekson, K. (2012). Identity, Ethics and Fan Privacy. In K. Larsen and L. Zubernis (Eds.), *Fan Culture: Theory/Practice* (pp. 38–56). Newcastle upon Tyne: Cambridge Scholars.

Busse, K., and Lothian, A. (2009). *Bending Gender: Feminist and (Trans)Gender Discourses in the Changing Bodies of Slash Fiction* [PDF]. Retrieved from http://queergeektheory.org/docs/Lothian_BendingGender.pdf.

Derecho, A. (2006). Archontic Literature: A Definition, a History, and Several Theories of Fan Fiction. In K. Hellekson and K. Busse (Eds.), *Fan Fiction and Fan Communities in the Age of the Internet* (pp. 61–78). Jefferson, NC: McFarland.

Driscoll, C. (2006). One True Pairing: The Romance of Pornography and the Pornography of Romance. In K. Hellekson and K. Busse (Eds.), *Fan Fiction and Fan Communities in the Age of the Internet* (pp. 79–96). Jefferson, NC: McFarland.

Fathallah, J.M. (2016a). Fandom at the Crossroads and Fangasm! by Lynn S. Zubernis and Katherine Larsen [Book Review]. In I. Willis (Ed.), "The Classical Canon and/as Transformative Work" [special issue]. *Transformative Works and Cultures, 21.* http://dx.doi.org/10.3983/twc.2016.0710.

Fathallah, J.M. (2016b). Transparency and Reciprocity: Respecting Fannish Spaces in Scholarly Research. *Journal of Fandom Studies, 4*(3), pp. 251–254. doi:10.1386/jfs.4.3.251_1.

Fiske, J. (1992). The Cultural Economy of Fandom. In L.A. Lewis (Ed.), *The Adoring Audience* (pp. 30–49). London: Routledge.

Hellekson, K., and Busse, K. (2009). Fan Privacy and TWC's Editorial Philosophy. *Organization for Transformative Works.* Retrieved from http://www.transformativeworks.org/twac/twc-citation/.

Jenkins, H. (1992). *Textual Poachers: Television Fans and Participatory Culture.* London: Routledge.

Jenkins, H. (2006). *Fans, Bloggers and Gamers: Exploring Participatory Culture.* New York: New York University Press.

Jensen, T. (2016). Let's Make It Personal! Ontological Ethics in Fan Studies. *Journal of Fandom Studies, 4*(3), pp. 255–274. doi:10.1386/jfs.4.3.255_1.

Jones, B. (2016, March 25). "The Ethical Hearse": Privacy, Identity and Fandom Online. *The Learned Fangirl.* Retrieved from http://thelearnedfangirl.com/2016/03/the-ethical-hearse-privacy-identity-and-fandom-online.

Kelley, B. (2016). Toward a Goodwill Ethics of Online Research Methods. *Transformative Works and Cultures, 22.* http://dx.doi.org/10.3983/twc.2016.0891.

Klink, F. (2017a, April 21). Fan Fiction vs. Fanfiction. *Fansplaining.* Retrieved from https://medium.com/fansplaining/fan-fiction-vs-fanfiction-6b6d092f4796.

Klink, F. (2017b, May 30). Towards a Definition of "FanFiction." *Fansplaining.* Retrieved from https://medium.com/fansplaining/towards-a-definition-of-fanfiction-178d4c681289.

Larsen, K., and Zubernis, L. (Eds.). (2012). *Fan Culture: Theory/Practice.* Newcastle upon Tyne: Cambridge Scholars.

Modleski, T. (1998). *Old Wives' Tales: Feminist Re-Visions of Film and Other Fictions.* London: I.B. Tauris.

Nielsen, E.J. (2016). Dear Researcher: Rethinking Engagement with Fan Authors. *Journal of Fandom Studies, 4*(3), pp. 233–249. doi:10.1386/jfs.4.3.233_1.

Popova, M. (2017). *"Slight dub-con but they both wanted hardcore": Erotic Fanfiction as a Form of Cultural Activism Around Sexual Consent* [Unpublished Doctoral thesis]. University of the West of England, Bristol.

Russ, J. (1985). Pornography by Women, for Women, with Love. In *Magic Mommas, Trembling Sisters, Puritans and Perverts: Essays on Sex and Pornography* (pp. 79–99). New York: Crossing Press.

Scodari, C. (2003). Resistance Re-Examined: Gender, Fan Practices, and Science Fiction Television. *Popular Communication, 1*(2), 111–130. doi:10.1207/S15405710PC0102_3.

Woledge, P. (2006). Intimatopia: Genre Intersections Between Slash and the Mainstream. In K. Hellekson and K. Busse (Eds.), *Fan Fiction and Fan Communities in the Age of the Internet* (pp. 97–114). Jefferson, NC: McFarland.

Zubernis, L., and Larsen, K. (2012). *Fandom at the Crossroads: Celebration, Shame and Fan/Producer Relationships.* Newcastle upon Tyne: Cambridge Scholars.

Slashing the Invisible

Bodily Autonomy in Asexual Fan Fiction

LÝSA WESTBERG GABRIEL

Introduction

In the dark and dusty corners of fandom, one finds something once as rare as a dodo in daylight: the asexual slash story. Out of more than 2.5 million fan works posted on the fan works hosting website Archive of Our Own (AO3), 7,647 use the asexuality tag, and only 862 works are left when we look only at slash fan fiction. The genre, however, has grown exponentially since the year 2000, where only a handful of asexual slash works were to be found on what was then the largest fan fiction hosting website, Fanfiction.net. However, the genre is older than its appearance on AO3 and other platforms would suggest; fans report that the term *Smarm*, coined in early fan spaces in the 1970s but rarely used today, was given to a genre which contained elements of asexuality, but as the definition of the term came to include sexual content it went out of use (noracharles, 2017, personal communication with the author).

Slash fiction offers a variety of sub-genres when it comes to orientation, gender, and body image, but for the main part the average work of slash fiction is about sex. Maybe not explicit or pornographic, but sex in one form or another is usually present, if only implicitly. So how is it that this small sub-genre of slash fiction seems to have picked up pace, becoming increasingly popular? What does it do differently to the standard variety of slash fiction? Who, in a genre which to a high degree is informed by sex and desire, would want to read slash fiction about couples who have no sexual attraction to one another? How is it even possible not to want sexual slash fiction? How is it even possible not to want sex? And where does the body go in all this? Does it even matter that fans discuss these questions in fan works and reader comments?

There are, of course, short answers to those questions—but none that fully explain what asexual fan fiction does for its authors and its readers. Nor do these answers explain how one of the core aspects of asexual slash fiction—bodily autonomy—is explored and negotiated by authors within the safe confines of a fictional relationship between two or more people—and later, amongst the readers and writers in archives and communities. Apart from offering answers to these questions, exploring what it is, exactly, that asexual slash fiction provides for its producers and audiences might help us increase our understanding of why slash fiction is so popular.

Examining slash within this context removes a critical research pitfall: looking only at slash as mainly porn/erotica because of explicit content. When it comes to slash fiction, gender, sexual orientation and relationship structures are under scrutiny—and asexuality-themed slash fiction is no exception. Though asexuality slash fiction has a limited back catalogue, it has a vocal (in a positive sense of the word) group of asexuality-interested authors, as well as supporters and readers across a variety of fandoms. Asexual slash fiction not only provides entertainment for its fans, but offers much more: it provides support, identification, representation, knowledge and an ongoing debate about bodily autonomy, and offers a response to the ways in which society appropriates the body and sexualizes it more than even the most imaginative slash fiction writer could.

Method

Based on a textual and statistical analysis of a hundred old and new fan works and the related conversations and discussions between authors and readers, this essay will explore how asexuality-themed slash fiction provides a much-needed opportunity for a debate on bodily autonomy in fiction as well as in real life. As fandom, asexual awareness in fandom and, not least, the development of the themes and issues under scrutiny in asexual-themed fan works appear to be closely intertwined, this analysis cannot be done without a quick overview of the history of asexuality, the history of asexuality-themed fan fiction and a general summary of core theory regarding society and the body.

In terms of the leading theoretical frameworks which appear in this essay, Cerankowski and Milks' (2014) work on asexuality provides a broad view on asexuality in context, and Foucault (1976/1978) on the history of sexualities. Simone de Beauvoir (1949/1953) and Susan Bordo (1993) each provide useful views on the body. Matt Hills (2002) and Henry Jenkins (2006) provide insight on fandom contexts, and Elizabeth Freund (1987) on reader-response criticism and the text. Quotes from fan works or fans adhere to the ethical guidelines in fan studies research as set by Thessa Jensen (2016) and Kali DeDominicis (2016); authors and readers are not quoted without permission and their fan fiction is only linked to with their explicit consent.

Vocabulary

It is impossible within the confines of one essay not to make only a general and shallow distinction between nuanced orientations instead of providing a detailed account of the true variety inside the asexual orientation. However, a short glossary covering the more common asexual identities and variations might be helpful to those who have encountered asexuality only briefly in real life or in the world of slash fiction.

This essay mainly uses "asexuality" as an umbrella term, as the orientation itself covers a wide spectrum; from the romantic to the aromantic, from the sex-repulsed to the sex-positive, from purely asexual and aromantic to the demi-romantic sex-positive. It should be noted that AVEN (The Asexuality Visibility and Education Network) in their census use the term "ace" rather than asexual as an umbrella term for people identifying somewhere on the spectrum (Ginoza & Miller, 2014). For further clarification and a deeper insight, AVEN's website[1] offers an in-depth explanation to the terms below, as well as a wide selection of other useful terms and information. It might also be useful to know that the asexual flag flies as three horizontal stripes in purple, white and black, just as some asexuals have chosen to wear a black ring to show their orientation.

Aromantic, *or* ***aro***: A person who experiences no romantic attraction. This does not prevent the aromantic from forming close, loving friendships with other people. Both sexual people and asexuals can be aromantic.

Asexual, *or* ***ace:*** A person who experiences no sexual attraction. An asexual person is able to love and connect emotionally in the same way sexual people do, just like they are able to get aroused or have orgasms. They simply never desire sexual gratification with a partner. Romantic asexuals experience romantic attraction. Some asexuals choose to engage in sex for the intimacy of it, or to give pleasure to a sexual partner.

AVEN: Asexual Visibility and Education Network. Asexuality information resource and online community for asexuals and others with an interest in the topic.

Cake: Better than sex. An inside joke in the asexual community.

Celibate/celibacy: The act of choosing to abstain from sexual encounters or gratification. A person who is celibate usually experiences sexual attraction during their celibacy.

Demi-sexual: Asexuals who experience sexual attraction only if they are closely emotionally connected to the person(s)/partner(s) in question.

Gray asexual**, or **gray ace: People who identify as fluctuating to some degree between asexuality and sexuality, also people who occasionally (but usually rather rarely and at a low level) experience some degree of sexual attraction.

Homo/hetero/bi/pan-romantic: Although asexuality is an orientation in its own right, romantic and gray asexuals might have preferences on which gender(s) they are romantically drawn to. Some asexuals are heteroromantic, others homo-romantic, bi-romantic, or pan-romantic.

Queerplatonic: A degree of commitment which is more than friendship, but not romantic. Although the term mainly has been used in asexual contexts, sexuals can be queerplatonic as well.

Sexual attraction: The innate desire to have sex with a partner.

Sexual desire: Libido, the need for sexual gratification.

Statistics and Numbers

On AO3, a search reveals that only 22 percent (1680) of the works tagged with "asexuality" are stories concerning heterosexual couples (Archive of Our Own, 2016b). In comparison, 63 percent of asexual-themed fan works feature a male/male couple, whereas female/female couples account for 11 percent (862) of the published asexual fan works. Parings consisting of more than two characters (tagged "multi," "gen," and "other"—which cover for instance poly relationships and platonic pairings) and stories with no romantic or sexual content make up 14 percent (1075), 21 percent (1584), and 8 percent (647) respectively. Some works do fall into more than one category, naturally skewing the number of works compared to categories.

Naturally, sourcing data only from Archive of Our Own does create a statistical bias. Not only is Archive of Our Own a relatively recent invention (first proposed in 2007), early asexual fan fiction is ultimately widely spread across the Internet, mainly hosted on earlier sites such as Fanfiction.net and LiveJournal, and at smaller, pairing-specific archives, which makes it more difficult to find. However, Archive of Our Own together with Fanfiction.net are the archival locations of most recent fan works, and therefore these sites offer a large selection of recent fandoms and themes, plus repostings of fan fiction that might otherwise be unrecognized if found only in their original locations. Additionally, there is another statistical bias to consider in that Fanfiction.net does not allow R and NC-17-rated fan fiction. With these elements in mind we must consider that AO3 and Fanfiction.net's numbers give only an idea of what is going on in primarily Western fandom spheres. The huge Asian fandoms, in particular the Chinese and Japanese fan communities, fly under the radar to some degree for obvious reasons. In Japan the social stigma of being a fanboy/girl/person does not encourage fans to be open about their interest:

> [C]ontrolling [the] otaku movement is no easy task, and the solution as I have seen it in Akihabara has been to simultaneously naturalize their image and marginalize their physical presence. The otaku image operates in increasingly contradictory ways. Variety shows featuring "otaku idols" (otadoru) appear next to reports of crimes perpetrated by otaku [Galbraith, 2010, p. 211].

Additionally, writing and reading slash is a punishable offence in China. Erika Junhui Yi writes about fan author arrests in China:

> Perhaps the most outrageous action taken against BL fan girls happened in 2011. The police in Zhengzhou Province arrested 32 slash fiction writers whose work had appeared on a Web site specializing in homoerotic content [Yi, 2013, para. 4, lines 3–4].

Given the rise in people who declare themselves asexual and/or disinterested in sex in Japan, it could be valuable in subsequent investigations to add to this statistic an account of the numbers of asexuality-themed fan fiction or doujinshi (Japanese fan-made comics based on a canon source), especially since a substantial number of works posted on Fanfiction.net and AO3 are based on Japanese pop-cultural canon.[2]

Invisibility and Exposure: Asexuality Then and Now

This essay is concerned primarily with the perception of bodily autonomy in asexual fan fiction. However, in order to contextualize these discussions around and within both academia and fandom, it is crucial to take into consideration that alongside the debates happening within fandom, asexual activists, researchers and pop culture trends have all contributed to the discourse on asexuality in real life before fans began to raise awareness of these debates. This section of the essay is therefore dedicated to providing a brief introduction to asexuality and notable events taking place outside fandom contexts, so as to gauge their impacts and effects inside it.

To begin with, from a purely biological perspective asexuality is defined as "an organism capable of asexual reproduction [which] is able to produce offspring in the absence of a mate. In asexual reproduction, the offspring is a clone of the parent and therefore results in low genetic variation in the species as a whole" (*Asexual reproduction.* 2016, para 2, lines 1–2). In sexology, however, it has a different meaning—one which is not necessarily entirely agreed upon yet, as the research field is quite young. Alfred Kinsey's groundbreaking research introduced sexuality as appearing on a scale, and created a new understanding of sexuality as fluid and not merely binary. His research showed that human sexuality varies greatly, and that humans are not purely either hetero- or homosexual. The Kinsey reports directed attention to both the bisexual and the asexual spectrum, thus acknowledging sexual identities that had long been overlooked or even denied. Kinsey mentioned in his reports (dated 1948 and 1953), a male group—X—which has "no socio-sexual contacts or reactions," including 1.5 percent of the male population (asexu ality.org, 2016, para 2). Kinsey wrote in *Sexual Behavior in the Human Female*, that the group X are people who "do not respond erotically to either hetero-sexual or homosexual stimuli, and do not have overt physical contact with individuals of either sex in which there is evidence of any response" (Kinsey 1953/1998, p. 472). The indications of a group of people with no response to sexual stimuli furthered research based on Kinsey's findings. One of the first articles on the topic was *Asexual and Autoerotic Women: Two Invisible Groups* by Myra T. Johnson (1977). Johnson refused the previous view of asexuality as being a result of a religious or traumatic nature, and made the distinction between asexual and autoerotic women. Furthermore, she directed attention to the oppression of asexuals due to the nature of their orientation's invisibility.

It has been more than thirty years since Storms (1980) developed a new theory, based on Kinsey's report, which argued that placing sexuality on axes and not on a scale allowed a distinction that Kinsey's scale did not: the distinction between bisexuality and asexuality, although this did not convince all researchers. In 2004, Dr. Anthony Bogaert published a series of research papers, demonstrating that around one percent of the British population identified as asexual, but although Bogaert's findings were supported by some key figures such as Dr. John Bancroft, a former director of the Kinsey institute for Research in Sex, Gender and Reproduction at Indiana University, other researchers from several fields disagreed with him. Until the Diagnostic and Statistical Manual of Mental Disorders (DSM-5) was revised, asexuality was included under the diagnosis of Hypoactive Sexual Desire Disorder (Q13 News Staff, 2014)—an argument which was disputed vehemently by asexuals across the world. Disregarding the academic kerfuffle and researchers who tried to erase their existence, asexuals gathered in the Asexual Visibility & Education Network (AVEN) founded by David Jay in 2001.

David Jay, then merely eighteen, encouraged asexuals across the world to meet and support each other. It was the need to discuss his experience that drove Jay to launch the network's website, AVEN.com, in 2006:

> For a couple of years I just assumed that I was broken. [...] I had spent the past four years struggling to realize that I was okay, and I didn't want other asexual people to have the realize the same thing [Hills, 2012, para. 9, lines 2–3].

Hitting the Internet at the exact right time, AVEN.com could easily be found by search engines, which lead to the network experiencing a perhaps unexpected rise in popularity. Suddenly, the invisible and silenced had a voice; a place to go where people understood the challenges of having no sexual desire in a Western society drenched in sexuality and the expressions of it:

> The website soon became a rallying cry: first for hundreds, then thousands, and later tens of thousands of people who felt alienated from the sexual stories and imagery that dominate our culture [Hills, 2012, para. 4, lines 5–8].

Asexuality has entered into what Jay calls the "third phase"; the budding normalization of asexuality, expanding mainstream's view on what is normal, however unusual. Cerankowski and Milks write in their introduction to *Asexualities: Feminist and Queer Perspectives*:

> … we need to recognize the ways in which asexual people are marginalized—or queered—in hypersexual societies […] synonymous with not only pathology and dysfunction but repression, aloneness, antisociality, repulsiveness, unattractiveness, and inhumaneness. The time has come to register the occlusion of asexuals within […] mainstream culture, with its "make it sexy" imperative and "hot or not" hierarchy, but also within feminist and queer culture; and somewhat shockingly, perhaps, within the fields of gender and sexuality studies as well [Cerankowski & Milks, 2014, p. 13].

Despite recent work and initiatives which support asexuals and recognize asexuality as an orientation, the decades-long debate epitomizes the core of the asexual orientation: at best, it is invisible, and at worst, it sees asexuals as "broken"—framing them as traumatized, dysfunctional victims of abuse or neglect, causing them to refuse society's compulsory imperatives regarding sexuality and sexual expression. Asexuals repeatedly encounter therapists, sexologists and psychologists who insist that there is something wrong with them; something which is, as AVEN's surveys show, far from the truth since only 22 percent of respondents identifying on the asexual spectrum wish to change their sexuality if they could (Ginoza and Miller, 2014). In general, very few asexuals (also known as "aces") have any urge to change what they are. AVEN itself addresses the issue like this:

> There is no litmus test to determine if someone is asexual. Asexuality is like any other identity—at its core, it's just a word that people use to help figure themselves out. If at any point someone finds the word asexual useful to describe themselves, we encourage them to use it for as long as it makes sense to do so [*AVEN Overview*, 2016].

One can sympathize with the "asexuality is not an orientation" camp, or with the asexuals themselves, but the attempt at scientific erasure is somewhat reflective of how asexuals have been perceived in general. Even in a

LGBTQ context, asexuals have been shunned, ridiculed, or accused by members of the LGBTQ community of co-opting their oppression. Asexuality, exactly because it exists in a society where the default setting is "have sex at some point," is overlooked and erased because society as a whole is tuned in to this preset ideology. On top of it comes the fact that romantic-aces (asexuals who feel romantic attraction) might be either heterosexual, bisexual or homoromantic—something which can be very confusing to some people. Additionally, asexuals who are not sex-repulsed might choose to have sex with their partner so as to enjoy their partner's pleasure. That, however, does not mean that an orientation which is able to "pass" is also non-existent. It means that it is harder to see, yes, but not that the asexual community is invisible.

In short: the asexual orientation is questioned, erased, ridiculed and at best, invisible. Is it then so surprising that many asexual readers and authors want representation in both media and fan works?

Society and the Body

One would think that gender would be unimportant in relations between asexuals, or in the way asexuals are treated. However, the male and female genders are still perceived very differently, as are their desires. Nonbinary genders and non-gendered identities are close to non-existent in a world which prefers the heteronormative-binary. Therefore, we need to approach the topic of asexuality and bodily autonomy with that in mind.

In her essay *Solving Desire* (2016), Alyson Spurgas highlights how even desire itself is gendered by examining the difference in treatments for what some might call sexual dysfunction. Twenty-six different FDA-approved drugs for men on the market all are aimed at the body; Viagra gets it up—it's a mere physical reaction. A male mind doesn't have to participate as long as his instrument works. In contrast, Addyi (a pink pill)—the single drug aimed at women—targets the mind to "remedy" the female-only diagnosis of FSIAD (Female Sexual Interest/Arousal Disorder), which is all about a "lack of receptivity" (Spurgas, 2016, para. 6). Thus, society and medicine leave us with a mandatorily heteronormative couple; the male as performer and the female as his pliant receptacle, both dysfunctional in the eyes of society if they do not adhere to this gendered, medically sanctioned norm. Heteronorm, mind.

The body therefore exists in both a biological and cultural context. Where the body is meant for recreation, only in the sexualized context is asexuality exposed—celibacy therefore becomes an option that is ridiculed by most. In popular culture, purity vows are something that is seen as a promise to be broken or lied about; sex is mandatory. It is implicit in today's Western society that the body ultimately must be used for intercourse at some point. That a person defines themselves as asexual is of no concern; to the uninformed, it merely means that the right, proper person has not yet emerged.

"The body is a situation," writes Simone de Beauvoir (1949/1953, p. 66), and being asexual and having one's body placed in a situation where its autonomy is removed by society—by doctors and psychologists, by boyfriends and girlfriends, by parents and friends—is not an envious one. Foucault (1976/1978) suggests that the body becomes a focal point for struggles over the shape of power, and in his chapter on the body and sex as domains he gives an extensive account of the ways society normalizes and controls the body and sexual behavior. Like de Beauvoir, Foucault notes how society takes over the body, something he calls society's "psychiatrization" of "perverse pleasure"; wider society carries out the socialization of procreative behavior and the control of it, normalizing behaviors which are seen as anomalies of the normative sexual act (1978, p. 105). Reproduction, sex and the normalization of the perverse thus become the family, and "the family is yet again the interchange of sexuality and alliance: it conveys the law and the juridical dimension in the deployment of sexuality" (1978, p. 103–114). He highlights the control and hysterization of female bodies in particular as being:

> A threefold process whereby the feminine body was analyzed—qualified and disqualified—as being thoroughly saturated with sexuality; whereby it was integrated in the sphere of medical practices, by reason of pathology intrinsic to it; whereby, finally, it was placed in an organic communication with the social body [...] the family space [...] and the life of children [p. 104].

Through this process, women have historically been regarded as having no sexuality and no voice of importance; they are merely receptacles for the male desire, and it gets worse if the woman is a woman of color. In contrast, however, Susan Bordo argues that "men's desires bear no responsibility, nor does the culture that subordinates women's desires to those of a man" (1993, p. 22). As a result of this process, it is often questioned why particularly female fans write slash fiction, how they write it, and what they get out of it. Some of the answers given to that from non-fans are as offensively uninformed as the heteronormative presets that society suffers. In *Let's make it personal! Ontological ethics in fan studies* (2016), for example, Thessa Jensen describes how even fan scholars use words such as "deviant," "perverted" and "ugly" to explain slash and its relationship to heteronormativity.

Henry Jenkins (2006) points out that slash is not a static genre and thus the reasons for writing it are also not static, but there are a variety of plausible explanations as to why fan authors of all genders[3] prefer to write about male/male couples. Including only men as protagonists in a work guarantees that both characters have agency, no matter if one is weak and the other strong—something which deconstructs the view of the heteronormative masculinity structures that normative society expects of them. It can be argued, of course, that writing strong female/female couples or equal heterosexual couples would allow the same frameworks. However, as Jenkins argues this would require strong female role models to identify with; females who have strong, rewarding relations with other females—females whose main purpose is advancing their own agency and agenda, rather than that of a man. "A woman," argues Jenkins, "having internalized the values of our culture, might feel that women are devalued per se, regardless of script, thus the woman-heroine becomes a worthless object of identification" (2006, para 21). Furthermore, Jenkins underlines that the relationships portrayed in a variety of popular media between the male hero and his male partners and friends is showed as stronger and more meaningful than any relationship he has with women. If fans had a similar number of female identification models—fully realized persons rather than decorative-but-mute bystanders to male heroism—who connect as meaningfully with the male protagonist, maybe heterosexual fan fiction would be vastly more popular.

When looking at the asexual person, however, no matter their gender presentation or ethnicity they exist under a similar socially-induced muteness. It can be suggested that the reason for this is that asexuals, like women, receive little concern from patriarchal society about their desires and wants. They must either be sexualized to fit in, or give over their desires (or lack of them) to the scrutiny of medical professionals and sexual partners—it is, after all, "only natural." So where does this leave the asexual reader and the asexual character, other than in a constant struggle to either ignore and suppress their own desires, or to battle society's notion of what desire is and of how sex is performed and expressed? The body is held hostage between orientation and expectation, and it is not an easy trap to get out of.

This is where it leaves us. As Foucault argues, "The deployment of sexuality has its reason for being, not in reproduction itself, but in proliferating, innovating, annexing, creating, and penetrating bodies in an increasingly detailed way, and in controlling populations in an increasingly comprehensive way" (1978, p. 106). Society wields its full power of medication, psychologization (here meaning the societal pressuring of the normal into a psychiatric context where it becomes suddenly abnormal) and stigmatization on those who attempt to evade the encoding power exercised on the supposedly autonomous domain of the body. In great parts of modern Western society, sexual repression of those who want to be free to explore their sexual urges and kinks has lessened in the past few decades. However, sexual repression and stigmatization of those who do not hand over their bodies to *some* kind of sexual identity or practice is still rampant.

This insidious form of repression looks different in different cultures, different for persons of color, and different for queer sexualities or non-binary genders, but it is still repression. There are varying degrees of tolerance to the sexualized—what of women, people of color, the poor and those who are class-marginalized? Non-male, non-heterosexual, non-white; there are so many ways to be wrong according to the norm, a notion shared by feminists such as Susan Bordo, who notes that "the 'generic' core is usually in reality a white or male body passing as the norm for all" (1993, p. 35). The debate around the appropriation of non-heteronormative bodies is ongoing across fandom spaces and it is within this additional frame that we need to understand asexual slash fiction. It can be suggested that the asexuality-themed fan authors, like many other authors in wider fandom, are actively trying to avoid the conflict-filled, heteronormative presets we know from daily life, thus remaining free to explore asexuality as a theme without having to deal with the deconstruction of the patriarchal/heteronormative context of M/F pairings. Further inquiries might help cast a light over their choice, but it is arguable that asexuality fan fiction—a genre which features and champions the representation of differing ethnicities, sexualities, relationship structures and genderqueerness—is perhaps inherently diverse.

The Rise of the Asexual Fan Work

Before 2000, almost all fan fiction led a secret life in places such as mailing lists and Internet Relay Chat, in closed archives hidden away from the public eye. Fanfiction.net was created in 1998, years before LiveJournal went online and a full decade before Archive of Our Own was built, and it provided fans with a relatively safe place to post their works on this new archive. Looking at the number of asexuality-themed works posted here before 2001 (the year AVEN was founded) it is a very small collection—consisting, in fact, of only a single piece of fan fiction.

Not even the organization of asexuals elicited any rise in numbers: between 2000 and 2005, no more than two asexuality-themed fan works were posted at Fanfiction.net. In 2006, when AVEN founder David Jay went online and out, this event created little impact on the fandom scene: five additional works on Fanfiction.net, one on Archive of Our Own.[4] Over the next couple of years, asexual fan fiction saw a minimal increase in numbers: an additional six works in 2006, ten in 2007, and nine more in 2008, bringing the total number of asexuality-themed fan works on AO3 and Fanfiction.net up to an unimpressive total of 32 fan fictions in almost as many fandoms. One would believe that the increased awareness about asexuality from scientists, psychologists and the general public would have a trickle-down effect on fandom.

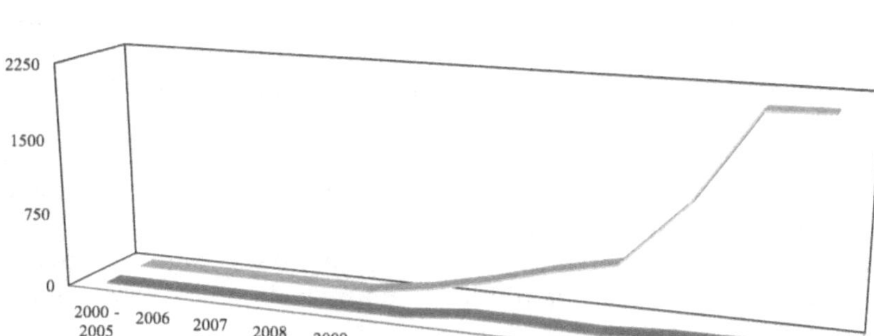

Graph 1: Asexuality-themed Fan Works on Fanfiction.net and Archive of Our Own, 2000–2016.

It is, however, not so—or rather it is, but it is a very limited effect. It is elsewhere we need to direct our attention if we want to find a plausible source or sources which are at least partly responsible for the exponential rise in asexual fan fiction.

Archive of Our Own came out of closed beta in November 2009, and made its opening towards the fandom users with a bang; the giant annual fan fiction exchange, Yuletide, moved to AO3 and users in the thousands were driven towards the new fandom-owned and run archive. Incidentally, this coincided with the rise in popularity of the blogging site Tumblr which opened in 2007. While Tumblr as a platform is somewhat less suited for fandom purposes, when paired with AO3's sudden burst of activity this combination of blogging and fan fiction posting became fandom's new OTP—its one true pairing.

Simultaneously, the BBC aired the first season of the TV show *Sherlock* (Gatiss & Moffat, 2010), featuring a Sherlock vastly more interested in the mind than the body. Additionally, the Warner Bros series *Supernatural* (Kripke, 2005) began introducing characters who openly declared that they either have no body, or do not care about them in general: demons inhabit the bodies they forcibly take over and angels (who are genderless) select the bodies they borrow regardless of gender. The theme of bodily autonomy repeated within *Supernatural* and the angels' canonical indifference to physical form was confirmed in the middle of 2011: Castiel, a seraph, confesses that he "spent time as a celestial wave of intent" (Kripke, Edlund & Singer, 2010), and later it is stated that Castiel, angel of the Lord, is "utterly indifferent to sexual orientation" (Gamble & Sgriccia, 2011), an instant that might be the sole line in the *Supernatural* series which kicks its asexual fans into action.

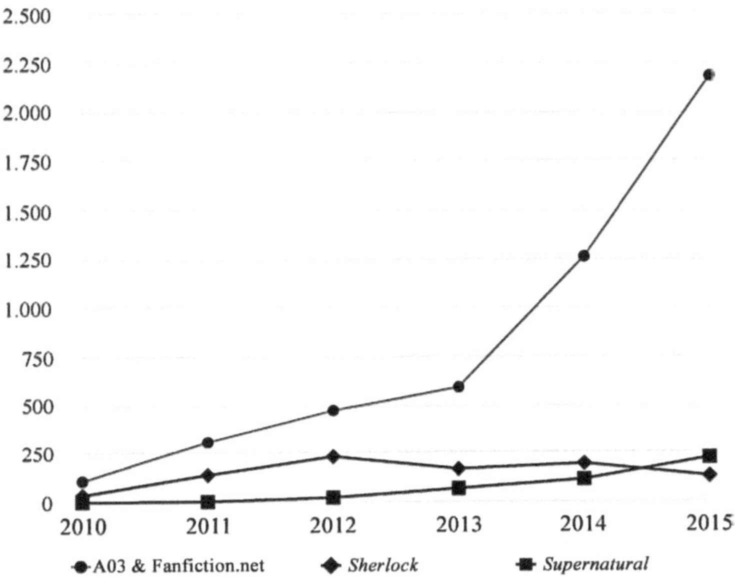

Graph 2: Number of Asexuality-themed Fan Works in the *Supernatural* and *Sherlock* Fandoms, 2000–2015.

The source of the surge in interest in asexuality-themed slash fiction could be located within the combined power of all of these circumstances and events. It might be that Jay's coming out and the creation of AVEN started the budding knowledge and awareness of asexuality, but it is from within fandom and media culture (especially on Tumblr) that new discourses and

Year	Event	Archive of Our Own (AO3)	Fanfiction.net (FF)
2000-2005	AVEN Founded – 2001	0	5
2006	Jay goes public	1	5
2007	Castiel appears in *Supernatural* – September	1	5
2008	AO3 comes out of closed beta – November	5	4
2009	[N/A]	3	14
2010	*Sherlock* premieres	92	14
2011	Castiel's "utterly indifferent to sexual orientation" quote – September	233	74
2012	*Sherlock* Season 2 airs – May	403	72
2013	[N/A]	537	57
2014	*Sherlock* Season 3 airs – January	1169	92
2015	Asexual Awareness Week – October	2088	94
2016	[N/A]	2104	59

Table 1: Numbers of Asexuality-themed Works and Corresponding Events Timeline.

ideas around asexuality in fandom bloomed. However, the annual Asexuality Awareness Week might indeed have had a small impact: there are currently 95 fan works in its corresponding tag (Archive Of Our Own, 2017).

In 2006, asexual slash fiction could be found across a wide range of fandoms, albeit in very small amounts, but it was concentrated predominantly in the fandoms of *Supernatural*, *Sherlock*, and to some degree the Marvel Cinematic Universe (MCU)—especially within the pairings of Clint Barton/Phil Coulson and Steve Rogers/Bucky Barnes. Despite works being spread across a number of small fandoms, on Fanfiction.net it was also possible to find a number of asexual fan works featuring persons of color—in this case, predominantly in the fandoms of Japanese manga and anime which gave ethnic diversity (or at least the implication of being non-white within the normative sexualized Western context) in asexuality fiction a relatively larger representation. It is worth noting that 30 percent of asexuality-themed fan fiction is comprised of a substantial number of works in non–Western fandoms featuring main characters of color, mainly Asian.

In 2010, everything began to change. Starting slow, the *Sherlock* fandom provided 34 out of 106 fan works, and when Castiel came out as being indifferent to sexual orientation and gender, the *Supernatural* fandom began to rise in popularity from 2011. Asexuality-themed fan fiction began rapidly increasing in numbers each year, topping 2015 off with 222 works, all but two of which were posted on AO3. Seen in relation to *Supernatural*'s whopping 145,000 fan works generated in 2015 alone, this small number pales in comparison—but to the people who identify as asexuals, it is an important contribution. It represents a small but pivotal possibility to see their desires, experiences, options and solutions represented in a fictional universe—to find a space where an asexual reader can find a mirror where their emotions and experiences can be examined, recast and explored safely.

Slashing the Invisible

Contemporary asexuality-themed fan fiction comes in all shapes and sizes; from a short 100-word drabble, to novel-length epic tales. In some fan works asexuality is the core of the narrative, in others it is merely mentioned in a passing sentence, having no influence on the overall story or its characters. A handful of authors use the biological definition of asexuality, telling stories about humans sprouting children. Others again confuse asexuality with celibacy. None of these discoveries are particularly surprising or shocking, but studying a number of fan works written between 2001 and 2016 posted on LiveJournal, Archive of Our Own and Fanfiction.net does, however, reveal some interesting trends.

Carrying out an analysis of more than a hundred fan works (half of which were selected on the basis of year written and number of comments, and half randomly) shows that not only does asexual fan fiction serve as entertainment, but also as a therapeutic tool for asexuals and as an informative channel to spread knowledge about asexuality. These are findings which coincide with the conclusions established by existing scholarly investigations into the function and operation of wider slash fiction spaces. What is more surprising is that a great number of asexuality-related fan works are set in a frame where it is not only the asexual character who might be in conflict with the sexualized society, feeling restrained, or caving under expectations when it comes to bodily autonomy. In almost 50 percent of all asexuality-themed works, the other person in the pairing is restrained as well; either by biology, circumstances, or location. The stories (independent of fandom) fall into six main themes, some of which overlap and thus subsequently skew the totals.[5] These categories are:

- **Pre-asexuality**—10%
- **"Cock cures all"**—25%
- **Label-but-no-impact-on-plot**—16%
- **Informative—**30%
- **Body-otherwise-bound**—50%
- **Third-wave fiction**—6%

Pre-asexuality (10%) mainly consists of fan fiction that in one way or another treats asexuality with a less informed approach—and it is worth highlighting that this group contains a great deal of fan fiction published before 2006. A lack of understanding about the complex issues and discourses around asexuality as an orientation is not entirely surprising, as this had hitherto been limited to the scientific sphere and to discussions conducted within offline groups. These works tend to show asexuals as beings who are celibate, or the author somehow connects social disorder with asexuality, or asexuality is confused with other orientations and gender issues. A few, however, do correctly identify and adhere to the biological understanding of the term and have their characters multiply by sprouting.

"Cock cures all" (25%) contains slash fiction stories which feature the asexual character realizing that they are not asexual after all; their partner's penis simply cured them of the condition. Some of these works might have characters who fall into the demi- or gray-ace part of the spectrum, and the reader response is at times not favorable when readers, who are either asexuals or allies, comment on this. These works might present or be perceived as presenting the idea that asexuality is curable or that asexuals are broken, or express the need to fit into society's demands—to have a "normal" life without the obstacles that an asexual invariably will meet in a world that runs on sex.

Label-but-no-impact-on-plot (16%) contains works that mention asexuality, but in which asexuality itself has little impact on the characters or the plot, if any.

Informative (30%) contains, as the label indicates, "information fan fiction"; works which at some point explain asexuality to the reader through the voice of one of the main characters. A part of these works also serve as a therapeutic outlet and contain autoethnographic elements.

Body-otherwise-bound (50%) is the largest group of works. These feature a pairing consisting of an asexual, gray-ace or demi-sexual character who is paired with a sexual character who is otherwise confined, disabled, incarcerated or bound—for instance, imprisoned. It is not uncommon to see the story set in the Omegaverse, or with characters merely living in a constraining environment—like a spaceship or a boarding school.

Third-wave fiction (6%) contains works which, one way or another, turn asexuality on its head, or feature a plot or characterization which deviates from the above-mentioned information works or bound-body works. It can be a deviation from the common pairing of sexual with asexual character, or it can be the meeting between asexual and non-human sexuality, as for instance between Kirk and Spock in Star Trek. Also included within this group are works which feature strong and out asexuals who defy sexualized society. Maybe it is in this group that we can find the future of asexual fan works; stories which, together with informative fiction and body-otherwise-bound works, cover asexuality and the asexual character through stages of realization, exploration and equality.

The pre-asexuality works are outdated, presenting little more than a snapshot of the development of the kinds of awareness and information on asexuality that fandom as a whole had at the time. However, analysing the groups of **informative** fan fiction, **body-otherwise-bound** fan fiction, and **third wave** fan fiction offer an insight into how authors and readers negotiate themes of bodily autonomy—both inside the fictional narrative and outside it. Ultimately, when examining these three groups of narratives, a clear progression in the portrayal and reception of asexuality, asexual bodies and relationships within slash fiction becomes visible.

Informative Fan Fiction

As discussed in the introduction to the history of asexuality introduced earlier in this collection, asexuality as an orientation has been hidden, overlooked or ignored for a very long time. Although the asexual individual often might pass as heteronormative, the lack of representation, validation and acknowledgment of asexual identities in general society is reflected in the way body and orientation are portrayed in asexual fiction. Often, the main pairing's sexual half is not aware of the orientation, or does not know much about it, which forms a recurring conflict within this subgroup of asexuality-themed slash fiction.

In Sidney Sussex's *To live for a moment in unison*, Clint Barton is falling in love with an asexual Phil Coulson, and seeks advice:

> He frowned at the little search text box, backspaced over the letters he'd already typed in, and entered what Phil had said earlier. Asexual.
>
> Clint didn't know what he'd been expecting when he hit the search button, but he was pretty sure he hadn't thought there would be five million hits.
>
> "Uh," he said aloud, scrolling up and down the first page of results. "Um, little help here, JARVIS?"
>
> "I suggest selecting the first result and working from there, sir" [2012, p. 10].

The author makes it clear that asexuality is defined by the individual in their notes for their work, and that their short story is not meant to offer instruction as such:

> [R]emember that one person's (a)sexuality is not necessarily anything like another's. Not everyone who identifies as asexual will have the issues presented here; some will have more, some fewer, some different. As usual, this depiction is taken from traits of my own and close friends (with permission); it's not meant to offend or to instruct, only to illustrate. This is told through experience, not expertise, so please don't read it as anything more [Sidney Sussex, 2012, Author's Notes].

Another example of this can be found in Inrainbowz's *Body and Soul, Free to Withhold* (2016), which is based on the author's personal experience. In *Body and Soul, Free to Withhold*, Shadowhunter Alec Lightwood struggles with his sexuality, thinking that sex is something he must have when his partner—wizard Magnus Bane—wants it. Alec never experiences any sexual desire, and thinks something is wrong with him. A friend comes to explain to him that it is not the case:

> "Do you know there are a lot of different sexual orientations?"
>
> It wasn't what he was expected at all. He stared at her.
>
> "Uh, what?"
>
> "You know, heterosexual, homosexual, bisexual."
>
> "And?"
>
> "And there's more" [Inrainbowz, 2016, p. 7].

What follows is a nice overview over the main points of being on the asexual spectrum and it is not strange that the short piece received many comments, in particular from readers who want to share their similar experiences and to praise the author for writing a piece that is both touching and informative.

These examples are not rare. On the contrary, the informative-type fan fiction undoubtedly has great importance and impact, creating the frame for discussion and reassurance between asexuals and other interested readers. Fan works within this group function as an outlet where information about asexuality and experiences—good or bad—are shared. Some of these works deal with the discovery of asexuality, others with the practicalities of everyday life as an asexual, or when one partner wants sex and the other does not. Others deal with the asexual character's encounters with ignorant, biased and rude people. These encounters are very similar to what the average asexual person experiences in everyday life; accidentally or intentionally uninformed or stigmatizing comments from doctors, parents, teachers, friends, and partners.

The importance of this type of fan fiction cannot be overestimated, nor can the therapeutic effect of being able to share one's experiences with a friendly group of like-minded readers. These works serve more than a singular purpose beyond being entertaining and touching stories which are pleasurable to read. The sense of community, the "perception of similarity with others, an acknowledged interdependence with others, [...] the feeling that one is part of a larger dependable and stable structure" (Obst, Zinkiewicz & Smith, 2001, p. 2), matters. There are several examples of asexuals coming out to the reader group, or readers asking questions to the author that they might not otherwise have gotten an answer to.

Body-Otherwise-Bound Works

Almost half of the studied asexual-themed fan works place the sexual character in a frame where his bodily autonomy is at stake. Since a significant number of the analyzed works contain this type of framing, it could be suggested that this may be the asexual (or asexuality-interested) author's method of making the pairing more equal and egalitarian. Smoothing out the differences in power and pressure from the surrounding society is similar to how slash pairings are used as a means to address gender inequality. There are many issues to write about for the average asexual: biological imperatives, relationships, equality, gender, orientation, love, power struggles inside the relationship, societal expectations, and medication of the non-normative body. One type of the body-otherwise-bound fan fiction combines them all; the Alpha/Beta/Omega trope. Commonly known as the Omegaverse, or A/B/O, the genre is very popular; some of these works have hundreds of comments, so it is interesting to explore how asexuality is portrayed within this subgenre of asexual slash fiction.

A/B/O stories are set within the context of a universe in which people's gender is any gender as we know them—plus the addition of a second biological sex layer. This new layer splits people into groups of either Alphas (sexually dominant and physically strong individuals), Betas (individuals who exhibit more "normal" human anatomy or have no special attributes), or Omegas (sexually submissive individuals who are physically weaker and capable of becoming pregnant). The Omegaverse also has its own set of tropes: true mates, mating bites and (sometimes enforced) knotting/breeding. It might not be easy to imagine how this hyper-sexualized genre could possibly offer anything to asexuality-interested writers or readers, but strangely enough this odd pairing makes for a challenging and complex dynamic in asexuality themed slash works.

Early A/B/O-fan fiction themes were heavily problematic with a focus on negotiating consent, usually featuring wholly submissive omegas struggling with the pairing's difficulties in dealing with their biological imperatives. It later developed into a field where the issues around gender equality, emancipation, sexuality and power were foregrounded. The genre grew up, so to speak, from a rape-kink into a meta-genre, where various expressions of power and bodily autonomy are negotiated. In that frame, it is not surprising that asexuality fan works set in this universe—where people are bound by biological constraints other than sexual orientation—are common; it levels the field for the characters by setting them on equal footing when it comes to having one's desire held in a tight grip by instinct and/or orientation. A large part of A/B/O-themed asexuality fan works fall into the two groups mentioned above: either they are informative fan fiction, or asexuality is mentioned in a passing sentence, playing no part (or in some cases, a misunderstood part) in the plot.

When they fall into the information works category, A/B/O slash fiction is often no different than other asexuality fan fiction. Common plots include an exploration of the situations faced by an ace character either coming out or having to explain their orientation to a partner; a plot centered around the negotiations between a partner who doesn't know about asexuality; or an ace who is shamed or vilified by a sexual society or insecure about how their relationship will turn out. In some cases, this turns out to be a cock-cures-all solution, or it shows an asexual character in reality being demisexual. In some of these works, the asexual partner ultimately agrees to appease the needs of their partner to please them. There is nothing wrong with those latter scenarios, of course, as this is the reality for many asexuals who try to navigate orientation and relationship in a world where more than 95 percent of the population is sexual (Kinsey, Pomeroy, Martin & Gebhard, 1953/1998).

Adherence to common plotlines, however, is not always the case. In mnwood's *Typecast* (2015), a *Supernatural* AU (Alternate Universe) story, Omega Dean Winchester and Alpha Castiel Novak are actors who are comfortable acting the parts of the opposite sex. Dean plays a character who is alpha and aromantic pan- or bisexual, whereas Castiel plays a romantic demi-sexual (labeled so by the author). Castiel has had his run of horrible relationships, and Dean none—by choice. In *Typecast* Dean is coming out as an Omega and gay—and although sex is a big part of what goes on between them Castiel never questions his own orientation, nor does he apologize for it or do anything to appease Dean unless he wants to. Contrary to most slash fiction, this story depicts an asexual character who becomes *less* attracted sexually as he gets to know his partner. However, Castiel welcomes his rut as it makes him want Dean sexually:

> Cas gets drunk on it, licking and kissing Dean's hole and swallowing everything he has to offer. He's never had desires like this before and likely won't again until his next rut, so he's going to make the most of it now [mnwood, 2015, pp. 185–186].

In *Typecast,* Castiel gets a new understanding of how it can feel for a sexual person to be with a demi- or asexual when Dean, tired of his partner's rut, lies back to eat ice cream and let Castiel take him again:

> He then reaches for the nightstand and grabs the gelato.
> "Oh," Cas says.
> Around a mouthful of melted gelato, Dean asks, "What?"
> "Is this how you feel when I'm not particularly interested in sex?"
> "That depends, how do you feel?"
> "Ignored. Like I have to do everything myself."
> "Aw, quit being so dramatic. So I made you do a little extra work, doesn't mean I'm ignoring you" [2015, p. 186].

Other popular asexuality themed narratives have featured characters experiencing anxiousness when presented with situations where they may be forced to live up to societal expectations—such as the joining of minds between an asexual character and their partner. The fear of being perceived as abnormal, or worse—of being accused of being disinterested in the relationship or having deceived one's partner—showcases how society's expectations in regards to presentation of sexuality weigh heavily on those who do not adhere to them. To fully understand how important these small clusters of asexual-themed fan fiction are to their readers in offering representation and recognition, it is important to examine the comments from readers.

Reader Response and Reception

Typecast is particularly well received for a variety of reasons: firstly, it features the most popular slash pairing on AO3, Castiel/Dean Winchester.[6] Secondly, it is one of the most popular tropes/genres within slash fiction: A/B/O. Thirdly, it is what this essay argues is a third wave asexuality awareness work: a story which progressively shows an asexual character to whom his orientation is not a source of pain or confusion, but one of acceptance. Works where there is a resolution to being a sexual/asexual couple are plenty, but there are few describing the asexual (or demi-/gray) character as one who is secure in his sexuality—one who never makes excuses or apologizes for it.

In *Typecast*, according to the author, Castiel is asexual but romantic, and Dean is aromantic, but bisexual. However, this choice was received very well with the readers, although the deviation from what is common in asexual-themed fan fiction also leads to some confusion among readers as to what was happening, with one reader reporting that she was a little confused by the "asexual Castiel" tag, asking whether Castiel is "grey-asexual, since he clearly responds to Dean with instant sexual attraction?" (Alessariel, 2015). The author explains:

> There are two reasons for Cas' sexual attraction to Dean. First, asexuality is a spectrum, and I'm writing Cas in this fic as more of the demisexual side of the spectrum. Additionally, this universe deals a lot with people's base (or animalistic) instincts, so Cas experiencing sexual attraction wouldn't be surprising to him even though it only happens to him rarely. And the second reason is that Cas is very much connected to the character he's playing, so during scenes he naturally reacts to situations the way that his character would react. That's why during the filming of the sex scene he was so immediately turned on. It will be addressed later, promise [*ibid.*].

Another reader raises doubts about how asexuality and A/B/O are portrayed when they are combined:

> So—you have this tagged as Cas is asexual and Dean is aromantic—and you've set up support for that with all the backstory and the current placement—but it seems that in this AU, the fact that they are true mates is going to somewhat over-ride both those settings?? [sic] Cas is getting unexpectedly horny, and Dean has already responded more to Cas than he expected. So far, it doesn't look like there is much romantic connection from Dean to Cas, but maybe eventually? [lizerd70, 2015].

This concern is subsequently acknowledged and directly addressed by mnwood:

> [...] to answer your question, yes, kind of—the fact that this is a/b/o somewhat changes the definitions of asexual and aromantic. BUT that doesn't mean it's going to be all rainbows and butterflies for Dean and Cas once they get together [*ibid.*].

Reader PorcupineGirl comments on the structure of the story and more or less sums up what it is that A/B/O-themed fan fiction does when it is combined with asexuality:

> I'm also interested to see how the aro/ace thing plays out in an omegaverse. In my mind, at least, there seems to be a third kind of attraction at work in omegaverses, the biological/chemical/scent thing. Which isn't necessarily in itself either romantic or sexual, but can foster either of those. But that's the type of attraction that actually

> drives people to mate/bond/claim/whatever (usually, obviously the rules of every omegaverse are slightly different), even though it usually is accompanied by or causes one or both of the others. So I'm curious how that type of attraction plays out in the absence of the other two. [...] (Or maybe your omegaverse functions totally differently, but it sure seems like scent attraction plays a big part here that's not quite equivalent to the others.) [PorcupineGirl, 2015].

This open discussion between author and readers is characteristic of much of the interaction that occurs in and around asexual fan fiction. It is rare to see rude comments; most often the author responds kindly and helps clear up definitions and misunderstandings, gently correcting people if a commenter is not aware that asexuality is an orientation. Generally, the commenters are curious, supportive and kind and, on occasion, the safe setting even gives readers the courage to come out as asexuals, or to consider that they might be. The fan base surrounding the authors and their works is often very welcoming and open about their sexuality and this, in addition to the narrative's resonance with everyday life and readers' experiences, is enthusiastically debated. This then adds to the sense of identity and community amongst the readers who share these experiences.

So Where Do We Go from Here?

Asexual slash fiction is still about sex. In some, the main characters have sex. In others, they don't. In some, they have cake. The difference between the works where the characters are both sexual, and those where one or both are identifying as being on the asexual spectrum, might be how the space in which the body is placed is itself placed under scrutiny—thus leveling the power balance between the couples. So when sex becomes unimportant, or its importance changes and takes a different form, is there anything this discovery can tell us? Perhaps that when sex is out of the picture, the core of slash fiction is all still about equality; about placing the conversation about body, relationship, power and love in a setting where heteronormative patriarchy cannot reach? Clearly, the asexual fan work has other agendas as well, such as providing support and raising awareness, but on the bottom line it is the typical story about a love between equals and seeing the conflict resolved that would otherwise have kept lovers apart.

Popular Omegaverse stories like mnwood's *Typecast* (2015) are not the only works which take asexuality and give it a twist. Other works feature interspecies couples who realize they would be happy fulfilling each other's respective biological urges twice a year and cuddling the rest of the time. Another work may feature a vampiric asexual who is into dominance and submission, making it clear that asexuals are not taking it lying down, but standing proud—preferably with whip in hand. The small rise in numbers when it comes to fan fiction featuring main pairings who are asserting their asexuality without shame or apologies might denote a change in how asexuality itself is being viewed and portrayed. This may even indicate a potential shift in the kinds of themes and empowerments that readers might find in the genre in the future.

The debate and negotiation of the coming-out part in asexual information and therapy fan fiction has been an important and necessary development, drawing away from the misunderstood and biology-based interpretations of asexuality within slash fiction. Judging from the comments on these works, writing, reading and sharing asexuality-themed works within an interpretive community empowers audiences and authors to negotiate their own relation to sexuality in a friendly atmosphere. Thus, asexuality themed slash fiction and its interpretive communities strengthen readers and authors alike, maybe helping them to become stronger and self-asserting individuals, proud to be asexual and standing strong knowing that they are not alone in fandom or in the world outside it. It can be argued that asexuality-themed fan fiction and its audiences participate in a profoundly positive cultural exercise—where media, asexual information networks and fandom passions combine, creating a lasting impact on our asexual awareness.

Notes

1. www.asexuality.org.
2. Although the author of this essay has lived in Japan and speaks Japanese, the language barrier prevents further investigation within the timeframe of this work.
3. Only around 35 percent of M/M slash fans identify themselves as heterosexual females, according to the 2014 AO3 census conducted by metastatistician centrumlumina.
4. As AO3 went into closed beta in 2007 and reopened in 2008, the works posted here dated prior to 2007–2008 are backdated and would have been posted elsewhere, and only later archived at AO3.
5. This overlap occurs mainly within the informative, body-otherwise-bound and third-wave groups of asexuality themed fan fiction.
6. Out of 1,409,146 works on AO3, 61,583 are Castiel/Dean Winchester slash—over 10,000 more than the second most popular pairing of Sherlock Holmes/John Watson with 49,240 works.

References

Alessariel. (2015, September 7). On Chapter 7 [Comment]. Archive of Our Own.

Archive of Our Own. (2016a). In *Fanlore*. Retrieved from https://fanlore.org/wiki/Archive_of_Our_Own.

Archive of Our Own. (2016b). *Search Results: Asexuality*. Retrieved from Archive of Our Own Search Results.

Archive of Our Own. (2017). *Asexual Awareness Week*. Retrieved from Archive of Our Own: Tag Search.

Asexual reproduction. (2016). Retrieved from the Biology Online website at http://www.biology-online.org/dictionary/asexual_reproduction.

asexuality.org. (2016). Research Relating to Asexuality. In *AVENwiki*. Retrieved from http://www.asexuality.org/wiki/index.php?title=Research_relating_to_asexuality.

AVEN General FAQ. (2016). Retrieved from the Asexual Visibility and Education Network website http://www.asexuality.org/?q=general.html.

AVEN Overview. (2016). Retrieved from the Asexual Visibility and Education Network website http://www.asexuality.org/?q=overview.html.

Bogaert, A.F. (2004). Asexuality: Prevalence and Associated Factors in a National Probability Sample. *The Journal of Sex Research, 41*(3), 279–287. http://dx.doi.org/10.1080/00224490409552235.

Bordo, S. (2003). *Unbearable Weight: Feminism, Western Culture and the Body* (2nd ed.). Berkeley: University of California Press.

centrumlumina. (2014). AO3 Census Masterpost [Blog post]. Retrieved from http://centrumlumina.tumblr.com/post/63208278796/ao3-census-masterpost.

Cerankowski, K.J., and Milks, M. (2014). *Asexualities: Feminist and Queer Perspectives*. New York: Routledge.

de Beauvoir, S. (1953). *The Second Sex* (H.M. Parshley, Trans.). London: Vintage. (Original work published 1949).

DeDominicis, K. (2016). *Fandom, Meta, and Public/Private Online Space: A Methodological and Ethical Approach*. Paper presented at the Fanstudies Network Conference, University of East Anglia, United Kingdom.

Fanfiction.net. (2016). *Search: Asexuality*. Retrieved from Fanfiction.net search results.

Foucault, M. (1978). *The History of Sexuality, Volume 1: An Introduction* (R. Hurley, Trans.). New York: Vintage. (Original work published 1976).

Freund, E. (1987). *The Return of the Reader: Reader-Response Criticism*. London: Methuen.

Galbraith, P.W. (2010). Akihabara: Conditioning a Public "Otaku" Image. *Mechademia, 5*, 210–230. Retrieved from https://muse.jhu.edu/article/400558.

Gamble, S. (Writer), and Sgriccia, P. (Director). (2011, September 23). Meet the New Boss [Television series episode]. In E. Kripke (Producer), *Supernatural*. Burbank, CA: Warner Bros. Television.

Gatiss, M., and Moffat, S. (Producers). (2010–). *Sherlock* [Television series]. London: Hartswood Films & BBC Wales.

Ginoza, M.K., and Miller, T. (2014). *AVEN Community Census 2014*. Retrieved from https://asexualcensus.files.wordpress.com/2014/11/2014censuspreliminaryreport.pdf.

Hills, M. (2002). *Fan Cultures*. Oxon: Routledge.

Hills, R. (2012, April 2). Life Without Sex: The Third Phase of the Asexuality Movement. *The Atlantic*. Retrieved from http://www.theatlantic.com/health/archive/2012/04/life-without-sex-the-third-phase-of-the-asexuality-movement/254880/.

Inrainbowz. (2016). *Body and Soul, Free to Withhold*. Archive of Our Own.

Jenkins, H. (2006). "Normal Female Interest in Men Bonking": Selections from the Terra Nostra Underground and Strange Bedfellows [Blog post]. Retrieved from http://web.mit.edu/21fms/People/henry3/bonking.html.

Jensen, T. (2016). Let's Make It Personal! Ontological Ethics in Fan Studies. *Journal of Fandom Studies, 4*(3), 255–273. https://doi.org/10.1386/jfs.4.3.255_1.

Johnson, M.T. (1977). Asexual and Autoerotic Women: Two Invisible Groups. In H.L. Gochros and J.S. Gochros (Eds.), *The Sexually Oppressed*. New York: Associated Press.

Kinsey, A.C., Pomeroy, W.B., Martin, C.E., and Gebhard, P.H. (1998). *Sexual Behavior in the Human Female* (3rd ed.). Bloomington: Indiana University Press. (Original work published 1953).

Kripke, E. (Producer). (2005–). *Supernatural* [Television series]. Burbank, CA: Warner Bros. Television.

Kripke, E., and Edlund, B. (Writers), and Singer, R. (Director). (2010, October 8). The Third Man [Television series episode]. In E. Kripke (Producer), *Supernatural*. Burbank, CA: Warner Bros. Television.

lizerd70. (2015, September 8). On Chapter 8 [Comment]. Archive of Our Own.

mnwood. (2015). *Typecast*. Archive of Our Own.

Obst, P.L., Zinkiewicz, L., and Smith, S.G. (2001). Sense of Community in Science Fiction Fandom, Part 1: Understanding Sense of Community in an International Community of Interest. *Journal of Community Psychology, 30*(1), 87–103. doi:10.1002/jcop.1052.

PorcupineGirl. (2015, September 11). On Chapter 9 [Comment]. Archive of Our Own.
Q13 News Staff. (2014, September 23). Is Asexuality an Orientation? *Q13FOX*. Retrieved from http://q13fox.com/2014/09/23/is-asexuality-an-orientation.
Sidney Sussex. (2012). *To Live for a Moment in Unison*. Archive of Our Own.
Spurgas, A.K. (2016, March 9). Solving Desire. *The New Inquiry*. Retrieved from http://thenewinquiry.com/essays/solving-desire.
Storms, M.D. (1980). Theories of Sexual Orientation. *Journal of Personality and Social Psychology, 38*(5), 783–792. doi:10.1037/0022-3514.38.5.783.
Supernatural Kink Community. (2016). LiveJournal.com.
Yi, E.J. (2013). Reflection on Chinese Boys' Love Fans: An Insider's View. *Transformative Works and Cultures, 12*. doi:10.3983/twc.2013.0424.

Icons of Self-Destruction

The Portrayal of Aggression and Abusive Behaviors in Band Slash Fiction

ÁGNES ZSILA *and* ZSOLT DEMETROVICS

Going Backstage: An Introduction to Band Slash Fiction

In a survey conducted by Boon and Lomore (2001) of admirer-celebrity relationships among Canadian young adults, 58.7 percent of undergraduates perceived that their favorite celebrities had an influence on their attitudes and values, whilst 46.7 percent of them reported that they engaged in one or more particular activities (e.g., acting, creative writing) because their idols shared the same interest. Despite the growing academic interest in exploring the association between fan engagement and creative practices, relatively little research attention has been paid to real person slash (RPS), which can be considered as an intersection of these two phenomena.

Band slash is a popular subgenre of RPS, which thematizes the romantic encounter of particular members of famous bands—mostly boy bands, as Thomas (2014) points out—often in a sexually explicit form. Based on the early observations reported in audience studies on the perceived high attendance of female enthusiasts in the fan base (Darling-Wolf, 2004) and gay culture (Fackler & Salvato, 2012; Moon, 1995) of famous boy bands, it might be assumed that the majority of band slash readers and writers are young, heterosexual, highly educated women, such as in the case of the proposed stereotypical profile of slash fiction fans.[1] Dyer (2004) reports that the narrative elements of band slash stories are generally based on interviews, biographies, and live performances of the musicians, which subsequently inspire fans to enrich their overall impression of their idols with speculative personal information in the form of creative, invented stories. As a result, band slash writers individually decide what information should be considered as truth, irrespective of the objectivity of the source, and interpret it accordingly in their narratives (Busse, 2006b). Page (2013) argues that social networking sites such as Twitter have become virtual "back stages" in recent years, where fans can find personal information about their favorite celebrities. However, the author also points out that these sites serve as a form of self-promotion instead of providing an intimate intersection between celebrities and their fans.

Boys' love genre (also known as BL or yaoi), the Japanese counterpart of slash, became popular rapidly in the early 2000s, which had a significant influence on the homoerotic writings of European fans as well as Asian fans (Welker, 2015). As a consequence, many band slash stories centered on Japanese and Korean boy bands. According to the prevalence of band slash fans in related online communities, it can be seen that J-pop/rock, K-pop/rock, and visual kei[2] band slash works have also attracted several fans from the anime-manga subculture.

The early concepts on fan cultures mostly emphasized the negative side of participation, and defined fans as pathological entities cherishing immature fantasies (Jenkins, 1992). By contrast, in the following years several academic essays argued that fan communities are developing and dynamic spaces (Thomas, 2006) in which members are encouraged to share their fantasies, ultimately establishing international collaborations between authors and readers of related works (Busse, 2006a). The increasing accessibility of the Internet had a great contribution to the global expansion of fan spaces, resulting in the construction of active virtual communities in which native and non-native English-speaking fans could meet and gain inspiration from each other's works (Black, 2004) while developing their writing skills.

Busse (2006a) argues that the discrepancy between public performance and the private lives of celebrities drives fans to create wishful fantasies which materialize in textual form. According to this, the role of male homoerotic narratives lies in the avoidance of rivalry, since female characters would cause tension in the writer/reader who may act out his/her own desires while engaging in narratives of intimacy and personal secrets (Busse, 2006a; Scodari, 2007). Fans distinctly separate the official and personal lives of their favorite stars in their works, and the secrecy surrounding the sexual identity of celebrities—that can be found in the majority of band slash stories—is used for this purpose (Busse, 2006a). In these fan narratives, the depicted band members are mostly heterosexual men (Kaplan, 2012), who may be married with children but who engage in homosexual interactions onstage in order to entertain fans (a practice which can be recognized during live performances as "fan service"[3]) while secretly being involved in a complex, often sexually-driven emotional bond with other band members. Their anxiety of being exposed in public for their sexual ambiguity is often expressed in angst stories, a subgenre of slash that depicts character and situational anxieties relating to the relationship of the main couple (Keft-Kennedy, 2008).

As with slash fiction as an overall genre, a wide variety of other themes can be found in band fiction, such as emotionally balanced stories exploring the everyday life moments of band members (termed "fluff") (Hellekson & Busse, 2006). Some band slash stories focus on sexuality instead of developing a detailed story background and these sexually explicit narratives are often labeled "PWP" ("Porn without plot" or "Plot? What plot?") (Tosenberger, 2008). The first sexual interaction between characters (referred as "first time" in fans' categorization) and a relationship developed between friends ("established relationship") are also popular settings in band slash stories. By creating physically and psychologically vulnerable characters in their stories, band slash authors make them more human and identifiable for readers. Therefore, they "reappropriate" the prototypical male characters (Kustritz, 2003, p. 371) and often make them more passive, sexually repressed, and emotionally vulnerable (Booth, 2014). External to the angst stories, several other slash subgenres provide space for more negative feelings, illustrating the darker side of reputation. Fan-created stories depicting physical and verbal aggression, rape, and sexual encounters in which either of the partners derives pleasure from experiencing pain and humiliation both within and external to BDSM situations also attract several readers (Roddy, 2011)—although hurt/comfort stories (in which a physically or emotionally hurt character finds comfort in his relationship) are also popular (McGee, 2005). These melodramatic stories often employ narratives that discuss psychological harms and related behavioral consequences such as abuse, emotional blackmailing, coping with terminal illness, and traumas. Self-destructive practices are presented in band slash works in the form of suicidal thoughts, attempted and/or committed suicide, and addictions (such as alcohol and/or drug addictions). Self-harming practices are rarely found in band slash stories, but these thematic elements are mostly derived from the observed prevalence of such behaviors in biographies of famous band members (Oksanen, 2012). If negative themes appear in the text, the author often warns readers in the header of the story, in tags or in the author's notes, which offers detailed information about the piece in order for a reader to assess whether they wish to proceed with the story.

There have been several studies which have explored the underlying motivations of creating homoerotic stories featuring fictitious and/or real persons (notably Hills, 2002; Jenkins, 1992 and Sandvoss, 2005). Focusing on psychological theories, Thomas (2006) emphasized that slash provides a space for self-exploration by creating plots that have a personal relevance for the authors. Sandvoss (2005, p. 121) argued that fans subconsciously derive pleasure from immersing in self-reflective narratives, since they are "fascinated by extensions of themselves." In a similar vein, Hills (2002) elaborated that fans gain pleasure from stories and textual representations which allow them to challenge the boundaries of their inner selves and external constructions. Busse (2006b) also underlined that slash works allow young readers in particular to explore their sexual desires in the safe place of fantasy. In the study of Lothian, Busse, and Reid (2007), fans also reported that slash works provided a virtual space for them to express identities that they have to repress in real life, and to act out their anxieties and personal problems through textual representations.

Despite the increasing research interest in the motivations of slash readers to engage in a highly self-reflective narration of secret fantasies involving their favorite musicians, the darker themes and elements around reputation has received relatively little research attention. The primary aim of this study is to explore the underlying motivations of band slash writers and readers who tend towards dark themes (e.g., aggression, emotional harm, suicide, addiction) in these fan-created pieces. In order to gain a more nuanced picture of this phenomenon, we investigate readers' reactions, motivations, and engagement from the perspective of band slash authors. Secondly, this investigation will explore the differences between popular and underground authors' insights regarding writers' motivation and readers' reaction from their perspective. By gaining a greater knowledge of fans' motivations from band slash authors, we can synthesize writers' and readers' experiences with the theoretical frameworks found in the existing literature of slash studies. All quotes and data contained within this essay are featured with the kind permission of the respondents.

Methods

Participants and Procedure

Eight band slash authors were asked to complete an online questionnaire containing both qualitative and quantitative questions. All participants were Hungarian women aged between 18 and 34 years (mean age = 25.25 years, standard deviation = 6.09) who published their works in Hungarian language. Furthermore, each author wrote band slash fictions featuring J-pop, J-rock, visual kei, K-pop, and K-rock boy bands. Half of the sample group could be labeled "Big Name Fans"[4] (according to their relatively large readership and productivity), whereas four authors reported that they published band slash stories mostly on their blogs to a smaller readership. However, we would prefer using alternative labels to refer to different author groups in this study, since the term "Big Name Fan" can have a pejorative connotation in fan conversations, and as emphasized by Hellekson and Busse (2006), popular fans often reject this label. Furthermore, authors who have a smaller group of followers than other writers in this sample may do so because they actively do not wish to publish their works to a broader audience. Thus, their relatively small readership base cannot be associated with the literary quality of their works. Moreover, stories featuring members of extremely popular bands attract more readers than pieces featuring two or more lesser-known musicians, irrespective of the quality of these stories. Therefore, for the purposes of this essay we will refer to band slash authors with a relatively large readership and productivity as "popular authors," whereas authors who do not write band slash regularly and have a smaller readership base will be labeled "underground authors."

Materials

The collected data included demographic characteristics, band slash writing activity (e.g., number of written stories, preferred subgenres), personal experiences with participants' favorite bands, and writing practices and feedback related to the dark side of band slash fiction. This latter section was separated into eight subthemes, which were selected on the basis of the existing literature on slash fiction contents (as identified by Hellekson & Busse, 2006, and Roddy, 2011), and on theoretical considerations following the data-driven argument of Rodriguez-Srednicki (2002) regarding psychological, physical and sexual abuse, and drug and alcohol use. We identified four major themes, comprised of eight subthemes.

Physical aggression and suffering:

1. Physical and/or verbal abuse
2. Rape
3. Illness and/or bodily suffering

Emotional harms:

4. Emotional blackmailing, intimidation, threats, constraint and coercion.
5. Humiliation and/or shaming.
6. Depression, anxiety and other psychological disorders

Self-destruction:

7. Self-destructive behaviors and/or suicide

Addiction:

8. Addictions: drug/alcohol, etc.

Respondents were asked to indicate through a multiple choice question which of the given themes appeared in band slash works they had written preceding the data collection, and participants could select more than one category. If the respondent answered positively to a theme, three recurring questions were asked:

1. "What motivated you to write band slash stories about this theme?"
2. "What kind of feedback did you get from your readers when you had written about this theme?"
3. "Why do you think your readers like your piece/pieces written about this theme?"

Results

Descriptive Demographic Data of Band Slash Authors

Demographic characteristics and information about band slash writing activity of the authors (sample size = 8) are presented in Table 1. The popular authors were older (between 19 and 34 years) than underground authors (between 18 and 28 years), and reported a higher level of education. Three of the four popular authors had a prestigious job at the time of the survey (jurist, resident doctor, researcher), whereas all of the underground authors were students. There were no relevant differences between the two author groups regarding marital status. Half of the authors were single, whereas half of them lived in a form of relationship. However, only half of the authors identified as heterosexual.

All of the popular authors had written more than 20 band slash stories and had on average more than 100 readers per story (calculated from the unique hits statistics of the web pages where they published their works). The majority of them published their stories on the current most popular Hungarian fan fiction website (Anime Fanfiction Style) and band slash fiction website (Rising Sun). The majority of them had written band slash for around six to nine years. In comparison, underground authors had written on average fewer than eleven band slash stories and had fewer than 51 readers per story (if website statistics were not available, authors were asked to estimate the size of their readership). None of them had written band slash regularly (more than 1–2 times per year). Three of them published their stories on their blogs, but half of them also published stories on dedicated websites.

	Demographic characteristics				Band slash writing activity			
Respondent ID*	Age	Level of education	Sexual orientation	Marital status	Number of band slash works	Experience of writing band slash (years)	Frequency of writing	Readership
P1	34	Higher education	Heterosexual	Married	21-30	6-9	Daily or almost daily	> 1000
P2	29	Higher education	Heterosexual	Single	31-50	6-9	Once or twice a year	501-1000
P3	19	High school graduate	Heterosexual	Single	21-30	3-5	Once or twice a month	501-1000
P4	29	Higher education	Bisexual	Married	> 50	6-9	Two or more times per week	101-300
U1	28	High school graduate	Bisexual	Engaged	1-5	< 1	Annually or less	10-50
U2	18	High school graduate	Bisexual	Single	6-10	< 1	Once or twice a year	No answer
U3	18	Grammar school	Heterosexual	Single	1-5	< 1	Once or twice a year	10-50
U4	27	High school graduate	Homosexual	In a relationship	1-5	< 1	No answer	< 10

Using a multiple-choice question, it was identified that the stories these authors wrote mostly angst (mentioned by four authors), hurt/comfort (three), and fluff (three). Furthermore, five authors had written "first time" stories, whereas only one had written "established relationship" narratives. Regarding bands, half of the authors wrote band slash stories about The Gazette and three wrote about Dir en grey members. They also mentioned similarly popular bands such as Alice Nine, Bangtan Boys, and other, comparatively underground K-pop bands (e.g., Exo, Infinite).

All of the authors have been fans of their favorite bands for more than three years. Three popular authors had been fans for more than six years (with P4 reporting having been a fan for over a decade) and the fourth author had been a fan for three to five years. Half of the underground authors had been fans of their preferred bands for six to nine years, and half of them for three to five years. Popular authors reported that they visited concerts staged by their favorite bands more frequently than underground authors; two attended concerts yearly and three had attended VIP meetings with the band members, where they could chat, take photos, and shake hands with their idols. In contrast, the majority of underground authors had never seen any live performances of their favorite bands; only one author had the opportunity to attend a concert. However, the attendance of fans may not be independent of their time constraints and financial status.

Motivations for Writing Band Slash Fiction

In order to explore the motivations of band slash writers, respondents were asked why they wrote band slash fiction. For the sake of anonymity, the real names and the pen names of the authors are withheld in the analysis, and personal codes are used (see Table 1).

All of the popular authors mentioned that they write band slash because they do not want to work with original characters and/or do not feel that they are ready for working with original characters. As P1 explained:

> I think real person slash is the most comfortable way of writing, because I do not have to create characters (problems with giving a name, how he should look) and work with fictional characters created by another author. [...] From this perspective, the difference between RPS and original is that in the former case, the majority of readers can identify the characters, whereas in the latter case, their identities remain secret.

Another popular author added that she and her readers are fans of the same musicians and bands, which provides a great opportunity to make friends. Underground authors mostly emphasized that they gained inspiration from their own adoration and appreciation for the bands. Furthermore, one author wrote that she was curious about homosexual relationships between particular band members (real or fictitious) that she found more sensual compared to heterosexual love. Another underground author reported that she found it challenging to write band slash, and this motivated her.

In summary, the general motivation of popular authors to write band slash fiction was related to their writing skill development. They wished to improve their abilities to create complex stories through real characters and structures (e.g., show business), which allowed them to practice their writing skills without investing large amounts of time and energy into generating original character plans or story settings. They reported that they preferred to increase their distance from real sources towards an original story through this step-by-step learning process, as was suggested by Lewis (2004) and Thomas (2006). Conversely, underground authors were inspired by their favorite musicians, and this appreciation was the primary motivation for them to expand their imagination of the musicians' true personalities behind the stage. These authors preferred to share fictitious, speculative or real information with similarly dedicated authors in order to express their enthusiasm and participation, and to immerse in a social network of fans with the same interest, which facilitates their social and individual self-construction, in accordance with the theories emphasized by Sandvoss (2005).

Exploring the Dark Side of Band Slash Fiction

In this section, we analyze the responses to the qualitative part of our research, which focused on the function of dark themes in band slash fiction, and the motivations behind creating and consuming band slash with troubling themes from the perspectives of both popular and underground authors.

Physical Aggression and Suffering

> "Is beating someone also part of taking care of them?" I am unable to ask this without irony.
>
> "Yes, it is" Aoi nods. "Only those can evoke such intense emotions in you who are important to you. If this had occurred one year before, he might have made me happy with a gesture like this. I mean, if he had tried to hit me."
>
> —Nanami, 2012

Theme one: Physical and/or Verbal Abuse

Six of eight authors had written band slash stories containing physical and/or verbal abuse. The motivations of popular authors to write band slash stories illustrating physical or verbal aggression were sharply different from the motivations mentioned by underground authors. Three popular authors found it challenging to portray physical abuse and considered their related works as a next stage in the development of their writing skills. Moreover, two of them wrote that aggression was a necessary stage in character development. This motivation reflected the general goals of popular authors which were related to their efforts to improve their writing skills.

In contrast, the reasons of underground authors for generating aggression in their narratives were more personal. One author, U1, claimed that she needed to release her negative feelings to turn them into her advantage in creating pieces. She wrote aggression in order to "dwell on the negative feelings, generated from real reasons." Furthermore, understanding human nature also appeared in the responses as a motivation. As another underground author, U2, exemplified: "If we hurt or humiliate someone, it gives a reason for another character to feel sorry for him, then he consoles the other, and their relationship begins to deepen." These motivations were in line with those reported by Thomas (2006), whose study observed that writing characters and narratives that are personally relevant to fans' own identities is of special importance for slash authors.

Regarding readers' reactions, both popular and underground authors reported similar experiences. They all stated that the feedback they received from their readers showed large variation. Two authors received mostly negative feedback on their stories portraying aggression, whereas only one author claimed that the majority of her readers liked her stories containing aggression, adding that her readers had curiously waited for her to continue these stories. Only a small minority of her readers felt that they did not wish to read about the suffering of others after a long day. In a similar vein, another author emphasized that readers' reactions are often dependent on the ending of the story, and positive solutions are always preferable.

There was a consensus between both popular and underground authors that the reason why their readers liked these stories relied in their closeness to reality and the potential for reader identification. One of them pointed out that a small minority of readers may perceive these narratives as a projection site for their own problems. However, another author noted that it is important to emphasize that meaningless violence (violence which does not contribute to the character development in the story) is rather undesirable. She argued that audiences wish to read about the progress and dynamics of the relationship between characters under the pressure of destructive circles and situations, since they are curious about the effects of violence on emotions. This effort was also recognized by Jenkins (1992), who suggested that fans seek to pursue more complex narratives and solve more difficult problems, and thus readers are here able to get more information about the characters through detailed psychological background stories.

Theme Two: Rape

Four authors reported that they had written band slash stories in which rape occurred. Three of them were popular authors, who claimed that the motivation for them to write rape in their stories was to add new, controversial elements to the narrative. One underground author also used this trope to deepen the relationship between the protagonists and to disrupt the monotony of the storyline.

Reader feedback on this theme was reported by only popular authors. Two of them wrote that they received mostly negative comments from readers, who felt sorry for the character that suffered sexual violence, but P4 reported that the reactions she observed showed great variety. As she remarked:

> [...] several core readers of mine told me that they did not even start to read the story because this theme was far too disturbing for them. However, other readers found it interesting how the personalities of characters and the dynamics of their relationship change, and how it affects the story.

Authors suggested that their followers read their band slash stories in which either of the characters becomes a rape victim because these stories are realistic, and they like plot twists and radical changes in the narratives which result in unpredicted outcomes. However, P1 argued that rape also has a special resonance with the readers, arguing "I think rape is a little bit arousing in the level of fantasies for all those who have not experienced it." She further argued that rape is a controversial theme in this aspect; readers may wish to participate in new experiences in the safety of fictional circumstances, but as a victim of rape they could only identify with a passive, helpless character that has no choice in this situation.

Nevertheless, the positive reframing of rape experiences in male/male homosexual fiction is not limited to slash. Rape also constitutes a main component of the boys' love genre, in which the stronger character rapes his partner, urged by the will to express his overflowing desire for him (Mizoguchi, 2003 & 2008). Therefore, it may be another common feature shared between these two male homoerotic subgenres, indicating that fans' needs and preferred narratives may not be so different in the genres of slash fiction and boys' love.

Theme Three: Illness, Physical Suffering

Similarly to rape, half of the authors (three of whom were popular authors) reported that they had written band slash in which either of the characters suffered from illness or had other physical health concerns. Their motivation to describe terminal illness, physical pain and injuries in their stories was mostly based on their studies, curiosity, and personal experiences from their professional life. For instance, P4 discussed that she had transformed some of her professional work experiences into stories.

All authors agreed that the reception of these works was notably negative in the majority of cases. They attributed this to readers' experiences, considering that a number of them were personally affected by these life events. Thus, reading about cancer or other terminal illnesses may have revived unpleasant memories for them. Authors reported that the most common reactions to these works were sadness, empathy, and pain. Furthermore, one author emphasized that her readers expressed strong emotional reactions to these themes, and a number of them told her that they cried while they were reading those stories. Despite the negative reception of stories describing illness and physical suffering, two popular authors noted that readers felt the need to identify with characters going through these kinds of tragic or challenging life events which could happen to anyone. As P4 remarked, "[My readers] like reading about things that could also happen to them because they can sympathize with the characters and [understand] their actions more deeply in the plot."

In prior studies, the motivation of gaining more knowledge about what can happen to oneself was identified as a main motive for media consumption in the field of media psychology (Rubin, 1983 and Weaver, 2003). The representation of physical health concerns in band slash fiction can be an important source of information for those fans who exhibit a high level of this motivation. However, P1 also added that despite the fact that illness and health concerns are not popular themes amongst band slash readers, they prefer reading about physical suffering more than psychological problems, because the latter is more inconceivable. This observation partly contradicts the commonly held assumption that heavy psychological themes are popular amongst band slash fans (Hellekson & Busse, 2006), but also highlights the diversity of fan reactions to the same narrative elements.

Emotional Harms

> Actually, I could have resisted. I could have walked away anytime but I didn't dare to do so. Kiyoharu made me addicted to him; he was like respiration for me, or like heroin for him. He destroyed my self-confidence, and I felt unable to exist without him. I have lost a part of myself, an important part that I could not replace anymore.—Rami, 2013

Theme Four: Emotional Blackmailing, Intimidation, Threats, Constraining, Coercion

More than half of the authors had written band slash stories in which emotional harms (e.g., emotional blackmailing, threats) occurred, the majority of whom were underground authors. Popular authors shared a consensus that their motivation for writing stories centering on negative emotional bonds was the challenge of writing about it; they wished to write about something that they had never written about before, which facilitated the development of their writing techniques. In contrast, the reasons of underground authors were again rather more personal. U1 reported that "the inspiration and the emotional charge" motivated her to write about such emotional harms. Another author noted that emotional burdens could also be a consequence of physical abuse. Furthermore, emotionally unstable characters could evoke sympathy in other band members in the story, leading to more complex relationships, as it was suggested by another underground author.

The majority of the authors who had written about emotional harms in their band slash stories reported that their readers found these themes exciting. As P4 recalled, "it evoked strong emotional responses in several people; they became attached to characters or began to hate them very much. Many readers described what they would have done in that situation." An underground author remarked that her readers were surprised and curious about the writer's motivation behind her reconfiguration of the real personalities and attitudes of their favorite musicians in her works. This curiosity may indicate that fans hold different fictional interpretations of their favorite stars' attitudes and behaviors, and they wish to explore other fans' representations by reading their stories.

Some authors pointed out that the reason why these themes attract many readers may be rooted in the realistic representation of emotional problems, which facilitates readers' identification with the characters. Furthermore, a popular author added that readers like reconsidering what they would have done in the same situation, whereas another popular author argued that it is easier for them to read about these emotions than to experience emotional distress personally.

Theme Five: Humiliation, Shaming

Half of the authors, three of whom were popular authors, reported that they had created band slash stories in which either of the protagonists suffered humiliation and shaming from other characters. All of the authors reported that their motivation to portray situations in which a character had been humiliated was to enrich his personality with additional traits and dark secrets. They argued that this twist in the plot is often unavoidable in respect of character development and has an integral role in the logical structure of the story.

Only popular authors could relay readers' reactions in relation to this theme, and two authors also emphasized that they did not receive many comments on this topic compared to other story elements (such as physical abuse) in their works, or within the same story. However, P3 reported that she received positive feedback from her readers, whereas P4 stated that her readers expressed sympathy for the victim in the majority of cases, although she noted that there are special conditions that could lead to positive reactions: "They found it particularly exciting in PWP stories in which humiliation was part of the sexual roleplay with the approval of both partners."

Kustritz (2008) drew a similar conclusion in her study regarding BDSM in slash fan fiction. She argued that the representation of sexual coercion and humiliation in slash stories may not carry the same meaning for all fans, and different perspectives are often present in fan conversations regarding this theme. In the current study, only one popular author presented some speculative reasons as to why fans read band slash stories in which humiliation and shaming occurs. P3 pointed out that readers may find realistic stories more engaging: "Life is not a fairytale. […] If [the humiliation of a character] is not gone too far, then it just makes the piece more realistic."

Theme Six: Depression, Anxiety, Other Psychological Disorders

Six of the eight authors reported that they had written band slash stories in which some of the characters had psychological problems. Popular and underground authors were equally distributed in this group. The motivational pattern of depicting psychological disorders in band slash stories was similar to the motivations found in Theme 4 (emotional blackmailing, threats, and other emotional harms) across the two author groups. Popular authors mentioned that they derived these experiences from their studies and professional life, whereas one author simply wished to write about this theme authentically. In contrast, underground authors' motivation was again more personal. For instance, one underground author confessed that she had similar problems at the time she had written her related pieces, and exploring these in her narrative helped her with the coping process. Another author found it important to portray male characters struggling with psychological problems, since it is against the commonly held assumption that mainly women are affected by these difficulties. U4 reported that she uses these narratives as a cathartic strategy to release her own negative emotions:

> There is nothing wrong with happy stories, since they are here to make our day after a pretty bad Monday. However, I can deal with the daily grind more easily with a negative story, since it "has never happened," although I keep convincing myself that it was "far worse, more crucial" what happened to my characters. The majority of my bad stories depict how the main characters can bounce back from horrible situations and do things that may the writer herself would never be able to do.

According to U4's argument, a possible explanation for band slash writers' motivation to create detailed psychological background stories of their favorite musicians in which they suffer from psychological harms could be that fans wish to cope with their own problems through the identification with strong and competent characters, who have a rich array of coping resources and social support. Thus, fans perceive these resources more accessible for themselves, which may facilitate the development of their own coping processes and frameworks.

Two authors noted that their readers found this theme depressing, and they subsequently did not receive much feedback on these works, while in contrast another two authors reported that their readers liked these narratives. However, no relevant difference was observed between popular and underground authors regarding these experiences. P2 added that her readers were surprised by the thematic content, and they appreciated the realistic representation of these problems in her pieces. P4 reported that some of her readers had queries regarding personal mental health concerns, hoping for suggestions from the author herself:

> Instead of particular feedback, they often ask questions—this is maybe due to the fact that some of my readers are aware of my professional background, or they are simply interested in this topic that much. Besides, many of them share their personal experiences in relation to this theme [e.g., psychological disorders of family members, acquaintances].

Two underground authors argued that their followers like reading realistic stories, which facilitates their immersion in the narrative. P2 explained: "[They like this theme] because it discusses common things that they might have already experienced or they think it can also happen to them." Another author added that these narratives help readers to forget about their own problems and to reconsider them after reading about characters who faced far worse situations. However, one popular author noted that in contrast to the positive reception identified by some of the respondents, her own readers are concerned with their own problems and do not wish to identify with characters that face more complex difficulties. In sum, reader reactions regarding this theme showed a mixed picture, which again indicates that fans can and do view the same narrative from different perspectives in band slash.

Self-Destruction

> You were completely knocked out when I found you in that separated room reserved for VIP guests. The owner called me saying that you were there and out of your mind. Well yes, they always call me in such situations; however, it is true that the owner is an old friend of mine and I was the one who had brought you there for the first time. I had no idea whether it was the alcohol that knocked you out that

much or something else, or maybe the combination of both, but I couldn't believe it was you.—Allesya, 2010

Theme Seven: Self-destructive Behaviors and/or Suicide

Six of the eight authors had written band slash stories in which self-destructive practices and/or suicide were presented, of whom three were popular authors and three underground. Both popular and underground authors mentioned personal and professional motives for writing about the self-destruction of famous musicians, with one underground author arguing that self-destructive behaviors reflect deep emotions in the narratives, representing suffering, pain, and unfulfilled desires. Furthermore, a popular author reported that observing the struggle of others in these stories relieved her pain and helped her to overcome her personal problems. Thus, she attributed part of her successful coping strategies to her identification with her favorite band members in the panorama of fictional struggles and obstacles.

In addition, an author who identified herself as a lesbian reported that she found it challenging when she wrote a special story featuring her favorite musicians in which either character sacrificed his physical health for the sake of a relationship. The author described in detail that her story was centered on the recovery of the main character after receiving sex reassignment surgery. This decision was made by the main character himself, who did not wish to become a woman but felt he had no choice after falling in love with someone who could not love him as a heterosexual man. The author considered this sacrifice a total destruction of the self, in which the reconstruction of sexual identity is deeply embedded in the context of contemporary social norms.

As seen, practical considerations such as the development of writing skills did not appear in the motivations in this theme. Instead, both popular and underground authors expressed a deep emotional involvement in these narratives, which were inspired by personal experiences in the majority of cases. This might indicate that band slash authors are more likely to write richly detailed plots depicting self-harming practices when they are personally affected. Writing about this theme in band slash might help authors and audiences to reconsider and positively reframe their experiences in the safe confines of fantasy, under more controllable circumstances.

Regarding readers' feedback, all authors reported that their readers had strong emotional reactions to stories containing themes of self-destructive behaviors. U3 stated that some of the most frequently observed reactions were "surprise, crying, freaking out, and other emotional responses." P2 reported that her readers did not understand the motivations of characters hurting themselves, whereas P1 stated that her readers were dissatisfied and wrote alternative solutions which would have led to a more optimistic ending. Furthermore, one author relayed that her readers reported feeling depressed and deeply touched by the narratives.

A popular and an underground author argued that band slash stories featuring self-destructive characters can be attractive for readers wanting to understand and explore the underlying motivations of self-harming practices, and for readers who wish to immerse more deeply in particular roles. P1 pointed out that readers often like this theme "because they would like to save the protagonist, and thereby, a little bit of themselves." In a similar vein, an underground author added that readers might need the love and attention of their environment as well, and in these stories they can become the one who receives careful attention through the identification with the self-destructive character who will be saved in the plot. This suggests that these narratives can facilitate the coping of fans with similarly destructive experiences through the identification with competent characters who successfully overcome their struggles.

Addiction

> I see her broken arms and wounded body. She is floating slowly, winks at me and then stretches herself out. I know the injected drug makes me see that. Seokjin told me that it wouldn't do me any harm if I tried it once. He has been an addict for at least half a year, because otherwise he could not have dealt with the death of his girlfriend who had died because of his actions. I told him "God forbid I ever try it." But now this is it. I couldn't let the loneliness embracing me. [*sic*]—K. Lee Anne, 2016

Theme Eight: Addictions (e.g., Alcohol and/or Drug Addictions)

Five of eight authors, three of whom were popular authors, reported that they had written band slash stories in which band members were addicted to substances (e.g., alcohol and/or drugs). Both popular and underground authors listed their motivations behind generating works featuring this theme as both personal reasons and reasons related to developing their writing skills. Two authors reported that they wanted to enrich the characters' traits with additional elements and to write band slash stories exploring addiction from a professional viewpoint. P4 admitted that her personal and work experiences motivated her to write about substance abuse, adding that this topic is extremely popular among band slash readers. Furthermore, an underground author remarked that she had never used drugs but she was always wondering what it feels like; her motivation, therefore, was to gain a deeper insight into this experience by identifying with the characters using drugs in the narrative. This motive is in line with those suggested by Jenkins (1992) regarding fan engagement in new, more complex narratives to further their understanding of the various themes featured within.

Comparing the two author groups, no relevant difference was found regarding readers' reactions to works featuring themes of addiction. P1 and U1 reported that their readers were relatively passive in their response (compared to the number of comments they received from their readership regarding other themes) and did not write any feedback on this topic, whereas P2 emphasized that her readers found the theme particularly realistic and honest in the context of celebrity life. One underground author said that a reader reported that she had cried and closed the document immediately, while her other readers simply found it depressing.

The authors suggested that this theme might be interesting for band slash readers for its naturalistic and realistic portrayal of addictions, and for the new experiences that readers can seek by identifying with characters having these problems. By observing the reactions of their favorite musicians in these stories, audiences might reduce their anxieties rooted in the fear of having the same experiences in their lives. Furthermore, they can identify with characters having a strong social support or other forms of help to overcome their difficulties, which might be lacking in the reader's life.

Discussion

The purpose of the current investigation was to explore band slash writers' motivation and reader reactions toward dark themes. There is a lack of empirical studies regarding real person slash, especially band slash, although further qualitative and quantitative research into fans' motivations and writing/reading practices would greatly extend our understanding of the positive and negative behavioral consequences of fan engagement. According to the statistics from Archive of Our Own,[5] real person slash is the fourth most popular subgenre after fan works located in the *Marvel*, *Harry Potter*, and *Sherlock Holmes* fandoms. Similarly, FicWad, which encourages the publication of both fan fiction and original stories, reported that the most popular category is Celebrities, with over 14,000 uploaded fan stories in this category (Kowalczyk, 2017). In recent years, considerable effort has been invested by media psychologists in studying the nature of celebrity worship (see Martin, McCutcheon & Cayanus, 2015, and Sansone & Sansone, 2014). These studies primarily focused on the negative consequences of high levels of celebrity worship (e.g., identity diffusion, sensation-seeking, addictive tendencies), whereas relatively little research addressed the positive impacts of fan engagement, mainly in the field of fan studies (Thomas, 2006). Building on this, the main purpose of our investigation was to gain a deeper insight into the positive and negative fan practices and coping efforts through creative activities in the emerging field of band slash studies. Drawing on the existing theoretical research in the field of slash studies, we conducted research directly into band slash authors' motivations, impressions and personal experiences with their readers, in order to provide a more nuanced understanding of this phenomenon, which allows for a data-driven argument on its implications.

As a result of this research, we were able to identify relevant differences in the demographic characteristics. Popular authors were older, had higher educational levels, and obtained prestigious jobs, similarly to the reports of Jenkins (1992) and Busse (2006a). Interestingly, only half of the respondent band slash authors reported that they were heterosexual. This relatively high proportion of non-heterosexual slash authors is similar to the findings reported in empirical studies conducted on boys' love fans, which demonstrated that only 47–66 percent of respondents identified as heterosexual (Levi, 2009; Pagliassotti, 2008; Zsila, Bernáth & Inántsy-Pap, 2015). This result could be attributed to the intersectional position of Asian band slash between the genres of slash fiction and boys' love. It could thus be considered either as a special characteristic of the present sample, or another indicator of the tension between commonly held assumptions and empirical evidence regarding the sexual orientation of slash fans, such as in the case of boys' love fans. However, more empirical research is needed to clarify this contradiction.

We could also identify relevant differences in writing techniques and habits, personal relations to preferred boy bands, and motivations between popular and underground band slash authors. However, no substantial differences were observed between the two author groups regarding their perceptions of reader reactions to dark themes. Regarding the motivations of writing band slash, the majority of popular authors stated that they had written band slash stories mainly because they found it too challenging to create and work with original characters. This is an observation in line with the suggestion of Lewis (2004) and Thomas (2006) that slash authors are motivated to improve their writing skills without needing to invest considerable amounts of time and energy into creating their own characters and fictitious story settings in this stage of their skill development. The popular authors reported preferring to pursue a step-by-step process through which they can increase their distance from real sources towards unique, complex original works.

Conversely, underground authors emphasized that their writing was a product of their appreciation for their favorite bands. They preferred to explore more (fictional or real) information about their favorite musicians, to broaden their self-knowledge by immersing in highly self-reflexive pieces featuring people they respect, and to express their enthusiasm in a supportive network of other fans with the same interest. Thus, the primary motivation for underground authors to create band slash fiction was to express their appreciation for the bands, and to explore themes and story settings which have a personal relevance for them, or which might remain hidden otherwise (e.g., a homosexual desire), in concurrence with the theories proposed by Thomas (2006). It might also be argued that underground authors gain inspiration out of the distance between themselves and their idols, whereas the popular authors drew on observations and personal impressions of their preferred bands in this creative process, since the majority of them had met their favorite musicians in person.

The most popular dark themes amongst this survey's respondents were physical and/or verbal abuse; depression, anxiety, other psychological disorders; self-destructive behaviors and/or suicide, followed by emotional harms such as blackmailing or threats, and addiction. We did not find any associations between the size of authors' readership base and the dark themes they preferred. However, popular authors indicated a relatively wider range of dark themes included in their repertoire of band slash writing compared to underground authors.

The main reported motivation for popular authors to write band slash stories centered around themes of physical aggression and suffering lay in cultivating strategies to develop their writing skills by illustrating emotions more expressively and thus contributing to character development. In contrast, underground authors reported that they intuitively drew on their personal experiences. Although all of the authors underlined that their readers enjoy identifying with characters who are facing common problems which could happen to anyone, meaningless violence without a clear function in the story was found to be undesirable—and positive solutions were always preferable and better received.

Readers commonly showed strong emotional reactions to the illness and physical suffering of characters. However, the authors pointed out that causing pain to others can gain a positive connotation in certain conditions when the approval of both partners is arranged, such as in the case of consensual sexual roleplay. Overall, the authors reported that their readers return to these themes due to their curiosity about life events that could also happen to them. By exploring works themed around these concerns from the perspective of the idols who they perceive as being strong and competent, they might reduce their own anxiety of being affected in these situations through a lack of supportive self-management techniques.

Regarding the theme of emotional harms, popular authors again argued that they gained inspiration from their studies and professional life. These experiences were transformed into a set of narrative tools, in order to make a major contribution in their narratives to character development and the construction of the story's logical structure. In contrast, the reported motivation of underground authors to dissect the theme of emotional harms in their band slash pieces was more personal. One author mentioned that she had experienced similar problems to those she generated in her works which informed the core message of the piece, whereas another author argued that writing out her negative feelings helped her to cope with them. She explained that this mechanism works by portraying far worse situations than the real ones, allowing the writer to place her own struggles in perspective. It was reported by the authors that their readers found the theme of emotional harms interesting, and they liked reading about it. Furthermore, readers often shared their personal experiences and discussed their problems with the author herself, particularly if she was perceived (or known to be) a competent helper.

Interestingly, professional and personal motivations intertwined in the further two major themes of self-destructive behaviors and addiction. When writing stories about the self-destructive and suicidal behaviors of famous musicians, both popular and underground authors reported that they gained inspiration from their studies, previous knowledge, and personal experiences. According to the authors' reports, themes of self-destruction and suicide evoked strong emotions in their readers who often cried, felt depressed, or offered alternative solutions that might have led to a more adequate way of coping with the problems depicted in the narrative. Authors also pointed out that these stories could be interesting—not only for those who are not directly affected by self-destructive behaviors but who wish to understand the underlying motivations, but also for those who have engaged in self-destructive experiences and who may want to save themselves by saving the protagonist from himself within the narrative. Thereby, readers can potentially associate themselves with fictional social support, empathy, and tenderness through their identification with band slash characters who have such a supportive background, which might also increase the efficacy of readers' coping mechanisms.

Similarly to self-destructive behaviors, the motives of popular and underground authors to write band slash stories focusing on addictions were based upon both the authors' personal and professional experiences and their observations of real-life celebrity culture. However, a minority of respondents suggested further motives, such as keeping the interest of readers by employing radical changes in the plot, or developing their writing skills. Authors remarked that band slash stories centered on addictions are popular amongst writers and readers who have never had experiences with drugs or other substances for providing a deeper insight into the lives of those musicians who may have experienced drug and/or alcohol problems.

Results of the present study indicate that authorial and audience interest in the dark side of band slash fiction may have an important role in the coping strategies of fans dealing with various psychological issues. For those who struggle with everyday or severe problems, these stories provide a site for projection in which they can reconstruct and reframe their concerns by projecting negative emotions onto their idols, and by placing them into challenging situations that actually represent the anxieties of the writer. Within band slash stories, these idols are portrayed as powerful and competent individuals who are able to successfully cope with their problems, since they possess a wide range of social and personal coping resources (e.g., success, appreciation, supportive band members, an empathic partner). These resources facilitate their successful coping in far worse situations than the writer/reader could imagine in her life. In spite of this fact, fans may perceive that their personal problems extend beyond their capacity to cope due to a perceived or actual lack of these supportive networks. However, they can observe and explore effective strategies to overcome their difficulties through the identification with their favorite musicians in band slash stories, such as finding information about seeking help, gaining knowledge of techniques which can help reduce stress (such as creative activities), and observing the consequences of different forms of adequate coping strategies (such as seeking professional help) and inadequate coping strategies (such as drug use).

In addition, band slash writers and readers create a special communicative sphere, established through a shared appreciation for their favorite bands, in which competent helpers and experienced fan authors encourage other fans to cope with their personal problems by offering an indirect assistance through their band slash narratives. While competent authors, who may have both a professional background and personal experience with these themes, use their knowledge to reframe and explore the experiences and difficulties portrayed in their stories, they also develop and integrate their self-knowledge within the text itself and within their relationships with and to their readers. The results of this investigation show that popular authors are in a more advanced stage of integrating this knowledge in their narratives and are using this to develop their writing skills, whereas underground authors focus primarily on the emotional impact of their works.

Although the current investigation was amongst the first qualitative explorations that addressed the role of dark themes in enhancing effective coping skills in band slash writers and readers, the present study is not without limitations. This study was conducted on a small sample of band slash authors, which was also specific for the cultural background (since the data collection took place in Hungary) and for the preferred boy bands. Therefore, the authors of this study are not representative of all band slash authors. Consequently, broader generalizations about writer/reader motivations are difficult to make, and a wider cultural comparison of Asian and European popular music and audiences fell out of the scope of this study. However, the analysis of cultural aspects in creating and reading band slash fiction narratives which focus on dark themes would contribute to a deeper understanding of both audience and author motivations in this niche genre. Nevertheless, the conclusions drawn from the present study may provide guidance for further empirical studies into the motivations of RPS fans to produce and read stories focusing on dark themes.

Large-scale studies are also needed to explore the associations of motivational patterns, personality traits and positive and negative psychological outcomes (e.g., depression, self-esteem) among fans. Given that research regarding the differences between fans is scarce, empirical research addressing these aspects would make a relevant contribution to the existing literature on slash fiction. By revealing individual differences between fans, the coping strategies and vulnerabilities within and in response to certain mental health concerns would be rendered more identifiable, which would make it possible to advance towards a better understanding of how slash fiction's authors and audiences use their inspiration and creativity to enhance their psychological well-being.

Conclusion

The aim of the present study was to work closely with authors of real person band slash fiction in order investigate the motivation of writers and readers in this genre to explore dark themes from an authorial perspective. The findings revealed several differences across popular and underground band slash authors regarding their demographics and motivations. The main motivation of popular authors to write band slash was to improve their writing skills, while underground authors wished to express their appreciation for the musicians, increase their self-knowledge through self-reflexive pieces, and immerse in the fan culture. In spite of the different motivational backgrounds of the two author groups, reported reader reactions showed no substantial differences regarding the depicted dark themes. Psychological harms and negative consequences (e.g., depression, addiction) were recognized as particularly popular themes among band slash writers/readers. Furthermore, it can be concluded that dark themes have an important role in this creative process and in fan engagement.

By exploring the imagined dark secrets of their favorite musicians, these authors and readers suggested that they could provide themselves with a rich set of coping resources, which can be used to help them overcome similar difficulties in their personal lives. Fans identify with strong and competent characters they respect, they reconsider and reframe their real-life experiences in fictional stories which are personally relevant to them, and they incorporate the observed strategies into their own coping process. This study highlighted the importance of this mechanism, which can possibly contribute to the psychological well-being of the authors and readers of band slash. Future research should therefore explore and address how this strategy may effectively serve fans in order to positively reframe their real-life experiences through their writing and reading practices.

Acknowledgments

We are most grateful to all of the band slash authors for their contributions in this study. This study was supported by the Hungarian National Research, Development and Innovation Office (Grant number: K111938). Ágnes Zsila was supported by the New National Excellence Program of the Ministry of Human Capacities.

Notes

1. See Busse, 2006a; Jenkins, 1992; Thomas, 2006 and Woledge, 2005 for further details.
2. Visual kei is a music movement in Japan, influenced by Western glam rock bands in the late 1980s. This movement also established a subculture, characterized by androgynous costume, make-up and hair styles, emphasizing the freedom of expression through fashion and gender ambiguities.
3. "Fan service" refers to acts or contents (in the case of visual and textual materials) which are created to please the fans. For instance, male musicians might entertain their female audience in live performances by engaging in implicitly homoerotic hints with each other (e.g. touches, glances).
4. Big Name Fans (BNF) are popular slash writers who have a relatively large readership base in a particular fandom or fan fiction community. Authors rarely identify themselves as BNFs; they instead allow readers to categorize them (Hellekson & Busse, 2006).
5. Archive of Our Own is an international project which archives fan creations (e.g., fan fiction, fan art, fan videos, etc.). The website has more than 170,000 users, who published more than 700,000 works online (Kowalczyk, 2017).

References

Allesya. (2010). *Háromszög* [*Triangle*] [Blog Post]. Blogspot.

Black, K.A., and McCloskey, K.A. (2013). Predicting Date Rape Perceptions: The Effects of Gender, Gender Role Attitudes, and Victim Resistance. *Violence Against Women, 19*(8), 949–967.

Black, R. (2004). Access and Affiliation: The Literacy and Composition Practices of English Language Learners in an Online Fanfiction Community. *Journal of Adolescent & Adult Literacy, 49*(2), 118–128. doi:10.1598/JAAL.49.2.4.

Boon, S.D., and Lomore, C.D. (2001). Admirer Celebrity Relationships Among Young Adults. *Human Communication Research, 27*(3), 432–465.

Booth, P. (2014). Slash and Porn: Media Subversion, Hyper-Articulation, and Parody. *Continuum, 28*(3), 396–409.

Busse, K. (2006a). I'm Jealous of the Fake Me. In S. Holmes and S. Redmond (Eds.), *Framing Celebrity: New Directions in Celebrity Culture* (pp. 253–267). London: Routledge.

Busse, K. (2006b). My Life Is a WIP on My LJ: Slashing the Slasher and the Reality of Celebrity and Internet Performances. In K. Hellekson and K. Busse (Eds.), *Fan Fiction and Fan Communities in the Age of the Internet* (pp. 207–224). Jefferson, NC: McFarland.

Darling Wolf, F. (2004). SMAP, Sex, and Masculinity: Constructing the Perfect Female Fantasy in Japanese Popular Music. *Popular Music and Society, 27*(3), 357–370.

Dyer, R. (2004). *Heavenly Bodies: Film Stars and Society*. New York: Routledge.

Fackler, M.F., and Salvato, N. (2012). Fag Hag: A Theory of Effeminate Enthusiasms. *Discourse, 34*(1), 59–92.

Hellekson, K., and Busse, K. (2006). *Fan Fiction and Fan Communities in the Age of the Internet: New Essays*. Jefferson, NC: McFarland.

Hills, M. (2002). *Fan Cultures*. London: Routledge.

Jenkins, H. (1992). *Textual Poachers: Television Fans and Participatory Culture*. London: Routledge.

K., Lee Anne. (2016, June 16). *Csillagok közt úszó bálna [Floating Whale Amongst the Stars]* [Blog Post]. Blogspot.

Kaplan, D. (2012). "Why Would Any Woman Want to Read Such Stories?": The Distinctions Between Genre Romances and Slash Fiction. In S.S.G. Frantz and E.M. Selinger (Eds.), *New Approaches to Popular Romance Fiction: Critical Essays* (pp. 121–132). Jefferson, NC: McFarland.

Keft-Kennedy, V. (2008). Fantasising Masculinity in Buffyverse Slash Fiction: Sexuality, Violence and the Vampire. *Nordic Journal of English Studies, 7*(1), 49–80.

Kowalczyk, P. (2017). 15 Most Popular Fanfiction Websites. Retrieved from https://ebookfriendly.com/fan-fiction-websites/.

Kustritz, A. (2003). Slashing the Romance Narrative. *The Journal of American Culture, 26*(3), 371–384.

Kustritz, A. (2008). Painful Pleasures: Sacrifice, Consent, and the Resignification of BDSM Symbolism in *The Story of O* and *The Story of Obi*. *Transformative Works and Cultures, 1*. doi:10.3983/twc.2008.0031.

Levi, A. (2009). North American Reactions to Yaoi. In M.I. West (Ed.), *The Japanification of Children's Popular Culture: From Godzilla to Miyazaki* (pp. 147–173). Lanham, MD: Scarecrow.

Lewis, D. (2004). Understanding the Power of Fan Fiction for Young Authors. *The Free Library*. Retrieved from https://www.thefreelibrary.com/Understanding+the+power+of+fan+fiction+for+young+authors.-a0114326743.

Lothian, A., Busse, K., and Reid, R.A. (2007). "Yearning Void and Infinite Potential": Online Slash Fandom as Queer Female Space. *English Language Notes, 45*(2), 103–111.

Martin, M.M., McCutcheon, L.E., and Cayanus, J. (2015). Celebrity Worship and Its Relationship to Television-Watching Motives: A Brief Report. *North American Journal of Psychology, 17*(2), 213–219.

McGee, J. (2005). "In the End It's All Made Up": The Ethics of Fanfiction and Real Person Fiction. In P.M. Japp, M. Mesiter, and D.K. Japp (Eds.), *Communication Ethics, Media and Popular Culture* (pp. 161–180). New York: Peter Lang.

Mizoguchi, A. (2003). Male-Male Romance by and for Women in Japan: A History and the Subgenres of Yaoi Fictions. *U.S.—Japan Women's Journal, 25*, 49–75.

Mizoguchi, A. (2008). *Reading and Living Yaoi: Male-Male Fantasy Narratives as Women's Sexual Subculture in Japan* [Doctoral Dissertation]. University of Rochester, New York.

Moon, D. (1995). Insult and Inclusion: The Term Fag Hag and Gay Male "Community." *Social Forces, 74*(2), 487–510.

Nanami. (2012). *A Nyomorultak* [*The Miserables*]. Anime Fanfiction Style.

Oksanen, A. (2012). To Hell and Back: Excessive Drug Use, Addiction, and the Process of Recovery in Mainstream Rock Autobiographies. *Substance Use & Misuse, 47*(2), 143–154.

Page, R.E. (2013). *Stories and Social Media: Identities and Interaction*. London: Routledge.

Pagliassotti, D. (2008). Reading Boys' Love in the West. *Participations, 5*(2). Retrieved from http://www.participations.org/Volume%205/Issue%202/5_02_pagliassotti.htm.

Rami. (2013). *Álarcok* [*Masks*]. Anime Fanfiction Style.

Roddy, K.E. (2011). Masochist or Machiavel? Reading Harley Quinn in Canon and Fanon. *Transformative Works and Cultures, 8*. http://dx.doi.org/10.3983/twc.2011.0259.

Rodriguez-Srednicki, O. (2002). Childhood Sexual Abuse, Dissociation, and Adult Self-Destructive Behavior. *Journal of Child Sexual Abuse, 10*(3), 75–89.

Rubin, A.M. (1983). Television Uses and Gratifications: The Interactions of Viewing Patterns and Motivations. *Journal of Broadcasting & Electronic Media, 27*(1), 37–51.
Sandvoss, C. (2005). *Fans: The Mirror of Consumption.* Cambridge: Polity Press.
Sansone, R.A., and Sansone, L.A. (2014). "I'm Your Number One Fan"—A Clinical Look at Celebrity Worship. *Innovations in Clinical Neuroscience, 11*(1), 39–43.
Scodari, C. (2007). Yoko in Cyberspace with Beatles Fans: Gender and the Re-Creation of Popular Mythology. In J. Gray, C. Sandvoss, and C.L. Harrington (Eds.), *Fandom: Identities and Communities in a Mediated World* (pp. 48–59). New York: New York University Press.
Thomas, A. (2006). Fan Fiction Online: Engagement, Critical Response and Affective Play Through Writing. *Australian Journal of Language and Literacy, 29*(3), 226–239.
Thomas, B. (2014). Fans Behaving Badly? Real Person Fic and the Blurring of the Boundaries Between the Public and the Private. In B. Thomas and J. Round (Eds.), *Real Lives, Celebrity Stories: Narratives of Ordinary and Extraordinary People Across Media* (pp. 171–185). New York: Bloomsbury.
Tosenberger, C. (2008). Homosexuality at the Online Hogwarts: Harry Potter Slash Fanfiction. *Children's Literature, 36*(1), 185–207.
Weaver, J.B. (2003). Individual Differences in Television Viewing Motives. *Personality and Individual Differences, 35*(6), 1427–1437.
Welker, J. (2015). A Brief History of Shōnen'ai, Yaoi and Boys Love. In M. McLelland, K. Nagaike, K. Suganuma, and J. Welker (Eds.), *Boys Love Manga and Beyond* (pp. 42–75). Jackson: University of Mississippi Press.
Woledge, E. (2005). From Slash to the Mainstream: Female Writers and Gender Blending Men. *Extrapolation, 46*(1), 50–65.
Zsila, Á., Bernáth, Á., and Inántsy-Pap, J. (2015). Yaoi-jelenség a magyar anime szubkultúrában [Yaoi Phenomenon in the Hungarian Anime Subculture]. *Médiakutató, Winter*, 55–65.

(Un)Sanctioned Bodies

The State-Sexuality-Disability Nexus in Captain America *Slash Fan Fiction*

Divya Garg

Introduction

Fan fiction has been in the news for some time now, coming out of the closet and away from the surrounding silences, secrecy and fears of ignominy associated with it until quite recently, though such perceptions remain. Due to this notoriety and fan fiction's association with smut and pornography, it may be even harder for slash fan fiction in particular to broach the walls of academia, although academic inclusion is not required to legitimize the existence of fan fiction. Despite being a derivative genre—fiction developing from fiction, in a way twice removed from reality—fan fiction often documents a marginal "history," according space to alternative voices and expressions. While slash has seen an increase in academic and popular interest because of its queering of mainstream heterosexual and heteronormative expressions of desire, one needs to go beyond the easy subversion of mere representation to understand the impact of the genre. One must examine the politics of the *kinds* of representation that fan fiction incorporates and explores within its liminal subcultural space. While fan fiction still remains largely dominated by stories of white cisgendered men in a homosexual relationship, its subversive capacity allows more and more narratives to claim space for wider non-normative forms of desire and expression. Thus, in order to question the kinds of subversion engendered within fan fiction, one needs to look at more than just the dominant interpretive paradigm within this space.

Exploring works located within the *Captain America* fandom (all media types) and primarily using fan fiction of the "Stucky" (Steve Rogers/Bucky Barnes) ship, this essay shall look at the articulation of non-normative bodies and desires within slash fan fiction, with particular respect to the State's regulation of these bodies and desires, and its production of normative bodies in accordance with its own national agenda. Largely basing my critique through the theoretical concepts of homonationalism and ablenationalism, I look at experiences of trans*[1] as a category that falls explicitly in the realm of non-normative and ambiguous sexuality and identity. As a text, *Captain America* forms an interesting standpoint for such a project because of its available readings of nationalism and State machinery at work. For the purpose of this investigation, the Marvel Cinematic Universe (MCU) has been taken as the canonical reference point of the text, though the comic origins have been kept in mind. Aiming for an intersectional incorporation of disability and sexuality studies, this essay shall argue that Steve Rogers' transformation into a super-soldier can be read along the lines of disciplining the transgressive body—whether trans, queer or otherwise. This essay also explores how Bucky Barnes' similar transformation and subsequent rehabilitation (whether successful or not) into normative society provides a more exploitative register of non-consensual disciplining; a nonconsensuality stressed through the visible marker of his Soviet-given metal arm. Bucky's disability goes beyond that which is visible on his person, yet the physical presence of his disability obfuscates the larger involvement of the domestic State, just like Steve's consent to be incorporated into the war machinery mythifies his.

Fan fiction, in articulating experiences of body dysphoria, ableism and trauma in light of the *Captain America* storyline, provides a script to read into the fissures of the dominant monomythic narratives of the homogeneous State and the bodies that it sanctions for the fulfillment and extension of its agenda. In the first part of this essay I shall explore how the script of transgenderism makes provision for such a rupture, primarily through the trope of Steve's transformation, focusing on experiences of body dysphoria. In the second half, I shall examine the discourse of disability, related to war trauma and otherwise, specifically in the character of Bucky Barnes.

Part I—"I just can't get this body to do what I want it to"[2]

When we talk about sexual subversion and non-normative bodies, it is important to look beyond the lens of representation, in order to examine the kind of experience and politics that representation seeks to make. When fan fiction queers characters, appropriating symbols for specific purposes, it makes political statements through such a project. The historical setting of the *Captain America* universe sets the background for a significant section of fan fiction which aims to do justice to period-typical attitudes to homosexuality and a different view of articulating sexual desire and gender identities. Language is the most directly affected feature of period-set fiction, as it not only points to the lack of appropriate terminology as it developed during the course of the LGBTQ+ movement, but also at the specific problem of war time censorship and anti-homosexuality laws in the military.

The good-looking, whitewashed versions of queerness that are being talked about even within the scope of slash fan fiction narratives points to the fault lines in this political project. The "Stucky" ship can be read to easily embody the symptoms of Jasbir Puar's concept of neoliberal homonationalism, which theorizes the emergence of a new normativity based on nationalism—namely, homonormativity. Homonormativity creates a norm of privileged homosexual subjects who emulate and achieve (rather than contest) the dominant heteronormative models of consumption and living. The State's recognition and incorporation of these selective queer subjects is contingent upon "parameters of white racial privilege, consumption capabilities, gender and kinship normativity, and bodily integrity" (Puar, 2007, p. xii). Homonationalism is therefore, the emergence of a nationalist homosexuality which is based on the recognition and inclusion of these privileged queer subjects at the cost of "the segregation and disqualification of racial and sexual others from the national imaginary" (Puar, 2007, p. 2). According to Puar, there are three symptoms of homonationalism which include sexual exceptionalism, queer as regulatory and the ascendency of whiteness. "Sexual exceptionalism" implies the acceptance of certain queer subjects at the cost of others within the fold of the U.S. national (hetero and homo) normativity. "Queer as regulatory" implies that treating queerness as a transgressive category by default, and thus a marker of resistance, relies on a certain notion of deviance from a "universal" non-normative, which normalizes biopolitics and hides the violence within the category of queer itself. The third symptom, that of the "ascendency of whiteness," highlights how by accepting certain queer identities at the cost of the exclusion of other ethnic communities, a white hegemony is consolidated. Puar writes, "Collectively, [these symptoms] continue or extend the project of U.S. nationalism and imperial expansion endemic to the war on terror" (Puar, 2007, p. 2).

This homonationalist thrust and the visibility of white queer heroes can be seen in the MCU and comic nationalist narratives, as well as the major stories of the white American heroes within fan fiction, hinting at the limits of the political subversiveness of "slashing" and even their particular popularity among fans. One marker of this popularity is the significant quantitative difference in the entries for the Steve/Sam ship and for the Steve/Bucky ship on major fan fiction sites and blogs (see Coker & Pande, this collection). Acting in opposition to selective, regulatory queer subjects is the increasing presence of trans*, ace and racially other characters in fan fiction, providing representation for those who are not so easily accommodated in the modern project of homonationalism. While the *Captain America* movies make big on the presence of the Howling Commandos—the most racially diverse strike unit in U.S. military history (including African American Gabe Jones and Japanese-American Jim Morita)—it is fan fiction that talks about the kind of political resistance and subversion that their existence signals of in a time of otherwise segregated units, literally and literarily moving beyond the silences of *don't ask, don't tell.*[3] In providing for colored characters' points of view and often their depiction in queer relationships, fan fiction undoes the homonationalist project that is inculcated by the canon. However, the limitedness of such narratives point to the trend of hegemonic dominance even within the subversive, counter-hegemonic space of fan fiction.

Additionally, in the chapter entitled *Docile Bodies* in Foucault's *Discipline and Punish* (1975/1977), Foucault describes how "by the late eighteenth century, the soldier has become something that can be *made*; out of formless clay, an inapt body, the machine required can be constructed" (p. 135, emphasis mine). The soldier's body is identified as the docile body which is affected through two registers, one of submission and the other of function, in order to produce a useful and intelligible body. The notion of docility lies at the center of these two registers, joining "the analysable body to the manipulable body" (pp. 135–136). Within the *Captain America* canon, Bucky Barnes and Steve Rogers can be read as having been transformed into docile bodies; while Steve is transformed, manipulated and rendered docile by volunteering for the supersoldier project (interestingly named "Project: Rebirth"), Bucky's docility as the Winter Soldier is rendered more literal through his depiction as a silent, brooding machine made to follow orders. The biopolitical dimensions of Project: Rebirth can be traced through the language used in *A Long Winter* (dropdeaddream and WhatAreFears, 2014a); Steve is reminded by Howard Stark of the financial consequences of "producing" him: "I made you. I *made you* what you are. Do you have any idea how much *you* cost?" (p. 14). Howard's language clearly dispels the idea of the heroic "emergence" of Captain America. The financial engineering rhetoric is also important because it brings attention to Steve's "un-being" before the State invested in him and erased his disability (scoliosis, color blindness, arrhythmia and asthma among others) as well as his identity, effectively making him into the ideal Foucauldian docile body. The *Not Easily Conquered* series by fan authors dropdeaddream and WhatAreFears (2014b) traces Steve Rogers' story over the Cold War years, highlighting the ineffectuality of a soldier like him in a war that was fought insidiously because he can function, but does not submit, fulfilling only *one* of the aspects of the State's desired docile body. While pre-serum Steve[4] might not have had enough screen-time in the movies, fan fiction's exploration of Steve's various ailments before his transformation brings attention to, and asserts, his disability—a transgressiveness that goes beyond the regulatory paradigm of queerness.

The transqueering of white heroes also undoes this homonationalist project by showing how only dominant marginalities are acceptable in the queer-friendly myth of America. Nonymos' *War, Children* (2015), for instance, features a pre-serum trans!Steve[5] who finds shelter with disabled war veteran Bucky. Steve's literal homelessness in the story succinctly captures the idea of the America that only accepts queerness which can be assimilated to its project of nation-building. As a trans man, Steve is unable to find shelter in any of the support systems that America has to offer its youth, and becomes the subject of further violence at the hands of the State emblematic, highlighting how the State not only fails its less dominant marginal subjects, but also adds to their oppression. Fan works which document an alternative history of queer experiences and identities, which has gone otherwise silenced and undocumented, allow for a truer "historical" telling. Narratives where the queerness of their protagonists interferes with the notion of national(ist) capabilities provide interesting ways to intervene into the canon's political incline. Within fan fiction, pre-serum Steve Rogers then becomes the queer subject who has the potential to subvert, while in post-serum Steve, the threat has been neutralized, setting him on the path of being a normative adult. The body and self become two separate states where the disjunction between the two can be used to examine the politics engendered by such a dysphoria. In post-serum Steve, the typically male conforming outside is non-threatening to the masculine and national order, while the inner self remains queer and transgressive. In Steve's articulation of his transgressive desires and state of being, fissures erupt into the dominant narrative of homonationalism.

As discussed earlier, representation is not entirely enough to qualify as subversion, and it becomes equally imperative to examine the kind of interpretive models incorporated within such representation. Replication of heterosexual paradigms, for instance, takes away from both subversive capacity as well as the uniqueness of queer desire. While the fandom often focuses on Bucky's physical and emotional transformation after his time as a traumatized, brainwashed assassin, Steve's transformation and the kind of response that it might evoke is often disregarded. For individuals who are themselves going through or looking for experiences of genderqueerness or transgenderism, Steve's body provides a site for the experience of body dysphoria.

Here, I use body dysphoria as distinct from body dysmorphic disorder (BDD) and gender dysphoria. Body dysmorphia is defined by the Anxiety and Depression Association of America (ADAA) as a "body-image disorder characterized by persistent and intrusive preoccupations with an imagined or slight defect in one's appearance" (*Body Dysmorphic Disorder*, 2014, para

5, lines 1–2). Gender dysphoria (earlier referred to as gender identity disorder or GID) is the anxiety and distress resulting from biological sex and personal gender identity differing. GID was included in the Diagnostic and Statistics Manual of the American Psychiatric Association in the 1980s, right after the depathologization of homosexuality, in a way to compensate for the deletion of homosexuality as a disorder while instating surveillance in order to prevent it (Puar, 2015). GID was replaced with gender dysphoria in 2013, acknowledging it as not being a disorder; especially relevant in experiences of transgenderism. *Body dysphoria*, then, follows the definition of gender dysphoria in the sense that there is a certain lack of correlation between the biological body and the desired/perceived (possibly but not necessarily gendered) body, and it is in this sense that fan fiction writers use it. In the case of Steve Rogers, the body is a complex site of warring desires. As an allegory for gender dysphoria, the serum would serve as a metaphor perhaps for the medical correctionism of the trans body according to the perceived/desirable identity, but as a body enhancement, the transformation is bound to carry its own set of anxieties which question the ethics of biopolitics.

As a sickly child of less than average masculine proportions, pre-serum Steve Rogers is conventionally unattractive. It is interesting to note that largely borrowing from the canonical depiction of sassy Steve, fandom Steve is also mostly comfortable in his body, though he acknowledges that others do not find him attractive. He would not necessarily be seen to display either body dysmorphia or body dysphoria. Skinny!Steve fan works then choose to show a Steve Rogers who is less than the perfect self that America chooses to identify with. The tag "Big Steve who did not experience Magical Puberty and still has ailments" on *The Stucky Library* blog acknowledges the existence of fanonical identities that retain the "lesser" aspects, perhaps providing hope for readers who carry similar experiences of "inadequacies." At the same time, an emphasis on the skinny trope can also signify the fetishization of a body type. Fan fiction is more varied than any one depiction; the plurality of the experiences available stands for the very existence of the multi-faceted experiences of individuals and the availability of corresponding multiple narratives in which to explore and reframe this.

Sincerely, Your Pal (2015) by fan author lettered, which is written entirely in epistolary format as correspondence between Steve and Bucky during the war, captures some of Steve's anxieties about his body. About mid-way into their exchange, Steve and Bucky articulate their desire for each other, and Steve's anxiety with respect to his physical transformation is based on the fact that Bucky fell in love with him when he was his "skinny" self. While the war correspondence itself is interesting in terms of how censorship required the two to be inconspicuous because of the anti-homosexuality laws and attitudes of the time (hence providing an example of fan fiction documenting alternative history), the concern about physical appearances is important to note because it is so often ignored in both canon and fanon. In the story, in a letter dated November 24, 1943, Steve iterates that his body has changed and that while he appreciates the fact that Bucky liked him as who he was in his conventionally unattractive self, he is wary of Bucky being attracted to a type and hence not finding him attractive in his new body. Steve tries to come to terms with his own dysphoria by the fact that his new body desires Bucky the same way his old one did, making him feel at home in his new body:

> Sometimes I feel like a whole nother [*sic*] person & the one way I know I'm not is I'm still yours ... when I imagine us together sometimes it's with my old self & the way you touch me sets me on fire. But sometimes it's with my new self & it's just as good, because I want someone to touch all the new parts of me & I want it to be you. You make me feel like me. But I know what you like. I've seen all the dames you were sweet on & they were a certain type.... Different people are attracted to different things, that's just the way that people are [lettered, 2015a, p. 83].

Steve's concerns are less of body image issues and more along the lines of coming to terms with his own new body, as well as about his fears regarding his new body being desirable to Bucky.

This line of thought of body transformation and how it affects desire and experiences of desire is developed further in the next work of the series, *War Is Over if You Want It* (lettered, 2015b), which is in the form of a dream that Bucky is forced to envision. A captive Bucky is asked to imagine that he is sent home from the war and everyone he loves is there, the fulfilling fantasy of homecoming that he never got. In the fantasy, the Steve that Bucky remembers—whom he *re*-creates—is his pre-serum self. Bucky's experience of his own body dysphoria (literally embedded into his subconscious) related to the loss of his arm and the modifications done to his body are coalesced with Steve's body changes and his desire for him. The voice of an unnamed operative from HYDRA (a cult organization bent on world domination which became the science division of the Nazis in the MCU) tells him:

> "You still have your arm," says the voice.
> He told me Steve is dead, but I still feel it sometimes. That *missing limb* [lettered, 2015b, p. 2, emphasis mine].

The pre-serum version of Steve that does not exist anymore becomes a metaphor for Bucky's actual missing limb; both of these have been erased as part of the war effort. The whole dream sequence is full of ruptures where Bucky remembers "real" things. When Bucky is told to imagine a time when everyone he loves is present *and* he has his arm, it shows how these two things are interconnected; because Bucky doesn't have the one, he doesn't have the other—his body change is, therefore, related to Steve's. The experience of physical loss is qualified by the experience of loss of desire. While Steve's desire for Bucky in his new body helped him deal with his dysphoria, Bucky's experience is a negative parallel of that same qualification. He cannot come to terms with either his own transformed body in a traumatic miscomprehension of the body horror of his situation, and neither can he completely come to terms with Steve's new body, and his desire and love for him in that body.

At the end of the narrative, the dream becomes a nightmare where Bucky's fears regarding post-serum Steve are realized. Steve suddenly becomes "enormous" and tells Bucky that he doesn't need him anymore. The moment fractures the dream sequence and Bucky remembers when he actually met Steve, in the middle of the war and while he still loved him, he wasn't who he wanted. The story shows a complex understanding of body and desire. Unlike most fan fiction where Bucky loves—and more importantly, is *able* to love—Steve, in whichever body, here we see an experience that does not conform to the expectation of love and desire coinciding with experiences of body configuration and trauma. This delineation of desire and dysphoria helps readers to understand the issue of consent from which these two transformations stem. Steve's body transformation may be the doing of military experimentation, but it was still his choice. In contrast to this is Bucky's similar experimentation by HYDRA, which results in his super strength and metal arm, but which also constitutes a whole other experience of trauma. Bucky's hatred and/or his inability to accept Steve's new body also provides a more nuanced reading of the consent of the act of Steve's volunteering into the super-soldier program.

If we examine Steve's transformation in accordance with the Gramscian idea of hegemony through consent and hegemony through coercion, it illustrates the idea of manufactured consent. While the former is generated through non state apparatus such as education and media, the latter involves direct state intervention—such as through the police and military. Bucky's transformation into a super-soldier is the result of direct intervention of the (foreign) State through literal, physical and mental coercion. Steve's indoctrination can be read on the basis of the work of war propaganda. Steve's desire to "prove himself" because of the perceived inadequacy of his body, however, gives his act a certain personal agency which must be acknowledged, and becomes an important idea in the transqueering allegory of his experience. Steve's act of disobeying orders in order to rescue Bucky and the other captured soldiers in the canon, a moment often stressed in fan fiction, provides one instance of his exercise of that active choice, which helps retain his autonomy in the face of his State-induced hegemonic production. The first part of the *Not Easily Conquered* series (dropdeaddream and WhatAreFears, 2014b) is centered around the emergence of Sergeant Barnes' thirteen incendiary letters written during the war, in an AU (alternate universe) where Steve survives World War II and his life provides a documentation of the Cold War era, McCarthyism and the history of the gay rights movement in America. In the narrative, the first letter is quoted right after an official historical account of Steve's rescue mission. The juxtaposition of Bucky's autobiographical account of love and desire, with a biographical account of Steve's daring act, points to the same register of love therein. Bucky's letters and the narrative style of the story, as well as Steve's consequent actions in the story, embody sites of rupture in the dominant narrative providing space for counter-hegemonic impulses. The creative space to explore emotionally charged and complex concepts of "worthiness," identity, disability, trans* and State/individual autonomy allows fan authors to assert experiences of identity in a framework that not only retains individual agency but also does justice to it.

A noticeable trend in the *Captain America* fandom allows readings of Steve's transformation as an allegory for trans* experience and to study body dysphoria in light of his responses to the physical change wrought through a scientific change. Falling in the category of "historical AU" fan works, it maps out the complexity of queer experience, replete with obsolete terminology which provides for an engagement with how identities were affirmed in a time when terminology was less fraught. Within the confines of fan fiction, Steve's *genderedness* is deliberately located within his body. In fan narratives where he identifies as a "fairy," his articulation is defined by the need to see his body as powerful and pleasurable in a particular context. Steve's inhibitions about his body are replaced by a pride in those very aspects that make him "girly," dainty and delicate, because he is able to claim a certain identity as a result of this very physical perception. He revels in his status as a "fairy" because he is able to use it to bring pleasure and power to himself and validate his experience of liking men. Such a claim is at once contradictory to the modern usage of the term and perception of such an identity. Steve's precise need for a reclamation of effeminacy is important in an age and atmosphere when progress is counted by mainstreaming identities, at the cost of excluding or demonizing others. It also provides us with a script into reading genderqueerness, given that such few forms of representations are available in mainstream culture, as well as in subcultural forms such as fan fiction. However, Steve's experience is shown to be only an individual one, and does not speak either for trans* or genderqueer individuals in general, iterating the complexity and subjectivity of experiences of sexuality and gender. While for Steve, in certain fan narratives, feminization is closely associated with having a body that others can clearly perceive as feminine, there are mentions of other people—transgendered and genderqueer people who dress in drag or become "girly" despite their otherwise masculine bodies.

Queer is a broad spectrum and slash fiction's historical AUs try to interpret queer experiences in a time when alternate identities were articulating themselves, both in public and private. Models of thinking and behaviors are therefore circumspect to otherwise problematic paradigms, and subversion within these forms therefore needs to be evaluated differently. Models of feminization in assertion of trans* identities are complicated, and these depictions themselves are often problematic. However, Steve's gradual coming into his own and coming out within fan fiction, provides for a realistic experience that may stand true to others; in certain instances, fan authors express their personal experience as "author's notes" along with their story, making the fandom space a more interactive, interpersonal and political way to share and engage with identity discourses.

Steve's body dysphoria in some fan narratives begins when his desires for sexual and social roles conflict with each other. With the news of the war breaking out, he wants to be a soldier and provide his body in service of the nation, but the soldier's body does not correspond to the idea of the feminine body. The nexus of ableism and sexuality needs to be examined in terms of the State's idea of a "normal" body. As Puar writes in *TSQ: Transgender Studies Quarterly*, using Dan Irving (2008) and Aren Aizura's (2011) argument, "neoliberal mandates regarding productive, capacitated bodies entrain trans bodies to recreate an abled body not only in terms of gender and sexuality but also in terms of economic productivity and the development of national economy" (in Puar, 2014, p. 78). Steve's body and (bodily) experience can be read in accordance to this argument. His body, the way it is, cannot accommodate the State's demands on it as well as his own desires, leading to body dysphoria in his subjective. Steve's active transformation into the State-desired body, through literal State intervention in the form of military experimentation, visibilizes not only the politics around human weaponization and the ethics of bio-engineering, but also the erasure of certain gendered and sexualized bodies in the production of the kind of abled body that is required for the nation-State. In the canon of *Captain America: The First Avenger* (2011), the first time Steve is rejected from an enlistment center, the stamped "4F" literally declares his body to be "unfit" for the purposes of the State and this is often reiterated in fan fiction. This process is repeated until Steve signs up for a program that will ensure that his body will be made fit, scientifically.

The language of *making* is in direct contrast to the language of *becoming*, which refers to the process of coming to terms with sexual and gender identity; the register of *becoming* can be used to subvert and counter the dominance and mechanics of *making*. Garner uses Deleuze and Guattari's notion of becoming to highlight how "becoming is both an ontological and an ethical position that involves movement from stable, "molar" entity to indeterminable, "molecular" nonidentity, extending beyond the limits of dominant corporeal and conceptual logics" (Garner, 2014, p. 30). The collusion of Science and State to produce conventionally, economically abled and disciplined bodies is evident through the literature of homosexuality and mental institutions. Gabrielle Owen writes, "One of the ways in which biopower regulates and disciplines trans phenomena is by locating them in the presumably pliable stage of adolescence, where State intervention appears to be developmentally natural and necessary" (Owen, 2014, p. 22). In emergency states such as war, a similar pliability can be noticed as the State infantilizes its subjects even as it makes it mandatory for them to participate in its agenda. Extending this argument, Steve's willing participation in the machinations of the State, in a story that mentions his acknowledgment of being a part of the war machine, points to the kind of Gramscian hegemony through consent involved even through direct State apparatus. While Steve's desire to fight in the war is generated because of the machinations of propaganda and civil society, the State facilitates it by indoctrinating him directly into the program and employing physical, biomechanical machinery which will make his body a suitable fighting machine, visually affecting a physical culmination of its agenda. Fan fiction then portrays a situation where the disciplined body is allowed to break out from this narrative of collusion. Steve—in his reclamation of his identity, in "becoming" who he wants to be—renders visible the systematic suppression of certain bodies and the working of the project of biopolitics, and resists that suppression.

The superhero costume itself is another site of this contention. In the exhibition entitled *Superheroes: Fashion and Fantasy* (2008), Margaret Harrison's segment *Censorship and Superbodies: the Creative Odyssey of Margaret Harrison*[6] featured representations of Captain America in drag. Michael Chabon discusses the role of superhero costumes:

> the costume—as different from the dull garb of our former existence as we have become from those abandoned selves—forms a kind of magic screen onto which the repressed narrative many be projected. No matter how well he or she hides its traces, the secret narrative of transformation, of rebirth from the confines of the ordinary, is given up by the costume [Chabon, 2008, cited by Munson, 2011, p. 4].

It is the costume that announces the identity of the hero, yet while it does allow for representation of certain repressed narratives (for example, the desire and ability of the common man to be able to save many) it also comes at the cost of other repressions. Superhero costumes have always been remarked upon for their unpractical and sexualizing nature, especially when it comes to female superheroes. However, they have always remained flashy and glamorous in order to appeal to the masses. Captain America, as the nationalist superhero literally draped in the American flag, becomes an important symbol for this repressive and expressive ideology. The Captain

America uniform is often discussed within fandom as a marker of both unrealistic military wear as well as in terms of the kind of subversive potential its bright primary shades of red, white and blue elicit in their association with stereotypical ideas of "gay"ness, identifying easy targets for violence. The immediate linking of the nation's colors to the act of violence towards certain communities recalls the nation's role in not only allowing for that violence in certain places while also making use of those very individuals for its own nation-building/asserting ends, but also in the legitimization of this project of violence. Chabon continues in the same essay:

> Superheroism is a kind of transvestism; our superdrag serves at once to obscure the exterior self that no longer defines us while betraying, with half-unconscious panache, the truth of the story we carry in our hearts, the story of our transformation [Chabon, 2008, p. 22, in Muson, 2011, p. 5].

Fan fiction reveals, to a certain extent, that this kind of transvestism is actually not subversive. It takes away the very potential for subversion that was implicit in the expressive freedom of donning a mask or a costume, as in the case of Captain America it is legitimized by the State itself and given only for the State's purposes, and largely in other superheroes' cases as well. *Captain America: Civil War* (2016) can be read in exposition of this. While Team Cap seeks to assert autonomy from State apparatus to some extent, Team Iron Man wants there to be further accountability and adherence to the State agenda. It is interesting that it is the literally State-produced hero rather than the "self-made" man (the signifying myth of capitalism) who rebels against the government, explicating Captain America's ideological position which falls in line with Steve Rogers' idea of doing right. Also, as soon as superheroes are recognized and/or sanctified by the State to any extent, they become part of the State's arsenal.

On the other hand, the idea of Captain America in drag becomes explosively subversive. It queers the idea of the nation's symbol and the nation's constitution and projection of itself as a body of able, cisgendered, heterosexual maleness. Both fan art and paintings (such as those of Margaret Harrison) do this even more obviously by providing representations of Captain America—the ideal masculine hero—in a distinctly un-masculine way, bringing to the surface a dysphoria that exists now in the mind of the viewer, especially one who has been normativized. If the superhero's costume is the politico-cultural fabric of the society that he stands for, then the queering of his costume engenders a deeper suspicion of that society and the political contingent that "he" is meant to stand for. This moment of the absolute annihilation of the dominant narrative is only articulated within the confines of the fan narrative.

Part II—"I'm Schrodinger's fucking Assassin, open the box, you never know what state I'm going to be inside"[7]

A post on Tumblr, the popular social media and microblogging platform where users are able to interact and form communities, went something as follows:

> **Anonymous asked: bucky has a disability??** [*sic*]
> [Reply]: *he doesn't have an arm* [MzMinola, 2015].

What this post reveals is that Bucky's disability is easy to forget because he is still able to fully function in a nationalist productionist narrative, especially enabled through the availability of an enhanced prosthetic which masks the history behind its induced "availability." A lot of fan fiction, for instance, completely undoes any such anxiety about the political purposes of the metal arm by having the prosthetic given by the American government in acknowledgment of Bucky's services in the war, or as a gift from Tony Stark—the most capitalist superhero in industrial America and the superhero universe. The highly problematic paradigm of an "arm" given in exchange for services rendered for the militaristic goal of American imperialism highlights the production and assimilation of the able-disabled body into the mythically inclusive and enabling nation. Bucky's narrative in the canon, then, works in tandem with the script of ableism as well as what Mitchell and Snyder (2015) term as ablenationalism.

Ablenationalism, like Puar's concept of homonationalism, outlines the idea that certain "disabled" identities are included in the American mythos at the cost of other disabled identities, in order to attest to the inclusivity of American statehood and establish the State's upholding of its mythic paradigms of liberty, equality and fraternity. Fan fiction which stresses Bucky's rejection of the arm in honor of his services, such as Nonymos' *War, Children* (2015), then pave the way for reading into this ablenationalist narrative. Mitchell and Snyder argue in *The Biopolitics of Disability: Neoliberalism, Ablenationalism and Peripheral Embodiment* (2015) that the attitude of American exceptionalism relies on the belief that disabled individuals have been successfully integrated into post-industrial society. However, the tolerance of some disabled individuals invisibilizes the exclusion of others. This privileged minority is called the "able-disabled." While canonical Bucky would fall under this category as he is *enabled* by the super-strength and the advanced prosthetic, fan fiction provides a deeper view into his status and experience as a prisoner of war, especially focusing on mental trauma as an aspect of his disability. The MCU canonical storyline sees Bucky first captured by HYDRA and experimented on during World War II and afterwards his capture by the same organization and transference to the Soviets, roughly for a period of 70 years. Bucky's torture is both physical and mental, however, and the extra abilities given to him obfuscate his physical disability and the effects of that torture. That Bucky is forcefully made into the Foucauldian "docile" body or Mitchell and Snyder's able-disabled subject, is made evident in painful detail in fan stories where HYDRA trains him to only retain aspects of the self that are useful and non-threatening to their own ends, going as far as breaking his molar teeth, removing his body hair, denying him touch and feeding him through tubes. The HYDRA production of Bucky is then similar to the State's imagined end, a point ironically highlighted in *Captain America: The Winter Soldier* (2014) where S.H.I.E.L.D (Strategic Homeland Intervention, Enforcement and Logistics Division), the American governmental intelligence agency that maintains global security, turns out to be infiltrated by HYDRA; an easy way out of the responsibility of the American government in Bucky's predicament. The tactics of surveillance and eliminating threats before they're formed through the use of artificial biopolitical power was part of the arsenal of the "good guys" but is only rejected after the nefarious involvement of HYDRA is realized. The canon does away with the ethics of the use of biopower in their ready solution of Nazism, the convenient source of all evil.

Within the tropes of fan fiction for this fandom, one major trope is the modern veteran narrative where Steve and/or Bucky are both vets. Varying storylines include one or both of them falling on hard times, calling attention to the often deplorable situation of veterans after their homecoming through the character plots of them being homeless, physically/mentally/sexually abused, or resorting to sex work. Ablenationalist workings allow access to services and resources to the able-disabled category which can produce meaningful labor, hence falling into the category of the "deserving poor." Snyder and Mitchell argue in *Ablenationalism and the Geo-Politics of Disability*:

> Disability Studies maps the coordinates of these populations [individuals not recognized as part of the "deserving poor"] in order to deepen an understanding of the degree to which disabled people find themselves "locked in or locked out" of meaningful cultural interactions with others [2010, p. 114].

Veterans suffering from PTSD and physical disabilities, who are unable to adapt to civilian life and contribute productively to the nation, may be seen as part of this population. Vet AUs in fan fiction deal in depth with these experiences and give insights into the politics of disability. In Nonymos' *War, Children* (2015) the kind of national socio-political isolation faced by Bucky, a veteran of Afghanistan, forms a stark illustration of this kind of literal locking out. In *War, Children*, Bucky has been isolated from his family and friends as well as from "normal" society through the work of his uncle—the Secretary of State, Alexander Pierce—who highlights the responsibility of the American political system directly working for the isolation of certain marginalities (both queer and disabled), and the apathy of the general public. By creating narratives that are not only able to articulate this isolating, exclusionary process of able-nationalist dictates, but which can also provide ways of overcoming the same within its narrative scope, fan fiction becomes a form of resistance to the ways of ablenationalism.

More often than not, it is Bucky Barnes who is the exhibitor of these marginalized traits, in a clear extension from the second *Captain America* movie where his body becomes the site of the soldier's suffering, both physical and mental. A brainwashed assassin whose memories are regularly erased through electroconvulsive torture, Bucky visibly carries the marks of his status as a prisoner of war in the form of his metal arm. In this context, a history of the characterization of Bucky through the comics reveals that this was a conscious theme therein. While Bucky originated as a teenage sidekick to make superheroes more relatable to their major audience, emulating the Batman and Robin paradigm, he went on to become someone more different later, considering it was wartime. Despite this, both the MCU and comics have not done justice to his character: in the first move, *Captain America: The First Avenger* (2011), Bucky gets a screen-time of roughly 13 minutes in the entire film and in the second film, *Captain America: The Winter Soldier* (2014), he has a total of five dialogues. It is in fan fiction that we discover his family, friends, thoughts and feelings, turning him into a real character rather than a trope to fulfill a purpose.

The war motif is what holds the narrative through the comics, the movies and even fan fiction; one cannot do away with the fact that Captain America and Sergeant James Buchanan "Bucky" Barnes are soldiers and everything gets defined by that leitmotif. In the comics, Bucky's character was killed during the war as he was in the movies, stayed dead for four decades and was brought back to life as recently as 2004 in the avatar of the "Winter Soldier." It is this comic arc that gets immortalized in the movies because, as Abraham Reisman puts it:

> The Winter Soldier has resonated with people because his archetype is a heady brew of mental health struggles, classic espionage tropes, America's poor treatment of veterans, an attempt to reckon with the violence of superhero comics, and male bonding so powerful that it's regularly read as homoerotic [Reisman, 2010, para 3, lines 2–5.]

All these things find fruition and representation in fan fiction, thus in a way legitimizing these feelings or at least allowing for a substantive involvement with these issues. It is in fan fiction that the darker historical links connecting the "Winter Soldier" title to actual historical war crimes[8] are done justice to and where PTSD experiences are intensively dealt with, such as in the "recovery" and "post-winter soldier" tags within fan fiction archiving, specifically.

Bucky's experimentation is easily categorized as falling under an external enemy, reducing the culpability of American imperialism. Bucky's Winter Soldier provides a direct parallel to Steve's super-patriot act, where the only difference between the two transformations and superbodies is that one was ordained by the American government and was undertaken voluntarily, while the other was a clear act of torture and brainwashing. However, Bucky's literally manufactured consent can be seen as a foil to Steve's conditioned manufactured response to the call of his country. A common trope within fan fiction has Steve's act of volunteering for Project: Rebirth portrayed as being done in order to be able to join Bucky in the war. Speranza's *All The Angels and The Saints* (2014), for instance, re-writes this act in the language of religiosity, calling his transformation a miracle in light of his love for Bucky, and such an interpretation undoes the nationalist thrust of the very formation of the icon of "Captain America." In some fan fiction, Bucky compares his love for Steve with Steve's love for his country, creating an interesting parallel behind the idea of rebirthing. While Steve is killed and resurrected in the name of his country, in works like the massively popular and influential *Not Easily Conquered* series (dropdeaddream & WhatAreFears, 2014b), Bucky reads his own actions as a hero being done for the sake of one person alone. The nationalist discourse is then challenged by the discourse of homosexual love and desire. Similarly, Steve's departure in the series from the goodness of the ideal hero, as he tears the world apart and turns to violence in his search for Bucky, operates in stark contrast to the given dimensions of his character. This gives him an agency beyond that ordained by the limiting narrative of the nationalist agenda of the canon, also highlighting the difference between Steve Rogers, the man, and Captain America, the national identity. While MCU Steve and Bucky may provide only limited scope for the political possibilities of storytelling, fan fiction Steve and Bucky provide multiple subversive ways of surpassing and resisting these defined boundaries.

Fan works such as BetteNoire's *The Murder Ballads* series (2015) provide an alternative narrative to the resulting polarized impetus of the biopolitical production of the hero and the villain/victim, where Bucky *chooses* to fight for "the enemy" (and later, as a hired mercenary) as the Winter Soldier. Bucky realizes the futility of killing in one country's name as good and the other as evil, and calls fighting for HYDRA merely as switching "one set of assholes for the other" (BetteNoire, 2016, p. 37). *The Murder Ballads* series underscores the culpability of every governmental system in the creation and sustenance of oppressive regimes and practices for the same imperialist ends. Bucky's acceptance of this allows him (and the readers) the scope to see through this culpability and create a semblance of choice for himself.

Another aspect that is stressed in order to create a very different view of Bucky is his survival instinct. In *I'm Friends with the Monster* (2016), Bucky became what he did—a super-efficient soldier working as a hired mercenary after killing off his erstwhile masters—in order to survive his harsh conditioning and torture, and as Steve informs him "surviving is not cowardice" (p. 45). Snyder and Mitchell write that "in part, these resistance strategies manifest themselves as necessitated survival strategies in response to violence and orchestrated campaigns of neglect" (2010, p. 114). Bucky's character and behavior in the story can then be seen as a way of coping with, and responding to, the exclusionary tactics of the ablenationalist State. By creating a persona that is able to enjoy his work and likes being the best at what he does, Bucky is able to assert self-agency within the mandates of neoliberal ablenationalism. At the same time, the effects of his rigorous training and torture are manifested in the form of his violent reactions to anything perceived as a threat, his extreme mistrust of others, his tendency to disassociate and his inability to assimilate with the rest of the world. Bucky's absolute refusal to become "normal" then is another instance of not giving into the ablenationalist environment embodying an "alternative strategy of non-normative living" (Mitchell and Snyder, 2015, p. 77).

Throughout the story, all the Avengers insist on the foreignness of Bucky, both in his distinctness from superheroic behavior and his "super"-humanness when he appears as just a killing machine. In a lot of fan fiction, Bucky's "Russianness" is emphasized, through his language or affiliation with aspects of Russian culture, or he is made to be Russian entirely. Since Russia is the eternal Cold War enemy of the U.S., it perhaps inadvertently serves to remind us of the un-Americanness and foreignness of Bucky—in contrast to the very American Captain America—not necessarily in a negative way in fan fiction. The Avengers provide the patriotic foil of national(ist) superheroes, the clear "good" guys, while it is insisted that Bucky can never be counted as one of the Avengers because of his deliberate refusal to fall in line with either their values, methods or their intentions. The MCU delineation of Bucky is completely different from such a projection, as is witnessed in the latest *Captain America* movie (*Captain America: Civil War*) where Bucky is visually and thematically associated with the Avengers, fighting on the side of Team Cap on the issue of the Geneva Accords and the superheroes' right to autonomy. The movie completely bypasses the issue of biopolitics and nationalism in light of Bucky's history, as well as the queer potential of his relationship with Steve.

Ways of resisting the thrust of ablenationalism include an insistence on focusing on the intersectionality of disability studies with queer and feminist discourses. Anti-normative ways of representation in cultural markers of a society, such as cinema and digital discourses, point to the failure of the inclusionary claim of nationhood. The fanon interpretation of Bucky's relationship with Steve often develops from the consequences of Bucky's inability to be included in the requirements of the able-disabled construct of production and consumption in the neoliberal market economy. The recognition of homoeroticism and fulfillment of queer desire in the homosexual relationship between Steve and Bucky is able to challenge the dominance of heteronormative paradigms of existence and sustenance, the necessary form of the reproductive ablenationalist State. Such a positivist outcome of disability narratives arising out of actualization of non-normative sexual identities and desires goes beyond the political end achieved by an oppression-discrimination model of disability.

However, not everything is easily conducive to the positivist critique of homonationalism and ablenationalism. Normative aspects of neoliberal dictates are also often replicated within the domain of fan fiction. Fan narratives often result in the reproduction of the normative family structure by portraying Steve and Bucky in the role of caregivers by adopting a pseudo-family in the form of other wayward children similarly excluded by the ableist heternormative State. More often than not, these adoptive families include individuals similarly marginalized by the dominant models of race, sexuality and gender. In this context, the family narrative is further complicated. Is such fan fiction subversive by allowing for the existence of an alternative family structure which challenges the heternormative paradigms of the dominant model, or does it add to the normativity of the same model by adhering to the mandates of homonormativity? Another trend in the *Captain America* fandom features Steve and Bucky forming a family with adoptive kids in the figures of minors belonging to certain racial, ethnic and sexual minorities, often the products of the failure of the American foster care system. Perhaps the answer lies neither in the normativist paradigm, nor in the complete annihilation of the hegemonic model, but in the questioning and engaging with the politics of such a narrative.

The trend of "bamf"[9] Bucky Barnes who delivers justice according to his own wishes, is resistant to the model of national(ist) heroism propagated by the American State, continuing on his ruthless path of vengeance, often suffering from a severe case of PTSD and even addiction. Stories focusing on Barnes' subjectivity and the aftermath of his torture at the hands of HYDRA also deal carefully and sensitively with the issue of sexual assault and trauma and its effect on the sexual and emotional lives of survivors, unsettling perceived notions of disability and trauma. A focus on artistic!Steve and Catholic!Steve within fan fiction tropes also complicates Steve's subjectivity, highlighting the divide between Captain America, the symbol, and Steve Rogers, the person; an important political project of a significant amount of *Captain America* fan fiction. Similarly, the inclusion and treatment of identities rejected by the monolithic homogeneous cisgendered White America, such as the homelessness of children rejected by the system, highlights the *abjectness* of their personhood where "the term [abjectness] refers to the process by which identificatory regimes exclude subjects that they render unintelligible or beyond classification" (Phillips, 2014, p. 19). However, "abjectness" as Kristeva sees it can be used to challenge the normativization by the system, as it "disturbs identity, system, order" (Kristeva, 1982, p. 4). Does the alternative family structure achieved at the end of such narratives then allow some hope for the thriving of non-normative and otherwise excluded marginalities, or does the familial spin of the narrative nullify the radical thrust of slash fiction's political project?

By complicating easy categorization into "resistant" or "complicit" narratives, slash fiction allows a more thorough engagement with interpretive models which unsettle the objectives of institutional systems of writing and art. Reading slash fan fiction in an analytical way, which challenges the dominant models of oppression and existence and highlights the exclusionary practices of the State, allows fan fiction to grow more subversively as a critical space. The *Captain America* comics and movies have generated significant scholarship, because of the myriad ideological connections that the project lends itself to. The *Captain America* fandom, however, allows for newer ways to delve into these workings and raise questions regarding the same, as well as providing space for more subversive engagements with the text through the creative and participatory realm of fan culture. Fan fiction need not imitate either canonical writing institutions or those of academia, and therefore, reading fan fiction asserts the revolutionary politics of its very aesthetics and non-utile teleology. The mainstream may be regulated by the constraints of what is considered socially acceptable, what is dominant and what "sells," but by allowing for non-normative experiences, the subcultural space of fan fiction questions these oppressive limits and gives voice to the otherwise suppressed. If fan fiction provides the stories that fans want to see, in ways they wish to enjoy them, the project of the "fan-as-intellectual"[10] should be to dismiss the register of utility alone and to embrace the very iniquity of fan fiction, to read these stories in ways that go beyond their examination with respect to the canon alone, and to acknowledge them as texts of pleasurable personal and political subversion in their own right.

Notes

1. I use the asterisk in order to connote the definition of trans* that includes not only identities such as transgender, transsexual, trans man, and trans woman that are prefixed by trans- but also identities such as genderqueer, neutrois, intersex, agender, two-spirit, crossdresser, and genderfluid (Tompkins, 2015).
2. lettered (2015a), p. 82.
3. Don't Ask Don't Tell (DADT), instituted by the Clinton administration in 1994, was the official U.S. State policy banning lesbians, gays and bisexual people from military service

until 2011. While the policy stated that closeted homosexual people would be allowed to serve and proceedings for investigation of sexual orientation would not be started without tangible proof (unlike the earlier situation where any hint of "queerness" was enough for a dishonorable discharge and court-martial orders) it still functioned on the paradigm of criminality, offense and silences. The U.S. military is one of the spaces where homophobia has been clearly regulated by the State, and a history of the laws (or lack thereof) governing homosexual behavior/personnel reveals the extent of this problem. The racial effects of the policy have often been ignored. Using Fear's statistics in "Draft Bill Spurs Debate" Puar writes, "From a glance at the demographics, one could deduce that those most likely to be forced into closeting by the 'Don't Ask, Don't Tell' policy given their disproportionate percentage of enlistment in the U.S. military, are men and women of color" (Puar, 2007, p. 50).

4. Pre-serum!Steve implies a Steve Rogers who did not receive the superhero serum and is therefore still afflicted by several debilitating disabilities including scoliosis, arrhythmia, color blindness and asthma.

5. The "!" implies a certain identity of the character, in this case the sexual identity of transgenderism.

6. See Bolton & Koda (2008).

7. Quoted from BetteNoire's *The Murder Ballads* series (2015).

8. The term "winter soldier" comes from the Winter Soldier Investigation This was a project by the Vietnam Veterans against the Vietnam War in 1971, bringing attention to war crimes committed by the U.S. army. There was another such project looking into the truth behind the atrocities committed by the soldiers in Iraq and Afghanistan in 2006. The Winter Soldier investigation was made into a documentary which was barely picked up by any channels and the investigation did not see any actual trials—see Riesman (2016).

9. An acronym of the phrase Bad-Ass Motherfucker.

10. Hills created the concept of the fan-as-intellectual to encourage scholars in fan studies to accept that intellectual practices can occur outside of institutionalized settings, particularly within new-media settings (Dunlap and Wolf, 2010).

References

BetteNoire. (2015). *The Murder Ballads* series. Archive of Our Own.

BetteNoire. (2016). *I'm Friends with the Monster.* Archive of Our Own.

Body Dysmorphic Disorder (BDD). (2014). Anxiety and Depression Association of America [ADAA]. Retrieved from https://www.adaa.org/understanding-anxiety/related-illnesses/other-related-conditions/body-dysmorphic-disorder-bdd.

Bolton, A., and Koda, H. (2008). *Superheroes: Fashion and Fantasy.* New Haven: Yale University Press.

dropdeaddream and WhatAreFears. (2014a). *A Long Winter.* Archive of Our Own.

dropdeaddream and WhatAreFears. (2014b). *Not Easily Conquered* series. Archive of Our Own.

Dunlap, K., and Wolf, C. (2010). Fans Behaving Badly: Anime, Metafandom, Brutal Criticism and the Intellectual Fan. *Mechademia, 5* (1), 267–283.

Foucault, M. (1977). *Discipline and Punish: The Birth of the Prison* (A. Sheridan, Trans.). New York: Random House, Vintage. (Original work published 1975).

Garner, T. (2014). Becoming. In S. Stryker and P. Currah (Eds.), *TSQ: Transgender Studies Quarterly, 1*(1–2), 30–32. Durham: Duke University Press.

Johnston, J. (Director). (2011). *Captain America: The First Avenger* [Motion picture]. United States: Marvel Studios.

Kristeva, J. (1982). *The Powers of Horror: An Essay on Abjection* (L.S. Roadiez, Trans.). New York: Columbia University Press.

lettered. (2015a). *Sincerely, Your Pal.* Archive of Our Own.

lettered. (2015b). *War Is Over if You Want It.* Archive of Our Own.

Mitchell, D.T. and Snyder, S.L. (2015). *The Biopolitics of Disability: Neoliberalism, Ablenationalism, and Peripheral Embodiment.* Ann Arbor: University of Michigan Press.

Mods. (n.d). The Library [Blog Post]. *The Stucky Library.* Tumblr.

Munson. K. (2011). *Censorship and Super Bodies: The Creative Odyssey of Margaret Harrison.* Paper presented at the PCA/ACA National Conference. Retrieved from http://www.academia.edu/1355117/Censorship_and_Super_Bodies_the_Creative_Odyssey_of_Margaret_Harrison.

MzMinola. (2015, November 10). Bucky Has a Disability?? [Blog post]. Tumblr.

Nonymos. (2015). *War, Children.* Archive of Our Own.

Owen, G. (2014). Adolescence. In S. Stryker and P. Currah (Eds.), *TSQ: Transgender Studies Quarterly, 1*(1–2), 22–24. Durham: Duke University Press.

Phillips, R. (2014). Abjection. In S. Stryker and P. Currah (Eds.), *TSQ: Transgender Studies Quarterly, 1*(1–2), 19–21. Durham: Duke University Press.

Puar, J. (2007). *Terrorist Assemblages: Homonationalism in Queer Times.* Durham: Duke University Press. Reviewed in Mendoza, V.R. (2009). *Journal of Asian American Studies, 12*(1), 128–132. https://doi.org/10.1353/jaas.0.0032.

Puar, J. (2014). Disability. In S. Stryker and P. Currah (Eds.), *TSQ: Transgender Studies Quarterly, 1*(1–2), 77–81. Durham: Duke University Press.

Reisman, A. (2016). The Story Behind Bucky's Groundbreaking Comic Book Reinvention as the Winter Soldier. *The Vulture.* Retrieved from http://www.vulture.com/2016/05/bucky-winter-soldier-history.html.

Russo, A., and Russo, J. (Directors). (2014). *Captain America: The Winter Soldier* [Motion picture]. United States: Marvel Studios.

Russo, A., and Russo, J. (Directors). (2016). *Captain America: Civil War* [Motion picture]. United States: Marvel Studios.

Speranza. (2014). *All The Angels and The Saints.* Archive of Our Own.

Snyder, S.L., and Mitchell, D.T. (2010). Introduction: Ablenationalism and the Geo-Politics of Disability. *Journal of Literary & Cultural Disability Studies, 4*(2), 113–125. http://dx.doi.org/10.3828/jlcds.2010.10.

Tomkins, A. (2014). Asterisk. In S. Stryker and P. Currah (Eds.), *TSQ: Transgender Studies Quarterly, 1*(1–2), 26–27. Durham: Duke University Press.

Not So Star-Spangled

Examining Race, Privilege and Problems in MCU's Captain America *Fandom*

CAIT COKER *and* RUKMINI PANDE

Introduction

Despite its vocal support for social justice, both fandom and acafandom continue to ignore the way race and privilege work within slash communities, especially how the vast bulk of fan fiction and art remains devoted to prioritizing white cis-bodies.[1] Fans often defend this "default," pointing to the lack of nuanced, fleshed out non-white characters in texts that attract fandom attention. However, as the Western English-language media texts that have been part of the traditional sources for media fandom have become more diverse, this argument has begun to be disproven. One example that has been enacted most recently and vividly has been in the context of the Marvel Cinematic Universe (MCU) fandom, focusing around the character of Sam Wilson. Introduced in *Captain America: The Winter Soldier* (2014)—and appearing in *Avengers: Age of Ultron* (2015), *Antman* (2015), and *Captain America: Civil War* (2016)—Wilson is Steve Rogers' close friend and ally. The popularity of the character and his relationship with Steve has caused a significant ripple in the competing "order" of Steve/Tony (Stony) and Steve/Bucky (Stucky) pairings. Sam's character and background speaks directly to all the things fandom has claimed it wanted from characters of color—diversity, acknowledgments of PTSD and trauma, even literalizing social justice through a brief mention of Sam's thwarted political run in the comics' canon. However, he is nonetheless continually erased or attacked (most infamously when a Big Name Fan in Stony fandom declared that he "had to be" part of HYDRA) specifically because he is Black, enacting narrative violence on the Black body that is an echo of the literal violence repeatedly shown to Black characters both on screen and in real life.

Further, while fandom has written extensively about social justice issues in the MCU, these explorations have inevitably centered on the character of Steve Rogers, showing him to be attuned to all kinds of social injustices from LGBT issues to economic inequality, but only seldom do they tackle the issue of race. In these narratives, Sam is continually cast in a supporting role, which is problematic in its sidelining of characters who face real-life discrimination. We can see the problem illustrated through the numbers at AO3: at the time of this writing, Steve/Tony has 17,145 fan fictions, Steve/Bucky has 23,186 fan fictions, and Steve/Sam has 1,562 (and we might even compare this to how the Tony/Loki pairing has 5,740 or the Clint/Coulson pairing has 9,173!).[2] Over and over again, idealized (though admittedly sometimes problematic) romance is limited to the depiction and consumption of white bodies. The Black body as an object of desire, whether for characters or readers, becomes an exception—and a source of controversy. In this essay, we discuss the practical and theoretical gap in the scholarship regarding race and fandom, and consider how the field of fan studies continues to reinforce the notion of fandom norms as a white and only nominally queer space—effectively Othering both fans of color and the objects of their fannish affections.

Constructing Race in Fan Spaces

The place of race/racism in fan spaces and fan studies in the contemporary moment is simultaneously characterized by a great deal of discussion as well as a resounding silence. On the one hand, there is a marked rise in instances of fans leveraging the power of social media to amplify their concerns about how popular media texts handle issues of representation of historically marginalized individuals. These efforts have spanned Twitter campaigns like #OscarsSoWhite, which saw fans and popular culture commentators protest the exclusion of non-white actors from the major award categories for the second year running, and campaigns like #GiveElsaAGirl friend which encouraged Disney Studios to debut their first queer Princess in the upcoming sequel of the highly successful animated movie *Frozen* (2013). Within fan studies, there has been steadily growing interest in the related idea of "fan activism" which is seen to be a new form of non-political civic action by fans around issues as diverse as cyberbullying to the civil war in Darfur (Jenkins, 2012; Brough and Shresthova, 2012; Cochran, 2012; Kligler-Vilenchik, 2016; Kligler-Vilenchik, McVeigh-Schultz, Weitbrecht & Tokuhama, 2012). This formulation is also in line with historical characterizations of fan spaces, especially media or participatory fan spaces, as being inclusive and progressive in their ideals and communitarian ethos (Hellekson and Busse, 2006; Zubernis and Larsen, 2012; Coppa, 2014).

However, at the same time, there is also a rise in the volume around debates concerning the operations of race/racism *within* such spaces, particularly with regard to the reception of non-white characters and their presence (or lack thereof) in transformative fan works such as fan fiction, fan art, and fan videos. This is not to say that these discussions are new; non-white fans have regularly expressed their discomfort at the sidelining or racist treatment of chromatic characters within popular fandoms. However, as fandom platforms have changed from more closed forums like mailing lists to dialogic ones like Tumblr and Twitter, this criticism has been amplified (Pande, 2016).

Another trend that has contributed to this amplification has been a small but significant widening of roles for non-white actors in the popular cultural texts themselves—Sam Wilson (Anthony Mackie) in the MCU, Michionne (Danai Gurai) in *The Walking Dead* (2010), Finn (John Boyega) in *Star Wars: The Force Awakens* (2015), etc. The continued exclusion of such characters—who are now granted both canonical primacy and the archetypal roles that fandom has traditionally flocked to in terms of fan work—is now critiqued more vociferously than ever before. This critique is met with varying degrees of defensiveness and deferral, as fans who continue to elevate white characters (even where they do not have canonical primacy) excuse their actions through a number of strategies. These include blaming larger institutional racism in society for their biases, accusing non-white fans of being "political" in their choices of fannish objects and retreating to preference-based arguments that ignore structural trends. To advance preference-based justifications for the continuing erasure of non-white characters in fandom is to argue that individual fans are simply attracted to character archetypes—the complex villain, the misunderstood loner, etc.—which are inevitably given to white actors. By this reasoning it is Hollywood's racist casting practices that are to blame for fandom's exclusions, rather than the fans themselves. This argument ignores the fact that even in the case of diverse casts in source texts—most recently seen in *The Force Awakens* (2016)—fandom frequently elevates even side white characters at the expense of characters of color in central roles. Additionally, non-white fans who do critique patterns of erasure are often accused of disrespecting communitarian norms that advocate for non-judgmental attitudes towards which characters and pairings that individuals may be attracted to within particular texts.

In response to this, and in contrast to fan studies' interest in fan activism, there has been a marked reluctance within the discipline to talk about the operations of race/racism within such spaces in a critical and sustained manner. It is crucial to acknowledge that this reluctance is not just a matter of oversight or coincidence but one that is built-in to the critical apparatuses of the field. As Rebecca Wanzo (2015) asserts, "One of the reasons race may be neglected is because it troubles some of the claims—and desires—at the heart of fan studies scholars and their scholarship" (1.4). As Wanzo points out, the foundational texts of fan studies and a strong strand of continuing scholarship have a distinctly utopic tone to their framings of such spaces. However, these conceptual framings can only continue to remain stable when the operations of race/racism within these spaces are deliberately and repeatedly set aside.

In this construction, because of their status as minorities within Western media fandoms, non-white fans are seen to interrupt normative operations of such structures only in specific contexts when they *make themselves visible.* This has mostly occurred in moments of controversy where a flashpoint situation is reached, prompting a range of critical responses from non-white fans. Such flashpoints are sometimes pan-fandom events such as RaceFail'09, which was a broad-ranging discussion of racism in Science Fiction/Fantasy spaces (Klink, 2010); and sometimes fandom-specific instances such as the treatment of the character of Nyota Uhura (Zoe Saldana) in the *Star Trek* (2009) reboot movie (Scodari, 2012). This has the effect of framing the presence of non-white fans *only* in terms of controversy, or of "being political," as the rest of the time their fannish activities are subsumed into the larger (white) norm. Racial identity is then only seen to be a relevant factor for theorizations about Western fandom communities when it is seen to be specifically interpolated by the presence of a "significant" character or issue that foregrounds explicitly the operations of *non-white* racial identity. In this framing, because whiteness is not considered a racialized identity with specific effects, its operations on fandom structures can be presented as normative. It is therefore crucial to the argument of this essay to recognize that whiteness is an undeclared yet *structuring* force in both fandom and fan studies.

Some of the key challenges to this structuring logic have come, in line with Wanzo's challenge, from Black scholars who have questioned the figure of the generalized "fan" and highlighted the erasures it perpetuates (Warner, 2014; Warner, 2015a; Warner, 2015b; Johnson, 2015; Carrington, 2016). In his study, *Speculative Blackness: The Future of Race in Science Fiction*, André M. Carrington dwells on the ways in which despite there being "a generation of cultural criticism published about the ways in which popular texts resonate with the interests of attentive, actively engaged fans and academic researchers concerned with gender, sexuality, class, national identities, and changing technologies" (2016, p. 1), it has failed to provide the tools for dealing with the effects of racial identity, particularly Blackness, within the genre. As Kirsten Warner notes in her study of Black women fans of shows like *Scandal* (2012–present), "The stark reality is that the only people who are *allowed to be visible* within fandom and *imagined to be fans* by the media industries are White men and women" (2015a, p. 33; added emphasis). Further, in her discussion of the misogynoir and anti–Blackness present in *The Walking Dead*

(2010–present) fandom around the character of Michonne, Johnson examines the embedded racism in how science fiction fan communities interact with both the archetypes and narratives that non-white characters signify. She notes:

> Representationally, we see POC [People of Colour] as stock, archetypal figures whose primary purpose is to either forward the story arcs of white protagonists or as comic relief. This sidelining of POC stories and perspectives can be reflected in SF community practices that emerge as suppressive, oppressive politics. As such, these spaces have routinely been deemed hostile to POC who attempt to participate and engage in the imaginative worldmaking processes that are central to fandom's informal philosophy of communal creation as a key tenet of SF's ethos [2015, p. 266].

The "imaginative worldmaking processes" that Johnson references can be seen to be central not only to SF's ethos but to transformative fandom as a whole. The continuing exclusion of characters of color, and particularly Black characters, from this ethos then has to be taken as seriously as do claims about fandom's subversive potential. Our case study in this essay seeks to analyze the operations of race/racism in the context of the trends sketched out in this section by focusing on the character of Sam Wilson from the MCU. He is a character that embodies the narrative tropes that have historically been seen to be generative of significant amounts of fannish output—self-sacrificing heroism in the pursuit of justice, instant chemistry with a lead male character, snark in the face of danger etc. We examine the treatment of Sam Wilson both in context of the relatively low amounts of fan work around him and in the problematic ways he is depicted within the texts that do exist. We also interview a long-time fan of color about her experiences of race/racism within participatory fandom to further elucidate these operations.

Contextualizing Captain America, The Falcon, and Sam/Steve

Numerous studies in recent years have explicated the comic book character Captain America at length (Ahmed, 2013; Dittmer, 2009; Dittmer, 2013; Phillips, 2013 and Zarin, 2013, etc.) but few have closely examined the titular character's uses of and intersections with race, aside from the notable *Captain America: Truth* miniseries.[3] Created by Jewish comic book writers Joe Simon and Jack Kirby, the cover of *Captain America #1* famously featured the Captain punching Hitler on the jaw well before the U.S. entered World War II; though the cover was dated March 1941 it was published and on sale in December 1940 (Evanier, 2008, p. 50; Thomas and Sanderson, 2007, p. 21). After World War II the title ceased publication, barring a very brief attempt to resuscitate the character in the 1950s, until Stan Lee re-introduced the character in *The Avengers* in 1963. Under Lee's leadership, Marvel Comics had a quiet agenda of liberal progressivism; however, discussions of race in the book were largely limited until the appearance of the character Sam Wilson, The Falcon, in *Captain America* #117, cover-dated September 1969. Sam was the first super-powered African-American character (unlike Gabriel Jones, a non-powered member of *Sgt. Fury and His Howling Commandos*, or Black Panther, who was super-powered but from the fictional nation of Wakanda) and would take on an increasingly larger role in the book, such that the comic was re-titled *Captain America and The Falcon* for issues #134–192 and #194–222 (February 1971–June 1978).

In the comics, Sam is introduced as a social worker with an affinity for taming and training birds—particularly his falcon, Redwing; an ability which is later expanded from mere affinity to telepathic bonding. The character's name "Sam Wilson" is drawn from the familiar American iconography of "Uncle Sam," a national personification whose historical reach goes far beyond that of Captain America. Reputedly named after a real New Yorker named Samuel Wilson who supplied American troops with rations in the War of 1812, the legend and its uses has expanded greatly since then, not least in the propaganda images encouraging recruitment into the U.S. military during World War II and after (Hicks, 2006). This connection of nomenclature is often overlooked, but in terms of popular imagery it connects Sam even more powerfully to the American ideal, especially when he took over the cowl and shield to become Captain America himself in the comics in 2014.

The MCU's Sam Wilson was also introduced in 2014 in *Captain America: The Winter Soldier.* Wilson is memorably and charmingly portrayed by Anthony Mackie, and much of the character's popularity is inextricably bound up with that of the actor. While the first *Captain America* film had performed admirably, *The Winter Soldier* was incredibly popular and catalyzed MCU fandom in a way not seen since *The Avengers* two years before. Further, the predominant ships in *Captain America*'s MCU fandom had been Stucky and Stony; the Steve/Tony fandom found its initial roots in the wake of the comic event *Civil War* in 2007, and MCU fandom adopted this ship in the wake of Bucky's apparent death in *Captain America: The First Avenger* (Coker, 2013). The tense interactions and witty banter between Steve and Tony in the earliest promotional trailers for *The Avengers* seemed to imply a similar bond, but in the wake of the actual release of the first *Avengers* film in 2012, Stony deteriorated in popularity; after the release of *Iron Man 3* in 2013, a number of fans were disappointed that Steve appeared nowhere in the film, let alone in the wake of the seeming death of Tony. Sam's introduction in *The Winter Soldier* was thus read by some as a "replacement" role, a necessary part that should nonetheless have been filled by a more familiar character rather than one who is newly introduced. However, this point of view overlooks how Sam's character background is accordingly shifted for the purpose of the film: from social worker to a veteran of the Air Force now working at the VA (Veterans Affairs) to assist fellow returning soldiers in dealing with PTSD. Sam's first encounters with Steve all hinge on the common bonding of American soldiers returning home to civilian life, with explicit parallels made between Sam's lost wingman, Riley, and Bucky, and in fan fiction these parallels are often made more explicitly as lost lovers rather than lost comrades.

We might also appreciate the timing of these events in the real world: April 2014 saw the release of *The Winter Soldier* and the introduction of Mackie's incarnation of Sam Wilson; July 2014 saw the comic book version of Wilson take up the shield as the new Captain America, and August 2014 saw the Ferguson "Unrest," in which America's troubled history of systemic racism and injustice with the legal system culminated in another police shooting of an unarmed Black man and the multiple waves of rioting and arrests that followed. The turbulent problems of race in America have simply not been this "black and white" in decades, and we should find it similarly thought-provoking that in the wake of these episodes, another prominent African-American hero has appeared on our screens—Luke Cage, a character whose superpower is impenetrable skin, and who is, in other words, a Black man who cannot be shot by police. First appearing in Netflix's *Jessica Jones* (2015), promotional materials for his eponymous 2016 series feature him gazing stolidly at the camera, wearing a dark T-shirt riddled with still-smoking bullet holes, while throughout the show itself Cage symbolically wears a hoodie as his superhero "uniform" to visually reference the 2012 murder of Trayvon Martin.

Thus it is in this context of racial and political injustice, PTSD and national alienation that we have a fandom that writes Sam Wilson in a loving relationship with Steve Rogers, and a fandom that consistently tries to erase or deny Sam Wilson altogether. While many fans who do not ship Sam/Steve and/or consistently remove Sam from their fan works are unlikely to think of themselves as racists, or even meaning any harm at all, this does not mean that their actions should go unconsidered or unremarked. Rather, it means that we should look more closely at the ways in which Sam has been used (or abused) in fan works to uncover his reception in a popular fandom. Too often the narrative in fan studies has been to read fannish space as utopia, but sadly this does not hold true when characters and writers of color are involved. To quote Sarah Gatson and Robin Reid:

> Not to speak about race, gender, class, sexuality—or being pressured not to speak—in a fandom space ends up creating the image of a "generic" or "normalized" fan. Such a fan identity is not free of race, class, gender, or sexuality but rather is assumed to be

> the default. The default fanboy has a presumed race, class, and sexuality: white, middle-class, male, heterosexual (with perhaps an overlay or geek or nerd identity, identities that are simultaneously embedded in emphasized whiteness, and increasingly certain kinds of class privilege, often displayed by access to higher education, particularly in scientific and technical fields). We're being disingenuous if we pretend that these social forces do not exist and do not affect fandom interactions, with different effects in off-line and online fandom spaces [Gatson and Reid, 2012, 4.1].

The typical producer of slash material has a similar default of white and female; the typical slash fan work valorizes able cis-male white bodies, often to degrees that can quickly become disturbing (as, for example, the expansive numbers of Kylo/Hux fan works that rehabilitate the "Space Nazis" of *Star Wars: The Force Awakens* at the expense of that film's actual POC heroes Finn and Poe Dameron). In Sam/Steve fandom we particularly see the problematic dichotomies between utopic fan spaces (with their sincere belief in fannish social justice) and the real-world racial hegemonies that continue to be enacted even on beloved fictional characters.

This Is Not a Ship War: Pushback and Problematizing Fan Response

As mentioned above, some fans met Sam's introduction to the MCU with a wariness bordering on hostility, and in some cases, actual hostility. They felt that the introduction of Sam to Steve's life effectively blocked the appearance of Tony in the film, purposefully removing opportunities for that pairing. Numerous fan works in both fiction and video that rewrite *The Winter Soldier* as an AU directly substitute Tony for Sam; a fan vid by author and YouTube user ann2who illustrating her fan fiction "Hold My Hand" uses footage from *The Winter Soldier* interspersed with footage of Tony/Iron Man from other films. Scenes in which Steve is shown interacting with Sam are largely repurposed to show Tony instead, with Sam only having a couple of brief appearances. In the fan fiction itself, Steve is backed by the entire team of the Avengers during the events of the film, with Sam relegated to a literal supporting role. For instance, rather than Steve showing up to Sam's house with only Natasha as they are on the run, he appears with the team and Sam is issued an invite: "Can't say no to the Avengers, can I?" he asks as he "smirked" and takes them into his house (ann2who, 2015a). The film scene in contrast is very different; Sam's response to Natasha's "Everyone we know is trying to kill us" is "Not everyone," and he looks outside warily as he brings the pair inside. Later in the fan story, Tony looks up Sam's record; he brings up Sam's history with the Falcon wings, rather than Sam bringing it up himself. Sam is made utterly passive to the needs of the team—a plot point rather than a character.

Other fans complained about Sam Wilson's character more directly, especially in meta discussions. Big Name Fan scifigrl47, in a post that has now been deleted, but which has been preserved through the responses of other fans to her, wondered if Sam couldn't have been a secret HYDRA agent himself:

> They [*sic*] guy who just HAPPENS to be on Steve's run? The guy with a military background who just HAPPENS to know exactly what Steve is going through? That doesn't seem a little too coincidental to you?
>
> I love Sam. I want Sam. But the writing is awfully convenient. "I just met you, now you are the lynchpin in my plan to save the world!"
>
> I just wish that they would make some sort of effort to acknowledge the rest of the big world [pangurbanthewhite, n.d].

This controversial post launched, if not a thousand ships, then an increasingly ugly war in fandom between Sam supporters and Sam detractors. Unfortunately, fan rhetoric in the community relegated this schism to being merely a ship war, rather than a crisis centered on problems of race. Tumblr user potnaps put it succinctly, stating that the debate was

> … about stopping the erasure of yet another person of color in the Marvel fandom and preventing lies and false characterizations from turning into accepted fanon. That shit was way bigger than shipping and I've been bothered for weeks that people who reblog all kinds of social justice mumbo-jumbo obviously don't understand much of it when the point of the "Sam is not HYDRA" campaign flew completely over their heads. There are people refusing to participate in all the Sam Wilson love because they think they're contributing to a goddamned ship war. That was not a ship war, and it hurts and disappoints me to see it described that way because it means that I really am a minority here, and that so few people can relate to the perspective and feelings of a person of color in the fandom that our meaningful, heartfelt actions around protecting and preserving our heroes gets cheapened and invalidated with a descriptor like "ship war" [potnaps, 2014].

Declaring the problem a ship war wasn't so much revisionist history as wishful thinking: fans like to consider fannish space utopian, and racism doesn't belong in utopia—therefore the problem wasn't racism, it was ships. This line of thinking was white privilege at its finest (or lowest), with POC fandom as its casualties.

Unfortunately, this line of thinking is also inextricably bound up with representations of Sam (and his relationships with both Steve and the Avengers) in fan fiction and fan art. Functionally this makes room for fetishizing the Other alongside active Othering; for example, fan fiction which features interracial couples like Steve/Sam often rhapsodizes over differing skin tones, aestheticizing objectification in what is ostensibly celebration, and so passively politicizing the Black body. While many of these representations are intended to be laudatory, as in tags like "Sam Wilson is a gift" or "Sam is such a great bro," in reality they reproduce troubling stereotypes or reductions. We spoke to one fan author, Rubynye, about these issues; she is a fan writer and fan artist who has been involved in fandom for decades. She also observed that the backlash to characters of color goes back much farther than just MCU fandom:

> Oh, this stuff has gone on for a long time. [With regards to] to Black characters—I remember back in my *Star Trek Voyager* days in the '90s, reading stories where Tuvok spoke in badly rendered AAVE, not as a joke but because the author was thinking that's how Black people speak. [...] And of course the Uhura wars.
>
> I saw a fanart the other day of Sam crumpling the "Sam is such a great bro" tag between his hands. I like to think "Sam Wilson is a gift" was printed on the other side. "Both are good warning labels for 'in this story Sam is here for the benefit of the real, White characters, not as a person in his own right.'"
>
> And OH MY GOD all the stuff where they reduce Sam to a Magical Negro sidekick. [...] Over time I've been fortunate to build a dash that includes works about Sam for his own sake and actual fans of his, but it's not easy" [Rubynye, private communications with the authors].

We also asked Rubynye what the character provided her as a queer woman of color:

> Besides writing a pairing so obvious it started with a meet cute and closed out both movies [*The Winter Soldier* and *Civil War*], I really love Sam Wilson because he's a vet and works in mental health and fights intelligently (as a "human fighter jet," with strategy), all these things still not considered "typical" for a Black person to do that we are abundantly capable of doing. I love how he demonstrates that. Similarly, by giving him an attraction to men I can, among other things, talk about the existence of queer Black people, another group typically considered a contradiction. [...] Plus, getting to write someone who's Black means I get to use physical descriptors I inhabit: the texture of our hair, the deep tones of our skin, and so on. I can write a gentle resistance to the idea that White features are "normal" [*ibid.*].

However, in the wake of the release of *Captain America: Civil War*, fandom's reactions were divided and, indeed, mirrored the schisms between the characters. In a series of private posts on LiveJournal (which we were given permission to quote from), she shared her frustrations. In a May 2016 post entitled *The Discouraged Fangirl*, she wrote,

> MCU fandom is kind of painful right now. Certainly not a place to relax and have fun. _Civil War_ fractured the fandom. #GiveCaptainAmericaABoyfriend is just shipping wrapped in a thin and appropriative veneer of pseudo-progressiveness, as can be seen by the exclusion of Sam Wilson (among others) from candidacy [Rubynye, 2016a].

While in a way Rubynye's words reflect an attitude in fandom that is shared by many, they nonetheless emphasize the alienation that fans of color can and do feel in fannish spaces *every day*. And here, we feel it important to emphasize, once again, that this alienation is not a rare occurrence to a specific individual or a specific fandom, but is rather part of a systemic and ongoing process of erasure and gaslighting.

Tags and Tropes

In this section, we will analyze some structural aspects of Rubynye's experience of race/racism in fandom spaces. As has been demonstrated, these usually take the form of affective arguments that facilitate the continued projection of media fandom spaces as generally liberal and progressive in their politics, except for isolated events. This is also reflected in the informal arguments circulated within these spaces that it is "unfair" to target them for racist trends because their participants are largely powerless to effect change. It is also argued that castigating participants, who are already marginalized in terms of their gender and often their sexuality, for their choices in the realm of popular culture where they retreat to "escape" is an ineffective way to create the stimulus for change.

As we have argued, these choices and freedoms are also very heavily contingent on axes of identity apart from gender and sexuality. It is also not useful to frame these criticisms as "activism for change" as that construction places any fan work that does deal with non-white characters as automatically motivated by a desire to "score social justice points," rather than as participating in a communal fandom exchange of pleasure. As this essay focuses on digital fan practices, it is important to note how the digital infrastructure of fandom is not neutral towards such individuals. This is a key aspect of our arguments, as it is often claimed that such infrastructure allows fans with diverse needs from fandom texts (whether across the racial, sexual, or able spectrums) to co-exist in communal spaces. It is also often lauded for its organizational capacity that is reactive to specific needs of participants. A logical conclusion is that correct usage of such infrastructure allows for a successful curation of fandom experience. Busse and Gray (2011) note this usage, stressing fan creativity within it:

> [...] fans use wiki software, blogging platforms such as LiveJournal.com, or bookmarking sites like Delicious.com in very specific ways: Livejournal.com, for example, was never intended to serve as a story archive, yet many fans developed specific workarounds such as newsletters, announcement communities, and particular tagging and bookmarking systems to customize the site for their particular use [2011, pp. 434–435].

This careful curation of fan work can, however, create an echo chamber for its users, reenforcing narrative defaults rather than just straightforwardly celebrating diversity.

Alexis Lothian (2013) also notes the specific politics of fan archival activity highlighting how the establishment of standalone fan advocate organizations like the Organization for Transformative Works (OTW) and its affiliated influential fanworks archival website—ArchiveOfOurOwn.com (AO3)—has affected questions of the conservation of subcultural digital ephemera. Further, the rise of Tumblr as a platform for fannish activity has also lead to changes in the way fandom digital infrastructure functions. While there are certainly other platforms that also host fanworks such as Wattpad.com, Fanfiction.net and sites for specific fanworks from non–English language fandoms, Tumblr and AO3 are two platforms that have formed the basis of much of contemporary fan studies research.

The parallel processes whereby racial identity is both a structuring force while also being invisibilized in the workings of digital environments has been the object of study for several scholars in the field of internet studies and digital humanities (Everett, 2002; Nakamura, 2002; Sinclair, 2004; Taborn, 2007). The operation of racial identity in the digital structures of internet-enabled platforms is therefore often felt as an exception when it is named as such and when it enters into spaces read as "neutral" but in actuality where whiteness has been centered. These operations are largely parsed in rhetorical structures that query "Why are you bringing race into this?" as if this is an additive—and further, disruptive—aspect of experience in what was up until then a "universal" one. In this context, it is also vital to see how these structures affect the usage of subcultural, digital ephemera in media fandom spaces as well. The ways in which fanwork is accessed, tagged and archived with whiteness as structuring force becomes inescapably foregrounded even for users who might wish to curate and filter their experiences in accordance with commonly accepted fandom etiquette.

Following on from the analyses of fandom tagging practices as outlined above, it could be speculated that these practices allow users to select only the content they wish to see, allowing for the smooth operation of fandom axioms such as "Ship and Let Ship." However, in practice, these tagging structures often foreground the level of erasure that non-white characters undergo within such communal spaces. For instance, in the cases of both Tumblr and more fanwork-focused archival websites like AO3 that focus on fan fiction, tagging a piece of content is geared towards finding an audience for it. While fanwork is usually created for free, within a "gift economy" it is also created within an expectation of appreciative feedback and the accrual of positive social capital (Fiske, 1992; Hellekson, 2009; Scott, 2009). Both platforms allow the use of free-form tags, which means that any combination of words or letters can be used as a description. It must be noted here that Tumblr's frequently tweaked search algorithms, which order such tagged content, make definitive judgments about their functioning difficult and frequently outdated.

Nonetheless, in most cases fan-creators tag their content according to the source text it is based on, the characters that feature in it and the pairings on which it is focused. Further tags are sometimes used as warnings for specific aspects of the fanwork but these are more subjective.[4]

AO3 has a more structured tagging etiquette, and volunteer fans, called tag-wranglers, classify free-form tags as general tags if they reach a certain level of usage. The site also encourages the classification of fan work by the media text or texts on which it is based, as well as the specific characters and pairings. Warnings are optional, although certain ones such as those that signal issues of consent are classified as "Archive Warnings." If a user chooses specifically not to warn for such content, this information is also listed. Fan writers often use the "Additional Tags" section to write free-form descriptions of the content or use the "Author Notes" sections to list any additional information that they would like readers to know.

In terms of access to filtering options, Tumblr does not have a specific structure that allows users to block out content but there have been additional add-on programs created by other users, such as Tumblr-Savior, that allow specific content, if tagged, to be blacklisted. AO3 also does not have specific options to filter out pairings or characters listed within fan works, though this can be achieved through creative use of the general search feature. In this case as well, individual users have come up with add-ons specific to the site that allow for more targeted filtering, but these are not part of the site itself.

In theory, these strategies (if followed in good faith) are seen to be adequate for the smooth functioning of fandom spaces, allowing fans to seek out or avoid specific content. In practice however, racist aggressions remain very much inbuilt into these very strategies. Within AO3 for instance, there is no way of indicating which pairings are the focus of the story and which ones are merely referred to in the background. This has led to consistent complaints from fans of femslash pairings, which are often included in a tokenistic fashion in pieces of fan fiction that are mostly focused on juggernaut male slash characters. While this may be combated to some extent by these fans choosing specific fandoms where there is a primacy of women characters in fan works, such a strategy is generally not available to fans of non-white characters even when they have a primary role to play in the source texts (Pande and Moitra, 2017).

This may seem to be an inevitable reflection of broader issues of fandom racism but this structural visibilization also has specific effects. To refer back to Rubynye's reflections on the way specific tags become highly fraught for fans of non-white characters, "Sam is such a good bro" which seems celebratory of his role in actuality becomes a coded erasure and recognizable microaggression. Indeed on both Tumblr and AO3, the "Sam Wilson" tag becomes a battleground that makes the experience of being interested in his character on a fannish level an exercise in combating racism.

To examine the operations of this on Tumblr, it must be noted that tags are often used to start conversations or find content and like-minded fans of specific characters or pairings. While a level of disagreement over character and narrative is to be expected in such a large communal space, this is elevated to an entirely different level when it comes to non-white characters. In the case of Wilson for instance, it was found that a disproportionately large amount of the fanwork, meta-essays and headcanons that had Wilson tagged, featured him exclusively in a supportive and secondary role to white characters such as Steve Rogers. His positioning within the canon as a counselor for U.S. war veterans (being one himself) was also leveraged for the benefit the white characters around him, reminding one suspiciously of the "mammy" stereotype[5] that haunts Black characters in particular. While it may be argued that his secondary positioning in the canon itself leads to this sidelining, it must be pointed out that this "natural" sidelining only seems to affect non-white characters. Indeed, fandom's intense focus on white characters like Agent Coulson—who gets even more limited screentime than Sam Wilson and yet is tagged in 9341 pieces of fan fiction as part of a primary pairing on AO3—points to the hollowness of this line of reasoning.

On AO3, a curation of content around Sam Wilson's character proceeded along this secondary status as well. There was little point in searching for content by the character tag, as none of the top-rated works of fan fiction that had Wilson tagged featured him in any meaningful way. Narrowing down further, it was only within the specific pairing tag of Steve Rogers and Sam Wilson that there seemed to be any probability of finding work featuring the latter as a fleshed out character, echoing the findings in the previous section as well. In the process of attempting these combinations, it was made apparent in the tagging structures that there were more works of fan fiction focusing on the pairing of Steve Rogers and Darcy Lewis (a heterosexual pairing of two characters that have never even met in the MCU canon) than on *any* pairing involving Wilson.

To place this finding in more context, even if the possibility of Sam Wilson becoming part of the juggernaut pairing in the fandom or even coming close to the popularity of the main slash ships (again Steve/Tony currently has 17,145 fan fictions, Steve/Bucky has 23,186 fan fictions) is discounted completely, there still could be an expectation of his character gaining a relatively strong secondary status. This expectation would be buttressed by the knowledge that AO3 has a statistical bias towards hosting fan fiction focused on male character relationships. For Wilson to fail to be generative of more material than even that of a heterosexual pairing around characters who have never even met in canon is especially damning of his status within fandom.

This quantified proof of the systematic erasure of Wilson's character also must be put into context with the intertextual communal spaces of fandom that, as we have explicated earlier, foreground discussion of social justice issues. These discussions are particularly incisive when it comes to critiquing the failures of entertainment conglomerates like Marvel and DC to grant primacy to non-white characters in their franchises. It is therefore not surprising that fans of non-white characters would find the hypocrisy evident between these two positions to be jarring. It also must be noted that in terms of options to deal with these micro and macro-aggressions, there are few options to adequately "filter" experience. If the "Sam Wilson" tag itself never has any content with him in a primary capacity, the experience of exploring his character in the communal spaces of fandom loses much of its escapist or pleasurable potential.

Conclusions

What we hope to have shown with this case study is that fan spaces are not as utopic as conventional studies claim and are, indeed, far from it. The slash fandoms and pairings which are valorized as representative and progressive instead reinforce a problematic continuity of systemic racial inequalities, and "celebrations" of specific characters can be seen as anything but even-handed. While the case of Sam Wilson shows the divisions within slash-centric fandom in prime relief, he is only a single example, with the fannish responses to Uhura, Michonne, and Finn (among others) being just as problematic across other spaces and just as worthy of being examined more closely. We must likewise acknowledge that the rhetorics of fan-policing—whether direct fan shaming or discourse that minimizes or reframes protest—are used against fans of color as a silencing tactic, with broader implications for how we should reconsider the fannish "default."

Finally, it is also vital to note that though the move to more open-ended and dialogic platforms like Tumblr and Twitter have amplified these concerns, these articulations are not new. Non-white fans have consistently identified patterns of erasure and/or demonization that only come into effect in the case of characters of color—across fandoms, pairings and character archetypes. We urge that these critiques be seen in the form of a continuum, rather than framed as an occasional controversial flashpoint in otherwise smoothly functioning fannish spaces. This would facilitate the recognition of fan spaces as always already fraught environments for non-white fans and further, enforce a reconsideration of generalized "universal ideas" of "safe spaces" or "fans-as-marginalized." It is our contention that only by paying attention to the ruptures and "exceptions" within these ideals can fan studies produce nuanced scholarship that is appropriately reflective of its contemporary nature.

Notes

1. Fan studies has a conspicuous race problem, one we have examined in our individual and collective work, and one that our essay in this collection also interrogates. It would therefore be remiss of us not to observe that the title of the collection—*The Darker Side of Slash Fan Fiction*—holds within it a very specific racially coded connotation about what constitutes "light" and "dark"—one that is a linguistic carryover from western dualisms indicative of hierarchical power structures including, but certainly not limited to, race. Arguably, the phrase has been assimilated into popular usage (not least by the *Star Wars* franchise), and the symbolic meaning of words or phrases are used within fandom in innocence and ignorance. However, this doesn't change their history or their impact on people today. To talk about "the dark side" as synonymous with problematic or ugly content is to reflect the racialization of language and how it can be used as a weapon by some. Since we specifically talk about racism in fandom and fan fiction in the essay that follows, we felt that it would be appropriate for us to point out this dichotomy, and offer readers a chance to unpack how they perceive "darkness" in fandom and in academic inquiry.

2. All fan fiction data was collected on September 20, 2016.

3. See Ryan, 2011. The *Truth: Red White, and Black* arc ran as a seven issue series in 2003. It introduced the "secret history" behind the super-soldier serum that was used on Steve Rogers in the 1940s; it was developed after testing on African American soldiers. The testing had clear parallels to the real world Tuskegee Experiments in which, under the auspices of the U.S. government's Public Health Service, numerous African American men (and their wives) went untreated for syphilis despite being told otherwise. In the comics, the first iterations of the supersoldier serum give the men mutations that later culminated in death, and only one subject—Isaiah Bradley—survives, but his side effects are diminishing mental capabilities. By the present day of the story, Bradley and his family have largely been ignored by the U.S. government, but he remains a hero to the black community; montage images show his room covered in photos of Bradley with numerous famous Black men and women from throughout the twentieth century, including MLK, Jr., Malcolm X, Muhammad Ali, and Nelson Mandela. In the conclusion, Steve returns to Bradley the Captain America uniform that Bradley had briefly stolen from Steve in the 1940s to liberate a Nazi concentration camp (a sequence that suggests further parallels between the American government's history with eugenics and medical experiments and that of Nazi Germany) and they take a photo together; a visual reconciliation of America's ideals with its own past. Popular response to the series was laudatory; in his book-length study *Super Black: American Pop Culture and Black Superheroes*, Adilifu Nama wrote, "*Truth* admonished the reader to incorporate the experiences and histories of black folk that paint a different picture of the cost and quest for freedom and democracy in America" (2011, 118).

4. One of the most influential discussions is known as "Trigger Warning Debate 2009." Among the issues discussed were the highly personal nature of triggers and to what extent authors' responsibility to warn readers of potentially triggering themes extended. Some commentators saw the demands as a form of censorship, especially when multiple issues that ranged from consensual BDSM sex to sexual assault were being grouped together. The pejorative association of warnings with specific "morally gray" areas, such as pairings that revolved around individuals with high age differentials or uneven power dynamics were also discussed. These debates are far from over, though warnings or at least notes that warn readers that the writer specifically chooses not to warn, are now more common (Trigger Warning Debate, 2009).

5. The "mammy" is a racialized stereotype that portrays Black characters, and especially Black women characters, as desexualized caregivers that has its roots in U.S.A. slavery (Brown Givens and Monahan, 2005; Woodard and Mastin, 2005).

References

Abrams, J.J. (Director). (2009). *Star Trek*. United States: Paramount Pictures, Bad Robot.

Abrams, J.J. (Director). (2015). *Star Wars: The Force Awakens*. United States: Lucasfilm, Bad Robot.

Ahmed, M. (2013). Captain America, Watergate, and the Falcon: Rediscovering the American Dream? *Intensities: The Journal of Cult Media, 5*, 151–176.

ann2who. (2015a). *Hold My Hand*. Archive of Our Own.

ann2who. (2015b). *Hold My Hand* [Online Video]. YouTube.

Black, S. (Director). (2013). *Iron Man 3*. United States: Marvel Studios.

Brough, M.M., and Shresthova, S. (2012). Fandom Meets Activism: Rethinking Civic and Political Participation. *Transformative Works and Cultures, 10*. http://dx.doi.org/10.3983/twc.2012.0303.

Brown Givens, S.M., and Monahan, J.L. (2005). Priming Mammies, Jezebels, and Other Controlling Images: An Examination of the Influence of Mediated Stereotypes on Perceptions of an African American Woman. *Media Psychology, 7*, 87–106. http://dx.doi.org/10.1207/S1532785XMEP0701_5.

Buck, C., and Lee, J. (Directors). (2013). *Frozen*. United States: Walt Disney Animation Studios.

Busse, K., and Gray, J. (2011). Fan Cultures and Fan Communities. In V. Nightingale (Ed.), *The Handbook of Media Audiences* (pp. 425–443) Sussex: Blackwell.

Carrington, A.M. (2016). *Speculative Blackness: The Future of Race in Science Fiction*. Minneapolis: University of Minnesota Press.

Cochran, T.R. (2012). "Past the brink of tacit support": Fan Activism and the Whedonverses. *Transformative Works and Cultures, 10*. http://dx.doi.org/10.3983/twc.2012.0331.

Coker, C. (2013). Earth 616, Earth 1610, Earth 3490—Wait, What Universe Is This Again? The Creation and Evolution of the Avengers and Captain America/Iron Man Fandom. *Transformative Works and Cultures, 13*. http://dx.doi.org/10.3983/twc.2013.0439.

Coker, C.H. (Producer). (2016). *Luke Cage* [Television series]. United States: Netflix.

Coppa, F. (2014). Fuck Yeah, Fandom Is Beautiful. *The Journal of Fandom Studies, 2*(1), 73–82. doi:10.1386/jfs.2.1.73_1.

Darabont, F. (Producer). (2010–). *The Walking Dead* [Television series]. United States: AMC.

Derecho, A. (2006). Archontic Literature: A Definition, a History, and Several Theories of Fan Fiction. In K. Hellekson and K. Busse (Eds.), *Fan Fiction and Fan Communities in the Age of the Internet: New Essays* (pp. 61–78). Jefferson, NC: McFarland.

Dittmer, J. (2009). Fighting for Home: Masculinity and the Constitution of the Domestic in Tales of Suspense and Captain America. In L.M. Detora (Ed.), *Heroes of Film, Comics and American Culture: Essays on Real and Fictional Defenders of Home* (pp. 96–116). Jefferson, NC: McFarland.

Dittmer, J. (2013). *Captain America and the Nationalist Superhero: Metaphors, Narratives, and Geopolitics*. Philadelphia: Temple University Press.

Evanier, M. (2008). *Kirby: King of Comics*. New York: Abrams Books.

Everett, A. (2002). The Revolution Will Be Digitized: Afrocentricity and the Digital Public Sphere. *Social Text, 20*(2), 125–146.

Feinberg, S. (2016, April 27). After #OscarsSoWhite, the Academy Struggles with Diversity, Age and "Relevance." *The Hollywood Reporter*. Retrieved from http://www.hollywoodreporter.com/features/oscarssowhite-academy-struggles-diversity-age-885633.

Fiske, J. (1992). The Cultural Economy of Fandom. In L.A. Lewis (Ed.), *The Adoring Audience: Fan Culture and Popular Media* (pp. 30–49). London: Routledge.

Gatson, S.N., and Reid, R. (2012). Editorial: Race and Ethnicity in Fandom. *Transformative Works and Cultures, 8*. http://dx.doi.org/10.3983/twc.2011.0392.

Hellekson, K. (2009). A Fannish Field of Value: Online Fan Gift Culture. *Cinema Journal, 48*(4), 113–118.

Hellekson, K., and Busse, K. (Eds.). (2006). *Fan Fiction and Fan Communities in the Age of the Internet: New Essays*. Jefferson, NC: McFarland.

Hicks, T.A. (2006). *Uncle Sam*. Malaysia: Marshall Cavendish Corporation.

Jenkins, H. (2012). "Cultural Acupuncture": Fan Activism and the Harry Potter Alliance. *Transformative Works and Cultures, 10.* doi:10.3983/twc.2012.0305.
Johnson, D.D. (2015). Misogynoir and Antiblack Racism: What "The Walking Dead" Teaches Us About the Limits of Speculative Fiction Fandom. *The Journal of Fandom Studies, 3,* 259–275. doi:10.1386/jfs.3.3.259_1.
Johnston, J. (Director). (2011). *Captain America: The First Avenger.* United States: Marvel Studios.
Kligler-Vilenchik, N. (2016). Decreasing World Suck: Harnessing Popular Culture for Fan Activism. In H. Jenkins, S. Shresthova, L. Gamber-Thompson, and A. Zimmerman (Eds.), *By Any Media Necessary: The New Youth Activism* (pp. 102–148). New York: New York University Press.
Kligler-Vilenchik, N., McVeigh-Schultz, J., Weitbrecht, C., and Tokuhama, C. (2012). Experiencing Fan Activism: Understanding the Power of Fan Activist Organizations Through Members' Narratives. *Transformative Works and Cultures, 10.* doi:10.3983/twc.2012.0322.
Klink, F. (2010, May 17). *RaceFail: Race and the Fantastic.* Retrieved from MIT Comparative Media Studies/Writing: http://cmsw.mit.edu/racefail-race-and-the-fantastic.
Lackner, E., Lucas, B.L., Reid, R.A. (2006). Cunning Linguists: The Bisexual Erotics of Words/Silence/Flesh. In K. Hellekson and K. Busse (Eds.), *Fan Fiction and Fan Communities in the Age of the Internet: New Essays* (pp. 189–206). Jefferson, NC: McFarland.
Lee, S., Thomas, R., Kirby, J., et al. (2011). *Captain America Omnibus Volume 1.* [nk]: Marvel Comics.
Lee, S., Thomas, R., Kirby, J., et al. (2016). *Captain America Omnibus Volume 2.* [nk]: Marvel Comics.
Lothian, A. (2013). Archival Anarchies: Online Fandom, Subcultural Conservation, and the Transformative Work of Digital Ephemera. *International Journal of Cultural Studies, 16,* 541–556. doi:10.1177/1367877912459132.
Morales, R. (2009). *Captain America: Truth.* [nk]: Marvel Publishing.
Nakamura, L. (2002). *Cybertypes: Race, Ethnicity, and Identity on the Internet.* New York: Routledge.
Nama, A. (2011). *Super Black: American Pop Culture and Black Superheroes.* Austin: University of Texas Press.
Pande, R. (2016). Squee from the Margins: Racial/Cultural/Ethnic Identity in Global Media Fandom. In L. Bennett and P. Booth (Eds.), *Seeing Fans: Representations of Fandom in Media and Popular Culture* (pp. 209–220). New York: Bloomsbury.
Pande, R., and Moitra, S. (2017). Yes! The Evil Queen Is Latina. *Transformative Works and Cultures, 24.* http://dx.doi.org/10.3983/twc.2017.908.
pangurbanthewhite. (n.d.). People Would Rather Think… [Blog Post]. Tumblr.
Phillips, F. (2013). Captain America and Fans' Political Activity. *Transformative Works and Cultures, 13.* doi:10.3983/twc.2013.0441.
potnaps. (2014, May 17). That Was Not a "Ship War" [Blog Post]. Tumblr.
Reed, P. (Director). (2015). *Antman.* United States: Marvel Studios.
Rosenberg, M. (Producer). (2015). *Jessica Jones* [Television Series]. United States: Netflix.
Rubynye. (2016a, May 27). The Discouraged Fangirl [Blog Post]. LiveJournal.
Rubynye. (2016b, August 19). Do I Still Deserve This Icon? [Blog Post]. LiveJournal.
Russo, A., and Russo, J. (Directors). (2014). *Captain America: The Winter Soldier.* United States: Marvel Studios.
Russo, A., and Russo, J. (Directors). (2016). *Captain America: Civil War.* United States: Marvel Studios.
Ryan, J. (2011). Truth Made Visible: Crises of Cultural Expression in "Truth: Red, White, and Black." *College Literature, 38*(3), 66–96.
Scodari, C. (2012). "Nyota Uhura Is Not a White Girl": Gender, Intersectionality, and Star Trek 2009's Alternative Romance Structures. *Feminist Media Studies, 12,* 335–351. doi:10.1080/14680777.2011.615605.
Scott, S. (2009). Repackaging Fan Culture: The Regifting Economy of Ancillary Content Models. *Transformative Works and Cultures, 3.* http://dx.doi.org/10.3983/twc.2009.0150.

Sinclair, B. (2004). *Technology and the African-American Experience: Needs and Opportunities for Study*. Cambridge: MIT Press.
Taborn, T. (2007). Separating Race and Technology: Finding Tomorrow's IT Progress in the Past. In A. Everett (Ed.), *Learning Race and Ethnicity: Youth and Digital Media* (pp. 39–60). Cambridge: MIT Press.
Thomas, R., and Sanderson, P. (2007). *The Marvel Vault: A Museum-in-a-Book with Rare Collectibles from the World of Marvel*. [n.p]: Running Press.
Trigger Warning Debate. (2009). In *Fanlore*. Retrieved from http://fanlore.org/wiki/Trigger_Warning_Debate_(2009).
Wanzo, R. (2015). African American Acafandom and Other Strangers: New Genealogies of Fan Studies. *Transformative Works and Cultures, 20*. http://dx.doi.org/10.3983/twc.2015.0699.
Warner, K.J. (2014). The Racial Logic of Grey's Anatomy: Shonda Rhimes and Her "Post-Civil Rights, Post-Feminist" Series. *Television New Media, 16*(7). doi:10.1177/1527476414550529.
Warner, K.J. (2015a). They Gon' Think You Loud Regardless: Ratchetness, Reality Television, and Black Womanhood. *Camera Obscura, 30*, 129–153. doi:10.1215/02705346-2885475.
Warner, K.J. (2015b). ABC's Scandal and Black Women's Fandom. In E. Levine (Ed.), *Cupcakes, Pinterest, and Ladyporn: Feminized Popular Culture in the Early Twenty-First Century* (pp. 32–50). Urbana: University of Illinois Press.
Whedon, J. (Director). (2012). *The Avengers*. United States: Marvel Studios.
Whedon, J. (Director). (2015). *Avengers: Age of Ultron*. United States: Marvel Studios.
Woodard, J.B., and Mastin, T. (2005). Black Womanhood: Essence and Its Treatment of Stereotypical Images of Black Women. *Journal of Black Studies, 36*, 264–281.
Zarin, B. (2013) The Advocacy of Steve Rogers (aka Captain America), as Seen in Hetrez's "Average Avengers Local Chapter 7 of New York." *Transformative Works and Cultures, 13*. doi:10.3983/twc.2013.0443.
Zubernis, L., and Larsen, K. (2012). *Fandom at the Crossroads: Celebration, Shame and Fan/Producer Relationships*. Newcastle upon Tyne: Cambridge Scholars.

When the Omega Empath Met the Alpha Doctor

An Analysis of the Alpha/Beta/Omega Dynamics in the Hannibal *Fandom*

LAURA CAMPILLO ARNAIZ

This essay is dedicated to Dr. José Luis Martínez, DO, Ph.D., and his brilliant team, who saved my life after two surgical malpractices.

Introduction

SHELDON: I meant ALL women are slaves to their biological urges. Even you. You're a slave.
MRS. DAVIS: I'm a what?[1]
SHELDON: I'm just saying at a certain point in a woman's menstrual cycle…
MRS. DAVIS: Whuh-ah! Woah! You can't talk about that, either, Dr. Cooper. Your language is entirely inappropriate, and I'm gonna advise that you shut your mouth right now.[2]

As Kristina Busse argues in *Pon Farr, Mpreg, Bonds and the Rise of the Omegaverse*: "There can't be only one explanation for why fans enjoy Alpha/Beta/Omega fan fiction, or even one description that encompasses all the stories" (2013, p. 321). Indeed, it would be difficult to explain what motivates fans to write and read this type of fan fiction, since Alpha/Beta/Omega (A/B/O) stories do have a wide spectrum and trying to identify reader engagement would be a tricky—not to mention presumptuous—field of research. However, the popularity, success and demand of these stories is evident; A/B/O ranks among the most popular kinktropes included in slash fan fiction, whether the narratives are loving and nurturing or dark and abusive. Meta-commentator destinationtoast has published some very relevant statistics about the use of tags by fan fiction writers on Archive of Our Own (AO3)—an open-source, non-profit, fan-run central hosting site established by The Organization for Transformative Works (OTW)—identifying that works marked with the Alpha/Beta/Omega Dynamics tag generally receive a significantly higher average number of kudos than the archive's overall median (destinationtoast, 2014, images 1 and 3).

In a modest fandom such as *Hannibal* (focused mostly on the 2013–2015 NBC TV series, but also on the Thomas Harris books and the several movies adapted from those), of 15,416 works filed at AO3 at the time of writing, 619 stories focus on an Omegaverse storyline, which represents a total of 4 percent of all of the *Hannibal* fan writing production on the website. In order to determine which fandoms were most actively producing Omegaverse fan fiction on Archive of Our Own, I conducted a search of the relevant Omegaverse tags (including "Other Tags: Alpha/Beta/Omega Dynamics" and similar and synonymous tags/subtags such as Alpha/Omega). This revealed that the *Hannibal* fandom appears to be ranked tenth out of the fandoms with the highest proportion of A/B/O-themed story generation on AO3, with the *Supernatural* (3,039), *Teen Wolf* (1,660) and the *Sherlock* (1,596) fandoms occupying the three first ranking positions.[3]

The *Hannibal* fandom's presence grew exponentially with the broadcast of the first episode, generating a significant output of Omegaverse-tagged fiction, with the majority of these stories tending to be of a very dark nature. This is nothing surprising given the themes and topics of the series, and taking into account that the main character is Dr. Hannibal Lecter, a genius psychopathic killer, cannibal and gourmet who ranks as the most famous villain in the American Film Institute's *AFI's 100 Years of Heroes and Villains* (2003).[4] In a more recent list published by *Rolling Stone* in 2016 regarding the "40 Greatest TV Villains of All Time," Dr. Lecter occupies a decent #18 position, making the first half of the list (Collins, 2016).

As a character, Hannibal Lecter may be familiar from movies such *The Silence of the Lambs* (1991), where he was portrayed to perfection by Anthony Hopkins who won an Oscar for his performance in the film. In the NBC TV series, which is focused on events years before *The Silence of the Lambs* and based on Thomas Harris' first thriller *Red Dragon* (1981), a younger Dr. Lecter (portrayed by Danish actor Mads Mikkelsen) has left his surgical practice and become a brilliant forensic psychiatrist. He is known for being an exquisite cook and patron of the arts, although his serial killer activities as the infamous "Chesapeake Ripper" are only known to the audience and uncovered too late by the rest of the characters of the TV series. Dr. Lecter develops a keen and dangerous interest in his antagonist, patient and "friend" Will

Graham, a gifted if mentally troubled FBI profiler played by English actor Hugh Dancy.

A loner who lives isolated with only the company of his rescue dogs, Will's ability to assume the thoughts and mental state of murderers is of great help to the FBI in order to solve particularly gruesome murder cases, although Graham's "pure empathy," as it is described in the series, takes a heavy toll on his sanity. Fueled by Dr. Lecter's vile and purposeful manipulations, Will is driven by his Machiavellian psychiatrist to the point of insanity, therefore losing all of his agency in the series and being incarcerated for Dr. Lecter's crimes at the end of Season 1. It is little wonder that a mentally unstable character such as Will—fragile, isolated and unhealthily attached to Dr. Lecter, in whom he trusts until the bitter end—becomes such an attractive character in Omegaverse narratives; he already appears in the canon as a naïve misfit who easily falls prey to Dr. Lecter's masterful machinations. The inherent power imbalance between these two characters, a canonical fact in the TV series, therefore becomes particularly significant and kinky in A/B/O dark slash fan fiction.

Given that this collection of essays explores non-normative eroticism within slash fiction and its associated online communities, and seeks to explore stories which create and maintain unequal paradigms, I have chosen two stories from the *Hannibal* fandom—*Sweet as Peaches on the Tongue* (2013) by Dangereuse and *Alter* (2014) by luvkurai—which, as a hundred many others, dynamite the concept of slash as a form of egalitarian romance. This essay will contend that readers and authors alike engage with these violent and abusive narratives to satisfy a host of very dark and controversial female sexual fantasies. Furthermore, it will explore the rationale of inviting feelings of powerlessness, unlovability and humiliation to paradoxically gain control over them and convert them into pleasure through writing and reading. However, it is firstly important to consider the following: what is A/B/O slash fiction anyway, and where did it come from?

Star Trek—*Always* Star Trek

Although the writers at *Fanlore* speculate that the A/B/O kinktrope originated in the *Supernatural* (SPN) fandom with the story *I Ain't No Lady, but You'd Be the Tramp* (2010) by tehdirtiestsock,[5] I would argue that its origin can very well be traced to the TV series *Star Trek* (The Original Series, 1966–1969). The first episode of the second season, *Amok Time* (1967), was written by the prolific and successful science-fiction author Theodore Sturgeon, who received (among others) the science-fiction Nebula Award and Hugo Literary Award. In the episode Spock is undergoing *pon farr*, a hormonal condition

Vulcans experience periodically throughout their adult lives; a biological imperative that forces them to mate or die. Captain Kirk is shocked by this revelation, but Spock explains that there are precedents in nature, such as "The giant eel birds of Regula Five [or] on your Earth, salmon, they must return to that one stream where they were born to spawn or die in trying [...]" (Sturgeon and Pevney, 1967).

Spock then, as Dr. Sheldon Cooper points out in the introductory quote, is a slave to his biological urges; urges he cannot control or escape. The idea of biological determinism is clearly introduced in this episode—an idea that is at the center of A/B/O fan fiction. As all viewers of *Amok Time* know, Spock never took T'Pring as his wife at the wedding ceremony in Vulcan, instead fighting Kirk (seemingly to Kirk's death), thus relieving himself of his mating lust through the battle. The resolution of Spock's *pon farr* with Captain Kirk, his disavowal of T'Pring and his very uncharacteristic beaming smile when he realizes that Jim is not dead, only helped to buttress the Kirk/Spock relationship further. In its essence, then, *pon farr* deals with a biological imperative that the characters cannot escape; a heat cycle that they must undergo, very much like primates, canines, horses and other mammals in the animal world.[6] This heat/rutting season in A/B/O fan fiction reveals a direct link with ethology that must be analyzed in order to proceed any further.

Ethologically speaking, if we think about a group of primates, the alpha is the highest ranking individual of the social group and has preferential access to food and sex. Betas are usually second in command to the reigning alpha, and omegas belong to the lowest caste of the social hierarchy. Omegas are expected to remain subordinate to everybody else, to be submissive and to stay at the end of the food distribution channel. These animals are usually used as scapegoats by the community, as outlets for frustration, and they are sometimes even alienated from the social group. Something obvious derived from this ethological description is that alphas and omegas can never interchange their roles; they can never be equals and will always remain in an immovable position of dominance/submission. If the alpha male dies, a beta will likely take the opportunity to take his place (or challenge the alpha during rutting season for the apex position) but omegas—bound by their status and biology—will always remain constrained in the lowest caste possible.

If we think back to *Amok Time* it is obvious that the female T'Pring takes the role of the omega of the episode, with Kirk and Spock acting as two opposing alphas when fighting for her during the wedding ritual. Captain Kirk, with the help of Dr. McCoy, is the winner of the battle and therefore remains the alpha of the USS Enterprise, whereas Spock continues as his second in command (beta), or, as some could argue, as his omega. This inherent inequality is crucial in A/B/O slash fiction; ruled and defined by their biological roles, human alphas and omegas traditionally interact in an inflexible social hierarchy based on the superiority/dominance of the alphas and the inferiority/submission of the omegas. As is the case with primates, the human protagonists of traditional A/B/O stories can never be equals, and their roles can never be interchanged. In this way, far from an idealized, egalitarian romance between its characters, Omegaverse is defined precisely by the contrary: by its inequality, classism, sexism, racism and an unbreakable social system in which the omegas are oppressed simply by being born omegas. Biological Determinism, therefore, is the notion which informs this ethology-based but fictional situation in A/B/O stories.

Biology Is Identity Is Destiny

Biological determinism was a concept established during the nineteenth century, and the notion owes much to pre-scientific ideas about European imperialism and the slave trade. Associated with the Italian physician Cesare Lombroso and his theories on phrenology and criminality, the concept fueled the birth of social Darwinism and eugenics. In the form of "Craniology," it was used to justify and defend the inferiority of women and rationalize, through a pseudo-scientific method, many sexist, racist and classist concepts. The idea, which is a fallacy that states that biology does absolutely dictate human behavior, resonated powerfully in Freud's statement "Anatomy is Destiny" (Freud, 1912/2014),[7] and it has lived through various resurgences during the last decades of the twentieth century in the fields of biology, neuroscience and politics. Examples of the highly contentious and bigoted ideologies of biological determinism would be to say, "Women are born to raise children and not go to work," "We can abuse animals because Nature put us humans in charge," or "People of African descent are inferior because of their higher risk of developing sickle-cell anemia." This concept surprisingly still appears in some contemporary attitudes nowadays, in TV talk shows, blogs and radio programs, among others.

Books shockingly written by women, such as *The Respect Dare: 40 Days to a Deeper Connection with God and Your Husband* (2012) by Nina Roesner, link the injunction "Wives, submit yourselves to your own husbands as you do to the Lord" (Ephesians 5:22, New International Version) with the modern professional woman and wife. To some, this results in a celebration of the husband/wife communication, and to others it results in a sexist book which preaches to women that they should be subservient to men, no matter the cost. The best-selling *Fifty Shades* trilogy "reveal[s] Christian's systematic use of abuse (e.g., stalking, intimidation, controlling behaviours, social isolation) to dominate Anastasia, consistent with national definitions of intimate partner violence" (Bonomi, Nichols, Carotta, Kiuchi & Perry, 2016, p. 140). Millions of readers[8] have been drawn to a narrative that depicts a violent, abusive and unhealthy relationship based on domestic abuse, which neglects the needs of the victim and disempowers her over time.

Real life cases (such as the one concerning accusations of domestic violence between musicians Chris Brown and Rihanna or the case of Amber Heard, who settled a domestic abuse case against Johnny Depp in 2015) have also made the news recently. Public opinion was divided after Ms. Heard released information regarding Mr. Depp's terrifying abuse, then finally released a joint statement with her husband published by the magazine *Variety* in which the couple stated: "Our relationship [was] always bound by love" (Khatchatourian, 2016, para 8, line 1). The examples given here not only reflect a lack of cultural understanding about the extremely complex and incredibly subjective reasons shaping why victims report that they loved or continue to love their abusers, but are also embedded in a societal narrative which upholds and maintains the patriarchal status quo. They exemplify an old but still deeply rooted view regarding the fact "Biology Is Identity Is Destiny."

This idea has been fiercely contested by feminists, particularly by Evelyn Reed. In her conference *Is Biology Women's Destiny*? which later was published on *The International Socialist Review*, Reed considers that "nature is held responsible for having condemned females to everlasting inferiority" (1971, p. 7), due to the fact that their reproductive organs and capacity handicap them and make their motherhood dependent on the superior male to provide for her and her young. Let us not forget that this pseudo-scientific argument which, as Reed denounces, "exonerates a sexist society and justifies the oppression of women on the ground of their biological makeup" (p. 8), was also held by none other than Charles Darwin—who considered women as being biologically inferior to men (Bergman, 1994, p. 2). Reed then asks the audience the following rhetorical questions: "why should women fight against their oppression and seek their liberation when their troubles flow from their genetic makeup? What good will it do to change society if women cannot change their biology?" (Reed, 1971, pp. 9–10). The author concludes that such thinking reduces humans to the animal level, and this is precisely the scenario that we have in A/B/O stories; humans reduced to their base animalistic behaviors and biological urges. Alphas take the role of studs and omegas the one of breeders: "purring and panting, covered in a thin layer of sweaty omega pheromones as his body surrender[s] to the mating."[9]

Meta-fiction on A/B/O stories has been widely written and published across a variety of fan spaces, notably by author norabombay who turned her nearly 10,000 word long meta-essay *Alphas, Betas, Omegas: A Primer* (2012) into her master's thesis. Although there is variation among the physiology, behavior and mating rituals between alphas and omegas in fan works, a general set of features are almost always associated with them.

Traditionally, alphas are larger, aggressive and very possessive. In darker slash fiction, alphas usually display an arrogant, derisive attitude towards almost everybody—rival alphas, betas and particularly omegas. They typically occupy the higher echelons of power, and are found working as politicians, CEOs, surgeons, and professors. Alphas undergo a rut cycle and they are extremely sensitive to the omegas' pheromones. When an alpha smells an omega in heat, he may make a formal courtship proposition if we find ourselves reading a gentle A/B/O story, or he may simply and bluntly rape the omega without any further concern or remorse if we are reading dark Omegaverse stories. The latter of these narratives are often accompanied by and filled with disturbing trigger warnings that include dubious consent, nonconsensual sex, rape, forced impregnation and sexual slavery. Since alphas have enlarged genitals with animalistic characteristics, it is usually the norm to find these stories also accompanied by warnings of bestiality, knotting and breeding.

If alphas have the upper hand in dark A/B/O stories, omegas suffer all kinds of abuse in these—physical, emotional and especially, sexual. Endowed with vestigial external sexual organs, omegas are smaller, submissive, nonaggressive and, in general, docile towards their superior alphas. They reek sexual pheromones when in heat, something which makes them easy prey for any and all alphas, so they usually try to mask their characteristic odor and omega status by using suppressants. These are usually chemical-based (such as pills, injections and deodorants) to prevent heat/hormonal activity—although some alphas can smell through them and may expose the omega, who is usually trying to pose as a beta as to avoid notice. In addition, omegas leak a messy sexual discharge when their heat is approaching. They can be impregnated and will deliver a litter of pups if their pregnancy comes full term. This scenario, loving and nurturing in gentle Omegaverse narratives, has a bleak side in darker slash fiction; alphas may literally buy virgin omegas with a dowry or settle an arranged marriage so that their thoroughbred alpha bloodline continues into the next generation. In some stories, omegas are so rare that they are kidnapped and presented to the tribal alpha leader for his personal sexual use, and in some others the unlucky omega is simply part of the trousseau of the previous household—something which objectifies and reduces him to mere chattel or a piece of furniture to be owned by his new alpha. Bought, hunted, rented, auctioned and sometimes even killed for fun, omegas are typically sexual slaves to the alphas in dark Omegaverse.

The key of the matter lies in that alphas and omegas share two unique traits: (1) their inherent social, emotional, physical and intellectual inequality and (2) their biological imperative to mate no matter the cost. When in rut or heat season neither can control their bodies or their urges, like the lust-blinded Spock of *Amok Time*. The scenario of the alpha/omega mating is full of tropes and clichés; it usually lasts around three to five days, during which neither party has control of themselves and will let their animalistic behavior and primal urges take over reason and logic. The alpha will breed the omega over and over again, and his knotting will ensure higher chances of impregnation. If the omega is unruly or doesn't submit to the mating, the alpha may use his superior strength and physical violence to subdue him; biting, clawing into him, pinning him down or forcefully raping him. There is pain, blood, tears and a great deal of suffering and agony involved in dark Omegaverse mating, so the next question that follows should be: why do female authors and readers love this dark kinktrope and write so much about it? The question is especially relevant since omegas undoubtedly stand for females in A/B/O slash fiction and they are as excessively mistreated as many women in real life situations—women who suffer all kinds of violence against them for the simple fact of being born a woman. The fallacy of biological determinism should presumably deter fans from writing, reading and reveling in these kinds of stories, yet dark Omegaverse slash fiction continues to attract women immensely. Why?

Sexual Fantasies

It is my contention that the great success of dark A/B/O fan fiction is owed to the trope's fulfillment of very dark and controversial female sexual fantasies.[10] In their study *In and Out of Daydream: Attachment Orientations, Daily Couple Interactions and Sexual Fantasies*, Birnbaum, Mikulincer and Gillath consider the obscure nature of sexual fantasies and the two questions these generate: "What are the underlying functions of sexual fantasies? And what guides their content?" (2011, p. 1398). Relying on Bowlby's Attachment Theory, they explain that when attachment figures are not reliably available during childhood, children develop defensive strategies for coping with their absence; attachment anxiety or attachment avoidance. "These early-developing working models," they argue, "guide interpersonal interactions over the entire life span. As such, they shape the regulatory functioning of the later-developing sexual system" (2011, p. 1399). These ideas reflect Stanley Siegel's in his book *Your Brain on Sex: How Smarter Sex Can Change Your Life* (2011b), and are explored in his series of articles entitled *Intelligent Lust* (2011a). One of these articles—*What Our Fantasies Say About Our Past*—is particularly relevant for this discussion; Siegel states that unresolved conflicts or unmet needs from our childhood are intertwined "into our sexuality, encoding them in the erotic images and narratives of our fantasies in an unconscious attempt to gain mastery over them, turn[ing] painful emotions into pleasurable ones" (2011a, para 5, line 2).

In my opinion, there are two main groups of phantasmatic manifestations which recur in dark A/B/O narratives and which can be defined as sexual fantasies. These fantasies are ones that slash fiction authors and readers explore together, in order to obtain control over them. Firstly, dark Omegaverse is defined by intense feelings of powerlessness or helplessness. By default an omega is a powerless, sometimes even illegal being, condemned by his biology to a permanent state of helplessness. He has no control over himself, his heats or his behavior, and needs a superior alpha to guide his life, offer protection and make decisions for him. Following Siegel's assertions, by inviting and experiencing these eroticized feeling of submission, discipline or humiliation as adults, as actively producing and consuming fans we paradoxically gain control over them, turning painful memories and frightening concerns into pleasurable experiences in an unconscious attempt to minimize their pain.

Secondly, dark Omegaverse is characterized by deep feelings of inadequacy and unlovability. By definition, an omega is not a partner to be loved, but a vessel to continue the alpha blood line and fulfill the many sexual needs of his alpha. His pheromone reeking is inconvenient; his constant cycles awkward; his uncontrollable sexual discharge embarrassing. Dark slash omegas have little to no self-worth or self-esteem compared to their superior alphas, and their existence is predicated at best on a genetic accident and at worst on a tiresome necessity. When we eroticize feelings of worthlessness or inadequacy, we come up with sexual fantasies involving submission, humiliation and abuse. Yet, once again, Siegel insists that by sexualizing and inviting these feelings, "we become in charge of [them] and through the sexual pleasure we receive, we weaken the impact of childhood pain" (2011a, para 28, line 10).

It is my assertion, therefore, that one of the possible reasons why authors and readers create and consume dark A/B/O stories could be that this genre offers the possibility of engaging with sexual fantasies to gain mastery over a host of deep-rooted negative feelings. These feelings of helplessness, humiliation, worthlessness and unlovability—feelings which almost all people have experienced at some point in their lives—are both explored and exploited in dark Omegaverse in order to allow fans to feel in control of them. This cathartic experience is anonymously and safely realized in websites around the Internet, where authors and readers can freely express and exorcize their darkest demons through these abusive, brutal and regularly non-consensual scenarios. The sexual gratification that authors and readers can obtain from this kind of slash fiction allows a liminal space which transforms painful memories and experiences into pleasurable, escapist, satisfying fantasies in which they are in control from beginning to end.

It may be worth considering if dark Omegaverse slash fiction, with its descriptions of excruciatingly detailed and shocking sexual fantasies, is a reflection of the social reality both fan fiction authors and readers have experienced within an unequal and discriminatory patriarchal society. Although this matter is open to discussion, negative representations of the self may ultimately be so ingrained in the cognitive makeup of authors and readers that they (consciously or unconsciously) seek opportunities to gain mastery over them, even if it is only in the realm of sexual fantasies and popular dark slash stories.

Sweet as Peaches on the Tongue

When selecting the stories for this study to explore these interpretive theories, I established the following criteria: firstly, I would only focus on stories published on AO3, since of the main fan fiction platforms available (LiveJournal, Fanfiction.net, Tumblr or Wattpad) AO3 is the best organized—and its tagging system allows the use of a powerful search engine to yield reliable results. Although AO3 may lack a major historical fannish presence compared to some older websites, the organization of tags, comments, bookmarks, kudos and hits permits easy searching and analysis of archival trends. Secondly, the stories selected for my study would have to have well over 1,000 kudos (a metric of reader approval—AO3's equivalent of a "like"), meaning more than a thousand different readers had read the story at least once and liked it. *Sweet as Peaches on the Tongue* (2013) has been bookmarked 399 times, has 1,730 kudos at the time of writing and has received 188 comments left by readers—the overwhelming majority of which are of a very positive nature.

Written by fan author Dangereuse during the first season of the NBC *Hannibal* TV Series, this is without doubt one of the most popular dark A/B/O stories in the *Hannibal* fandom. Inspired by another (now orphaned) A/B/O story, Dangereuse chose to make Will a minor, thereby increasing the kink factor and moral wrongness of the story—something she is very well aware of and extensively warns her readers about in a note at the beginning of the work. AO3 encourages creators to use a Warning System before publishing any work, the logic being that warnings can attract some readers who are looking for specific content and also alert and forewarn readers who are trying to avoid that content. Warnings are not screened by the AO3 management team and are left to the discretion of creators, but authors are urged to mark at least one, or a combination of the following, mandatory warnings when uploading a story:

(1) Chose Not to Use Archive Warnings
(2) Graphic Depictions of Violence
(3) Major Character Death
(4) No Archive Warnings Apply
(5) Rape/Non-Con
(6) Underage Sex

Many more warnings may be uploaded by fiction authors, making the specific content of their stories easy to search and find. In this way, reading experiences are both flexible and customizable to suit the needs of users.

Dangereuse chose two of the AO3 mandatory warnings when publishing her work ("Rape/Non-Con" and "Underage") accompanied by other warnings such as: "Taking advantage of a minor," "Humbert!HumbertHannibal," "Lolita!Will," and "Will is Hannibal's Nymphet" (Dangereuse, 2013, Author's Notes). By including these highly morally questionable trigger warnings, the author herself is consciously identifying her story as exceedingly problematic, something which may actually warn off—or attract, given the instant success of the story—any number of readers. As a matter of fact, several readers commented it was the literary allusion to *Lolita*[11] which caught their attention and made them read the story. It is not unusual to find underage characters in A/B/O slash fiction (after all, the younger the omega, the more fertile) and this kinktrope in particular, together with virginity, is very popular in dark Omegaverse fiction. There may be any number of reasons for this, but I feel a strong candidate may be the relatively young age of some fan authors and readers. According to meta-commentator and statistician centrumlumina, the majority of the respondents to her 2013 AO3 Census were among 16 to 25 years old, with the median age being in the 22–24 range (2013, para 7, line 3). Early, even teenage, sexual experimentation and intercourse (whether satisfactory or not) may well have lead many writers and readers to have a particular interest in exploring and reframing these issues in dark Omegaverse slash fiction.

Sweet as Peaches on the Tongue can be defined as the typical dark A/B/O story, wherein a rich alpha gentleman (Dr. Hannibal Lecter) comes across a very young, virginal omega (Will Graham) by accident. Hannibal is depicted as an alpha predator with a strong sense of entitlement; an arrogant serial killer on the prowl for a new victim in the poorest areas of Louisiana. He smells "the perfect little prey" standing at a fuel station: "an omega boy, no more than sixteen or seventeen" (Dangereuse, 2013, p. 4). Hannibal resolves to claim the boy and take him in his approaching heat, so he hunts Will back to his home, where Will's father (a beta) informs Dr. Lecter that his son is pure—meaning he's untouched and has never been through a heat.

In a mockery of a courtship ritual, Hannibal demands that proof of such a claim is satisfied. Will strips bare for him and Dr. Lecter examines him intimately, being satisfied that he is indeed a virgin omega. The dowry is settled—Will's father wants thirty thousand for his boy, but Hannibal makes a counter offer; "I will give you thirty-five under the condition that the courtship will be concluded today and his guardianship will be conferred to me—effective immediately" (pp. 13–14). Will's father is satisfied and the boy agrees to leave with Dr. Lecter. Will, who hasn't spoken a word during the whole story, not even when his most private parts were being inspected, speaks now to ask if he can take his books with him. The boy hasn't finished high school, and he is intent on getting his diploma, something Dr. Lecter forbids: "You will come to me with empty hands, as is tradition. I will provide. [...] You are mine now" (pp. 16–18). Hannibal's first kiss and his alpha saliva trigger Will's heat, so Dr. Lecter rents a bonding suite before reaching his home in Baltimore in order to take his boy. The mating process is described in excruciating detail; Hannibal disrobing Will, feasting on his young, virgin body, enjoying Will's tears from the pain of the first penetration and biting him forcefully on the nape when the boy can't take his knot—until Will finally submits. The story ends with the couple happily together in bed, with Will purring in submission and Hannibal possessively grabbing him in his arms.

From beginning to end, *Sweet as Peaches on the Tongue* openly revels in an explicit classism and a caste system where alphas are at the apex of the social hierarchy and omegas are commodities to be bought, bred and owned. The narrative is strongly rooted in notions of biological determinism—referred to in the story as "the natural order of things" (2013, p. 7), something which makes it quite impossible for the alpha and omega to be equal or for them to develop an egalitarian romance. Furthermore, the language used to describe, label and define the virginal Will—"a prey" (p. 4), "a fine peach" (p. 5), or "such exemplary stock" (p. 13)—debases him as a human being and reduces him to the status of a mere object. As the story is told from Hannibal's point of view, it's not just him who sees Will as a consumable commodity; as readers, we are equally encouraged to view Will on Hannibal's terms in the narrative. Some readers picked up on this narrative decision and wondered, as the story went on, if Hannibal would be able to resist such temptation or give in to it. Phrases such as "It's not unlike the response of a doe freezing in front of a superior foe" (p. 11) invite a sense of impending doom between the two characters, and establish a prey/predator dichotomy which reinforces their distinctive biological urges and the inescapable inequality between them. A few readers commented they were anxiously expecting for Will to be thrown into the hands of the proverbial wolf, and praised the author for making Hannibal so in character by not making the doctor view his mate as a person.

Dr. Lecter is depicted as a thoroughbred alpha; a snob and a possessive, selfish predator who will have his prize at any cost. He doesn't intend to love Will, to marry him or make him his bonded mate—he is only focused in satisfying his alpha lust in and on him, and to own the boy in every sense of the word. In keeping with the canonical character of the TV series, the Hannibal of *Sweet as Peaches on the Tongue* is a true sadist, who gets aroused at the sight of Will's tears and enjoys his omega as a plaything, leaving bites and other marks of ownership on his body. When Will's body doesn't respond as Hannibal was expecting during the mating, as an alpha Hannibal has no doubt that physical violence and domination are the right response: "It's necessary to take an omega hard at the first mating, to prove ownership and authority over a mate. An omega responds best this way; the highest possible chance of bonding occurring only when properly dominated" (2013, p. 23). In the end, despite the pain, tears, blood and futile pleas, Will does submit to the forceful mating and finally becomes a submissive omega, pleasing Dr. Lecter immensely.

The fact that Will virtually doesn't speak through the whole story—except for when he expresses his desire to continue studying, and a few whimpers, sobs and pleading when his heat blooms and he is being knotted—highlight his inferiority, vulnerability and thorough objectification. We know nothing of what the boy experiences, how he feels, or what he thinks of his parents selling him off to the first stranger that comes knocking at their door. As the story is written from Dr. Lecter's point of view, we don't even know how Will feels about Hannibal, or whether he is going to like his new life despite the happy ending of the story. I believe this narrative choice by Dangereuse is a deliberate action to highlight the plight and fate of the omega child as being just an expendable commodity in the caste hierarchy that she has created for her story; that Will has no say in the matter of his *omeganess*, and that his body, heat, virginity and life are not under his control, but belong to authority figures; first his parents and then to the superior alpha who literally buys him.

In his enforced omega silence, Will cannot consent to the mating. He is bound by his age, obedience to his parents, his genotype and the cultural expectations of "proper" omega behavior in front of a rich alpha suitor—all of which can be argued to be expectations of "traditional" femininity. Furthermore, not only is Will a minor, but he's also deprived of all logic by his heat, something which renders him irrational and speechless and culminates in him *seeking* Hannibal to relive himself of his hormonal stress. It is very common in dark A/B/O fiction to find the victimized, disempowered omega actually seeking and needing his alpha abuser in the mating frenzy; something which bonds the alpha rapist and the omega victim in a perverse relationship in which the characters are still depicted as happy and contented: "It's then when one of Will's sleepy sighs fades into a small, rumbling purr. […] [Hannibal's] omega is safe and sure and *his* in his arms" (p. 25).

I very much doubt that any author or reader (particularly one who identifies as female) would wish for a scenario like this to happen to them in real life, but the fact that it is written and enjoyed as a fantasy which provides great sexual pleasure is certainly remarkable. In fact, several readers unabashedly commented they were sexually enjoying the story. It is certainly shocking that the rape of a minor, one of the most controversial and certainly illegal issues depicted in *Sweet as Peaches on the Tongue*, hasn't deterred thousands of readers to like, read and comment on a story which deliberately creates and celebrates inequality between the partners, revels in abuse of all kinds, depicts non-consensual sex and then establishes a traditionally happy ending for the newly mated couple.

Of the comments received on this work and the discussion surrounding it, *Sweet as Peaches on the Tongue* received an extraordinarily high number of positive, encouraging and praising comments. Hundreds of readers applauded the author, her prose and detailed heat sex, complaining that they couldn't leave more kudos on the story. Many more asked for a sequel, requesting an even more docile, conditioned and even pregnant Will—and they felt untroubled by expressing these darker desires for the boy's bleak future. It is remarkable that only one commenter asked the author for Will's version of his story, so that readers could hear his voice and know his thoughts and feelings, but this was something which Dangereuse was reluctant to write—and never did. Similarly, it is interesting that only three other readers highlighted that the story was sad for a number of reasons—because Will had to leave school, because he had no option but to obey his parents, and because he was stuck with a selfish alpha who didn't care about his happiness. Dangereuse argued that that was *exactly* what she was going for—a melancholic ending which to her mind clearly didn't equate to the "happy ending" her readers were praising her for.

This difference of opinion between the hundreds of commenters and the author herself regarding the tone of the ending of the story may seem intriguing, but it's simple to clarify. The "melancholic" ending the author claimed to have written didn't fit the clichés, tropes and expectations of dark A/B/O fan fiction, thus its subversive undertone didn't come across properly at the end of the story. Given the purposefully sadistic and selfish characterization made by the author of Dr. Lecter, there were not enough cues in such a highly problematic, deliberately tagged and warning-labeled fiction to justify anything beyond a "melancholic" ending at all. However, the moment the underage, virginal Will is mounted, knotted and bred by his alpha, Hannibal is the winner of the sexual struggle, therefore laying claim and ownership over his mate forever. This is the inevitable, expected and desired ending of dark (and perhaps most) Omegaverse stories, so it is hardly surprising that the story was universally cheered for such a structurally satisfying ending.

Although it is true that Will dubiously cuddles up to Hannibal at the end of the story, in my opinion this was interpreted by readers as the character seeking comfort and protection from his alpha; the "normative" behavior of a freshly claimed omega, especially after such an intense first-time sexual experience. When Dangereuse consciously made Hannibal the narrator of the story, readers who were consistently encouraged to identify with his point of view had little choice at the end of the work to see things differently from Dr. Lecter's worldview regarding his legal, monetary and sexual ownership of Will. To sum up, *Sweet as Peaches on the Tongue* successfully reframes, yet inadvertently reinforces, patriarchal ideas of submission to a strong male as a difficult yet ultimately pleasurable route to safety, comfort and eventual happiness. It subverts the Romantic, egalitarian paradigm so typically associated with slash fiction by circumventing the complex paradigms of consent.

Alter

Written by fan author luvkurai, *Alter* (2014) is one of the most successful dark Omegaverse stories in the *Hannibal* fandom. It boasts 2,456 kudos at the time of writing, 564 bookmarks and 223 comments from readers. In justice to Dangereuse, these numbers may be so high due to the popularity of luvkurai's Tumblr blog; she was a very popular and active *fannibal* during the first season of the TV series, and her blog section *Smutty Anons* gained great popularity. Additionally, the success of *Alter* is also partially due to the fact that it took her almost a year to complete her case-based and lengthy story (25,230 words vs. *Sweet as Peaches on the Tongue*'s 8,452 words), so the slow updates attracted more and more readers. This story was chosen as it met all the established popularity criteria, and its summary gives us a glimpse of its intriguing plot: "God, as is somewhat characteristic of such a vast and preoccupied being, has made a mistake in the classing of Will Graham. Will should have been born an omega—Hannibal's perfect mate. Where god has failed, Hannibal will correct the error and perfect him" (luvkurai, 2014, p. 1).

Contrary to the typical scenario expected in a dark A/B/O story, in this story *both* Hannibal and Will are alphas—but Hannibal wants Will to be his omega; subservient and submissive to him only. Thus, Dr. Lecter devises a careful medical plan involving "hormone resituating" (p. 5), which implies several weeks of injectable hormone replacement therapy, a procedure that will change Will physically and emotionally. The expected outcome is that at the end of the non-consensual drug treatment, Will should become a true omega, wanting and needing to be bred, knotted and impregnated by Dr. Lecter. This story also establishes a proper natural order or social hierarchy whereby "alphas [want] to spread their seed, continue their line, have someone to take care of, and omegas [want] to be desired, to have babies, to be taken care of" (pp. 10–11). Biological determinism informs this story, although with his God complex and medical expertise the story explores the concept that Dr. Lecter will be able to *alter* the laws of nature and bend them to his very whim.

The story describes in detail the effects that the hormonal treatment is having in Will, who is none the wiser about its actual purpose as he trusts his friend and doctor wholeheartedly. Dr. Lecter first drugs Will's drink with Rohypnol to start the course of hormonal injections while he is asleep, and then tells Will that the remaining injections are just a little something to help him sleep. Given that in the TV series canon Will suffers from untreatable insomnia, it's not surprising that he accepts Dr. Lecter's help. The portrayal of Hannibal Lecter in this story is very much in keeping with his character in the TV series canon; a cunningly manipulative former surgeon/psychiatrist with a God complex who is obsessed with Will Graham, and who in this story guides his confused victim through the resulting biologically-induced existential crisis Will suffers as a result of the treatment with half-truths and half-lies. Although the story is not told from Dr. Lecter's point of view, Hannibal has a remarkable insight, and as a superior alpha he has already established his plans for Will, which include

> [leaving] bruises and leaking, bleeding bites all over Will's skin, marking him as *his*. Perhaps he will even forbid Will from working, from leaving the house unless accompanied by Hannibal himself. Perhaps he will need to beat Will's disobedience, swayed by remaining alpha hormones, out of him. [...] It will be his right, as Will's alpha—by biology and by law [luvkurai, 2014, p. 22 & p. 39].

The inequality between the characters grows exponentially as the hormonal treatment advances week after week, until the day Will finally confesses that he doesn't feel like an alpha anymore. Satisfied beyond belief, Hannibal informs Will that his status is altering and that he is indeed becoming an omega: "this omega that is truly and completely *his*. Controlled, *created* by him" (p. 28). Faced with Will's obvious confusion and shock, Dr. Lecter volunteers little information as to the reasons behind the change in Will's *alphaness*, but instead begins to caress and fondle him, seeking his omega pressure point until he elicits a docile omega response from Will, who becomes submissive and sexually aroused in Hannibal's arms. Dr. Lecter masturbates Will's erect—and still alpha—penis to a complete climax, which establishes the first and very dubiously consensual sexual intimacy between them.

Hannibal deceitfully declares that he loves Will whether he is an alpha or an omega, and that in his new *omeganess*, Will should consider Hannibal as his alpha, protector and provider. Will flees the doctor's office, though, and after missing a few appointments with him, Hannibal visits him in his house at Wolf's Trap where he finds Will about to enter his first omega heat, which has rendered him sweet, meek and pliant in the presence of an alpha. As a matter of fact, Will seizes Hannibal and kisses him several times, which pleases Dr. Lecter immensely. He gives Will the final "hormone regulator" injection and slips a powerful drug into his drink, knowing it will trigger Will's heat promptly. Hannibal leaves only to receive an urgent phone call less than an hour later, where a desperate Will begs him to return to guide him through his first heat.

Dr. Lecter triumphantly returns to Will's house, yet does nothing and takes no alpha initiative, determined as he is to hear Will beg him. And this is something that a heat-ridden Will does, begging Hannibal over and over again to take him, to mate him, to knot him. Although Will is still lucid enough to ask for the mating, his consent is clearly deeply questionable by the drugs he has been unknowingly taking against his will. This makes the mating between him and Hannibal a non-consensual act, something the author has warned as "dubious consent" at the beginning of her story. However, luvkurai is aware that her story could also be read as non-consensual: "I have this marked as dubcon, but the levels of manipulation present could very well allow it to be read as noncon" (luvkurai, 2014, Author's Notes).

As in *Sweet as Peaches on the Tongue*, the mating is violent and sadistic, with Hannibal reveling in taking Will's virginity by force:

> Although he would not want William harmed more than he can handle, and certainly never permanently, he would take a barbarous sort of glee from the knowledge that Will would feel him still inside him for days after their first copulation [...] Hannibal is harming Will, undoubtedly, but he doubts the omega is strong (or present) enough to do anything about it [luvkurai, 2015, p. 44].

The mating concludes with Hannibal reflecting how he owns Will, body and soul; his unique creation, forced down the chain of hierarchy by Hannibal's physical power and sheer willpower. Dr. Lecter reflects that now that he has defied the laws of nature, nothing can stand in his way—and that therefore, he's not an alpha anymore, but a true God. The Epilogue to the story is relevant in that we learn that Will is littered with bruises, marks and bites from his alpha, who takes him sexually on a daily basis. Hannibal does all the paperwork regarding Will's shift in status, since they're legally bonded now and registered as alpha and omega mates. Although Hannibal plans for Will to solely look after his household, he allows him at first to keep on doing some tasks at his former job at the FBI, until he is finally a fully stay at home omega. A reflection from Will during the Epilogue is of particular importance, as he reveals: "I haven't felt this good in a long time—ever, to be honest.

I suppose I have you to thank for it" (p. 48). With Will thanking his abuser for feeling "this good," and expressing his happiness over the blissful existence he now lives as an omega, the story comes to a "happy" end. We last see both mates in bed, with Will knotted to Hannibal as he promises to be good, submissive and never disappoint his alpha. Hannibal whispers a true "I love you" to his mate, and Will responds with tears in his eyes.

Something remarkable that readers of this story enjoyed immensely was seeing an alpha Will being "taking down a notch" and transformed into a meek, subservient omega by Dr. Lecter. This forceful and non-consensual re-education which leads to a happy ending makes both author and readers revel in the forced, imposed and very much desired inequality between the characters, as well as in the methods to achieve it; the non-consensual drug use, the emotional manipulation and thorough debasing of Will Graham to an inferior category in the social hierarchy. The terrifying icing on the cake comes when the abused, victimized and disempowered Will thanks his abuser for the new happy life he's now enjoying, and pledges to submit himself to Hannibal forever. So once more, a story of intimate partner violence and domestic abuse that no woman would ever want to live in real life, becomes a dark sexual fantasy for both author and readers to enjoy, *only* because they are in control of the fiction, plot and characters from beginning to end. I consider that the particular engagement of readers with concepts of manipulation and abuse in this fan work arises from the challenge of expectations the writer proposes at the beginning of her story; Will Graham cannot be an alpha in *any* alternate reality whatsoever, as his rightful canonical and fanonical place in A/B/O fiction is to be a subservient omega, especially to Dr. Lecter. Once more, by letting the narrative be guided mostly by Hannibal's point of view, the author makes readers sympathize with his classist, selfish and narcissistic desires towards Will, something which consciously inducts fans into the twisted relationship that both characters develop. The toxic relationship between the alpha/omega couple is further embedded in an atmosphere of problematic eroticism and sick home comfort, which is nonetheless perceived by the majority of readers as the perfect happy ending for Will.

This, too, is something especially problematic about fan perceptions of *Alter*; although the author was universally praised, blessed and acclaimed for her story, its hundreds of comments uncritically cheered an abusive dynamic which was perceived as sexy despite perpetuating mistreatment and domestic violence. As the story was being slowly written and updated, a number of users highlighted how badly they wanted Hannibal to succeed and to see Will mated with such a virile alpha as Dr. Lecter, whose arrogance and God complex was well characterized in the story. Many readers insisted that it was all a work of love on the part of Dr. Lecter, while others stressed that the forceful and non-consensual transition into *omeganess* was for the "greater good" of Will. As a matter of fact, several commenters highlighted that Will should stop working and be a house omega forever, scared of leaving home without his alpha by his side and feeling happy by simply doing the house chores. Curiously enough, of the two hundrerd and twenty three highly positive comments the story received, only three users made mild complaints about it; one would have liked to see a glimpse into Will's headspace, another considered Hannibal's sick love for Will didn't justify everything he did, and a very angry user flamed the author for forcing a non-consensual sex change into Will, even though the issue was flagged up and warned about at length at the beginning of the story.

As one of the most read, kudos'ed and praised dark A/B/O stories of the *Hannibal* fandom, luvkurai's *Alter* raises a number of contentious questions. One of the most relevant of these questions deals with female interest in dark fiction that exclusively aims at reproducing and celebrating the traditional standards and roles of femininity and a power paradigm where intimate partner violence and emotional, physical and domestic abuse play a key role in the story. That this genre of dark slash fiction is so popular and widely written, read and commented should not, in my view, be seen as a political stand advocating for or condoning these horrors women face every day worldwide. However, the fact that this Omegaverse kink trope consistently appears across all fandoms to the great enjoyment of the women who create and consume it should make us reflect on how women encounter discrimination across all backgrounds (educational, emotional, and sexual) and on the impact these experiences have on their psychological makeup. It should make us reflect on how fiction can work as an open fantasy field which allows us to explore and to try to gain control over the social practices which still impose and enforce similar patriarchal policies on real women in the modern world. If, as Siegel and other theorists propose, we develop and employ our fantasies as coping mechanisms, what might the pervasive presence and popularity of dark Omegaverse across so many fandoms suggest about modern experiences of, and attitudes and responses towards, the patriarchal power systems to which women are subjected?

Discussion

After the analysis and arguments I have developed in this essay, I could not agree less with Anne Kustritz's conclusions in her paper *Slashing the Romance Narrative*, where she proposes that

> in slash narratives, authors meticulously create an equality relationship dynamic in which characters are completely equal in everything from decision making to love

> making, and from patterns of dress to household chores to levels of attractiveness and financial security [Kustritz, 2003, p. 380].

In my opinion, this is a "meticulously created[d]" lie—one that is difficult to accept given how slash fiction as a genre has evolved to explore and accommodate the needs of its writers and audiences. Elizabeth Woledge, another pioneering scholar into the field of slash fiction, also argued that following on from her reading of Kirk/Spock fanzines, she believed slash fiction is centrally concerned with intimacy: "Thus, in today's highly sexual culture, the *intimacy* of intimatopic slash fiction is most remarkable" (Woledge, 2006, p. 111). Kustritz also concluded that women are attracted to slash fiction as it allows them a view of a coupled relationship "based upon mutual trust and egalitarian values" (Kustritz, 2003, p. 380). Although this may be typical of the types of slash stories these wonderful authors have read, this is simply not the truth about slash fiction in its entirety. It is not even half of the story.

In the 1980s, in a time where the Internet did not have the impact it has today in our lives and most slash stories were difficult to find—both within and outside of in printed fanzines (and those published were mostly of a romantic nature)—theorists Lamb and Veith (1986) created this politically correct egalitarian myth. Positing that truly equal relationships cannot exist within a patriarchal society due to the inherent power imbalance between males and females, they construed slash as acting as a dreamy fantasy where female authors and readers could explore, through the use of male bodies, the types of equal, egalitarian relationships denied to them by the biological and cultural power imbalances enforced on them by dint of their gender. In this academic account that was actively created and investigated by the first generation of fan fiction theorists several decades ago, women could escape social and cultural relationship inequalities and free themselves of both their traditional feminine roles and the marginalized desires, urges and bodily processes to which they are inherently, inescapably bound, as Dr. Sheldon Cooper reminds Mrs. Davis at the beginning of this essay.

Although it *is* true that there are indeed a great many slash stories with a loving, equal and nurturing relationship between the characters, it is my argument that scholars who continue to follow in these lines of assertion in modern slash fiction inquiries have cherry-picked slash stories to make them match this comfortable, tasteful agenda. Even in a fairly recent but popular fandom such as *Hannibal*, it was very easy to find two extremely dark and extremely popular works which feature an unequal, toxic and abusive relationship between its characters; stories full of explicit, non-consensual kinky sex depicting mistreatment, intimate partner violence and a satisfying "happy" ending to the delight of many readers. This kind of fan fiction was never accounted for by the first generation of slash academics, and the stories clearly subvert the gentle, Romantic and egalitarian paradigm where slash fiction has been unjustly shelved for too long.

It is my belief that beyond dark Omegaverse, darker slash fiction in general—the kind that abounds in the web (and the kind that's impossible *not* to come across today in websites, blogs, Tumblr and even on social media platforms like Twitter)—has often been purposefully left aside by academic authors. This is not because new researchers are unaware of its existence—quite impossible if they are good researchers—but because the implications of these dark stories are far too upsetting to consider. It is naturally safer to maintain and perpetuate the myth that women write and read slash because they seek the "egalitarian romance" they cannot find in real life. It is certainly far safer than to consider that thousands of women around the globe are finding sexual relief when writing and reading dark slash fiction filled with rape, abusive relationships, emotional manipulation, humiliation, non-consensual drug use, forced pregnancy, sexual slavery, bestiality, incest, daddykink, tentacle sex, amputation, suicidal thoughts and self-harm among many others issues.

To ignore these stories that fill fan fiction archives to the brim, and to ignore the discussions happening around them, is to do a disservice to slash fan fiction—and to give a lopsided, prejudiced and incomplete view about what slash authors and readers are really fantasizing about. The "egalitarian romance" myth regarding slash fiction is a myth that seemed to neatly solve the problematization of slash fiction in the first place—a "problem" that never was. The myriad ways in which women across the globe find sexual relief within their writing, readings and private fantasies should not be, but still remains, the object of academic, public or societal scrutiny. This mystery is really very easy to dismantle, if only one wishes to acknowledge and study dark slash fiction and its communities both within and external to the conditions in which they form with the necessary degree of critical and ethical academic rigor.

To conclude this essay, I believe that we as fans and scholars need to establish a new, all-inclusive definition and updated concept of slash fan fiction, one that takes into account the many romantic and egalitarian slash stories around, but which also includes the other side; the very dark, abusive and violent fan works—a set of subgenres in plain sight, permeating every fandom's collective imagination—which are so successful, popular and demanded around the Internet. In this way, we may be able to get the bigger, *real* picture about slash fiction and engage in an honest, open dialogue which includes audiences, authors and scholars and allows us to explore the developments taking place in the field of slash fiction. We have barely scratched the surface of the Omegaverse. Its tropes, themes and functions are more diverse and more resonant than we give it credit for. As fans and as academics, we must help provide the same visibility and authority to the thousands of dark slash works which populate the web as we have done to those who seek a more egalitarian paradigm over the last few decades. We must support and engage with slash writers who are unjustly ignored and neglected at best—and at worst, demonized and Othered. I believe that they have much to offer to the field of fan and popular culture studies, women's studies, queer theory, adaptation studies and many other research fields, if only we are willing to navigate, explore and understand the darkness in their stories.

Notes

1. Mrs. Davis is an African American woman in the series.
2. Molaro, Prady, & Holland (2013).
3. The *Supernatural* fandom still produces the highest number of A/B/O stories, something which contrasts with the statistics obtained by destinationtoast. In the search she carried out on AO3 using the same methodology, she discovered that the three first ranking positions of Omegaverse writing were occupied by the *Sherlock*, *Teen Wolf* and *The Avengers* fandoms, followed by *Supernatural* and *Supernatural* RPF. The discrepancies between these results are likely due to the fact that her research was carried out in 2013; the evolutions of both fandoms and A/B/O interest and production have changed dramatically since then.
4. It should be noted that in this list, Norman Bates ranks second and Darth Vader third.
5. For a timeline arguing the SPN fandom was the origin of this kinktrope, please refer to *The nonnies made them do it!* by netweight (2013).
6. In my opinion, this was the original seed at the core of the A/B/O kinktrope, which was later developed, explored and expanded in TV series such as *Supernatural* and *Teen Wolf*. The hybrid nature of some of these series' characters (vampires, werewolves, angels) who happen to operate in pack dynamics, was the perfect soil for the addition and development of extra kinks such as bestiality, knotting and an old timer in fan fiction, mpreg (male pregnancy).
7. For a brilliant refutation of this idea, see Alice Dreger's (2010) TED Talk *Is Anatomy Destiny?*
8. For the global selling impact of the book, see Meredith (2012), para 1, lines 1–2.
9. telera (2014), p. 25.
10. In their study *What Exactly Is an Unusual Sexual Fantasy?* Joyal, Cossette and Lapierre (2014) employed a quantitative data analysis to determine which sexual fantasies were rare, unusual, common, or typical from a statistical point of view. They discovered that only two sexual fantasies were found to be rare for women or men, while nine others were unusual. Submission and domination themes were not only common for both men and women, but they were also significantly related to each other. They consequently advise against labeling any given sexual fantasy as unusual, let alone deviant.
11. In Nabokov's infamous novel *Lolita* (1955), a middle-aged professor becomes sexually involved with his young stepdaughter after becoming unhealthily obsessed with her. While the fan story has no literary links to *Lolita*, I believe that the author chose these tags to warn readers that the story would feature an older father figure who was going to abuse and rape a younger character over whom he has power.

References

American Film Institute. (2003). *AFI's 100 Greatest Heroes and Villains*. Retrieved from http://www.afi.com/100years/handv.aspx.

Bergman, J. (1994). Darwin's Teaching of Women's Inferiority. *Acts & Facts, 23*(3). Retrieved from http://www.icr.org/article/darwins-teaching-womens-inferiority/.

Birnbaum, G.E., Mikulincer, M., and Gillath, O. (2011). In and Out of a Daydream: Attachment

Orientations, Daily Couple Interactions, and Sexual Fantasies. *Personality and Social Psychology Bulletin, 37*(10), 1398–1410. doi:10.1177/0146167211410986.

Bonomi A.E., Nichols, E.M., Carotta, C.L., Kiuchi, Y, and Perry, S. (2016). Young Women's Perception of the Relationship in Fifty Shades of Grey. *Journal of Women's Health, 25*(2), 139–148. doi:10.1089/jwh.2015.5318.

Busse, K. (2013). Pon Farr, Mpreg, Bonds, and the Rise of the Omegaverse. In A.E. Jamison (Ed.), *Fic: Why Fanfiction Is Taking Over the World* (pp. 316–322). Dallas: Smart Pop.

centrumlumnia. (2013, October 1). Age [Blog post]. Tumblr. Retrieved from http://centrumlumina.tumblr.com/post/62805734754/age.

Collins, S.T. (2016, February 9). 40 Greatest TV Villains of All Time. *Rolling Stone*. Retrieved from http://www.rollingstone.com/tv/lists/40-greatest-tv-villains-of-all-time-20160209.

Coon, G.L., Lucas, J.M., and Frieberger, F. (Producers). (2007). *Star Trek, the Original Series: Seasons One, Two and Three* [DVD]. Hollywood: CBS Home Entertainment.

Dangereuse. (2013). *Sweet as Peaches on the Tongue*. Archive of Our Own.

Demme, J. (Director). (1991). *The Silence of the Lambs* [Motion picture]. United States: Orion Pictures.

destinationtoast. (2013, August 25). It's Time for Fandom Stats: Omegaverse Edition! [Blog post]. Tumblr.

destinationtoast. (2014, October 12). Which AO3 Tags Are Used the Most? Which Get the Most Kudos? [Blog post]. Tumblr.

Dreger, A. (2010). *Is Anatomy Destiny?* [Video file]. Retrieved from http://www.ted.com/talks/alice_dreger_is_anatomy_destiny#t-11291.

Freud, S. (2014). *On the Universal Tendency to Debasement in the Sphere of Love*. Worcestershire: White Press. (Original work published 1912).

Fuller, B. (Producer). (2013). *Hannibal* [Television series]. Toronto: NBC.

Gray, J., Sandvoss, C., and Harrington, C.L. (Eds.). (2007). *Fandom: Identities and Communities in a Mediated World*. New York: New York University Press.

Harris, T. (1981). *Red Dragon*. New York: Dell.

Harris, T. (1988). *The Silence of the Lambs*. New York: St. Martin's Press.

James, E.L. (2012). *Fifty Shades of Grey*. New York: Vintage.

Jenkins, H. (1992). *Textual Poachers: Television Fans and Participatory Culture*. Abingdon: Routledge.

Joyal, C.C., Cossette, A., and Lapierre, V. (2014). What Exactly Is an Unusual Sexual Fantasy? *Journal of Sexual Medicine, 12*(2), 328–340. doi:10.1111/jsm.12734.

Khatchatourian, M. (2016, August 16). Johnny Depp, Amber Heard's Divorce Settled, Domestic Violence Case Dismissed. Retrieved from http://variety.com/2016/film/news/amber-heard-johnny-depp-domestic-violence-settlement-1201838239/.

Kustritz, A. (2003). Slashing the Romance Narrative. *The Journal of American Culture, 26*(3), 371–384. doi:10.1111/1542–734X.00098.

Lamb, P.F., and Veith, D.L. (1986). Romantic Myth, Transcendence, and Star Trek Zines. In D. Palumbo (Ed.), *Erotic Universe: Sexuality and Fantastic Literature* (pp. 236–255). Westport, CT: Greenwood Press.

luvkurai. (2014). *Alter*. Archive of Our Own.

Meredith, C. (2012, August 1). Fifty Shades of Grey Becomes the Bestselling Book of All Time. *Daily Express*. Retrieved from http://www.express.co.uk/news/uk/336759/Fifty-Shades-of-Grey-becomes-the-bestselling-book-of-all-time.

Molaro, S., Prady, B., and Holland, S. (Writers), and Cendrowski, M. (Director). (2013). The Egg Salad Equivalency [Television series episode]. In C. Lorre (Producer), *The Big Bang Theory*. Burbank, CA: Warner Bros.

Nabokov, V. (1955). *Lolita*. Paris: The Olympia Press.

netweight. (2013). *The Nonnies Made Them Do It!* Archive of Our Own.

norabombay. (2012) *Alphas, Betas, Omegas: A Primer*. Archive of Our Own.

Penley, C. (1994). Feminism, Psychoanalysis, and the Study of Popular Culture. In L. Grossberg, C. Nelson, and P. Treichler (Eds.), *Cultural Studies* (pp. 479–500). New York: Routledge.

Reed, E. (1971). Is Biology Woman's Destiny? *International Socialist Review*, *32*(11), 7–11 and 35–39.
Roesner, N. (2012). *The Respect Dare: 40 Days to a Deeper Connection with God and Your Husband*. Nashville: Thomas Nelson.
Siegel, S. (2011a, September 28). Intelligent Lust: What Our Sexual Fantasies Say About Our Past. *Stanley Siegel*. Retrieved from http://stanleysiegel.com/2011/09/28/what-our-sexual-fantasies-say-about-our-past/.
Siegel, S. (2011b). *Your Brain on Sex: How Smarter Sex Can Change Your Life*. Naperville, IL: Sourcebooks Casablanca.
Sturgeon, T. (Writer), and Pevney, J. (Director). (1967). Amok Time [Television series episode]. In G. Rodenberry (Producer), *Star Trek: The Original Series*. Hollywood: Paramount Pictures.
tehdirtiestsock. (2010, July 24). *I Ain't No Lady, but You'd Be the Tramp* [Blog post]. LiveJournal.
telera. (2014) *An Embarrassing Problem*. Archive of Our Own.
Tosenberger, C. (2008). "The Epic Love Story of Sam and Dean": *Supernatural*, Queer Readings, and the Romance of Incestuous Fan Fiction. *Transformative Works and Cultures*, *1*. doi:10.3983/twc.2008.0030.
Woledge, E. (2006). Intimatopia: Genre Intersections Between Slash and the Mainstream. In K. Hellekson and K. Busse (Eds.), *Fan Fiction and Fan Communities in the Age of the Internet* (pp. 97–114). Jefferson, NC: McFarland.

Pregnancy as Bondage

Impregnating the Cisgender Man in Works of Sherlock *and* Merlin *Slash Fiction*

JESSE ASHMAN

Introduction

In this essay, I will explore works which respond to a very specific kink; namely, what if cisgender men could get pregnant? This is a trope within fan works which allows for narratives that challenge, arouse and entertain the reader by a process of reimagining and subverting preconceptions of the body. I focus on texts which use the television series of *Merlin* (2008) and *Sherlock* (2010) as their starting points, not only because these are two of my favorite shows and fandoms, but also because they have a particularly rich male pregnancy (mpreg or m!preg) kink community.

Derecho (2006) asserts that fan fiction is a genre which is dominated by, and belongs to, women and the subordinate (p. 72) and there is an (incorrect though culturally ingrained) assumption that this subset of writers would be those who can become pregnant. Simone de Beauvoir highlights how a "woman's enslavement to the species is tighter or looser depending on how many births the society demands and the hygienic conditions in which pregnancy and birth occur"—for de Beauvoir, the womb itself is the catalyst for the subjugation of women (1949/2010, p. 69). Mpreg subverts this assertion and uses it for the creation of erotic works. In its most docile form, this means gay men being able to have biological children and a happy family unit as a result of this, creating a domestic narrative centered around the values of love and family. In its darker forms, mpreg becomes an explicit pornographic genre that purposely breaks taboos and plays with BDSM elements and multiple kinks.

Mpreg can and does exist in non-kinky forms; in a study of *Supernatural* (2005) fan fiction, Berit Åström identifies that mpreg fan fiction often represents a subset of domestic narratives, where the focus is not on the supernatural as it were, but instead on the domestic relationship—in this instance, between the main characters Sam and Dean Winchester (Åström, 2010). While these kinds of domestic texts do exist in the body of work around *Sherlock* (2014) and *Merlin* (2008), I will focus on texts which explore the bodily erotic, bonding (in both the restricting and reparative sense) and the painful experience of male pregnancy. In these texts the pregnant body is repurposed as male, confining and kinky. This gives us a specific type of erotica that focuses on the internal and a kink which can only exist within a digital world.

This essay uses fan works from the Archive of Our Own (AO3) community. AO3 is one of the largest contemporary fan work sites, which organizes fan works that may have been posted on other sites. For example, the *Merlin* mpreg fests (a version of a "kinkfest"—an online community writing event wherein participating authors all write on the same kink, in this case choosing from a variety of prompts given by the fest curators) are all posted on AO3 as part of that fan community (Merlinmpreg_mod, 2012). It is one of the preferred platforms of possibly the most prolific mpreg writer in the *Sherlock* fandom, Annabagnell, as well as the majority of writers in the *Merlin* fandom. Many of the fan works in these mpreg worlds are written as gifts for other writers, and as a platform AO3 allows users to search texts by who they are a gift for. AO3 therefore goes further than just being a platform for disseminating works; it provides a digital space for a kink community to develop.

Fan fiction allows us to find very specific kinks and tropes and AO3 makes this simple by having designated or freeform tags for each individual kink—such as the Omegaverse, birthsex, bp!Merlin (boy pussy Merlin) or pregnancy kink, all of which exist as separate tags within the mpreg genre. This has allowed AO3 to become the hub for all things mpreg. Additionally, if an author on AO3 no longer wishes to be credited for their work, they can abandon it and it will be attached to the generic author placeholder "orphan_account"—a feature which is particularly useful for people writing in taboo genres, as there is no permanence of the text being related to the author.

Using mpreg fan works published on AO3, this essay will chart the erotic uses of pregnancy as a BDSM practice in the texts and discuss how this relies on both the digital nature of the text and the tangible nature of the actor's body. It will argue that these works present a form of fetish that is, and can only be, present in fan fiction texts and posit the idea that this erotic potential in fact relies on the cisgenderness of the canon characters and the real-life actors that portray them. In the cyberspace realm of fan fiction, these bodies become an erotic battleground for the deconstruction of male and female reproductive systems by allowing for erotic, kinky, male cisgender pregnancy.

Eroticizing Pregnancy

What is added by mpreg to the worlds of *Sherlock* and *Merlin* is a queering and eroticizing of the internal mechanisms of the body by taking pregnancy and presenting it back to us as a point of erotic fascination or contact. However, pregnancy is culturally far removed from eroticism. The virgin/whore dichotomy explains the cultural reading of the pregnant woman as virginal; since a woman can only be read as either a virgin or a whore, the pregnant woman therefore becomes coded as the virgin. This stems from the most famous virgin of all, The Virgin Mary—who, as Rubin (2009) asserts, is both a core part of and an unavoidable presence within Western culture that dates back to medieval Europe (p. xxi). Our cultural perception of pregnancy for this reason is one linked to the ethereal figure of the pregnant Virgin Mary, and although the reality of pregnancy is that it is caused by sex in some form or another, pregnancy is coded in the West as a wholesome state of being a non-sexual entity. This extends to even the experiences of pregnant women themselves; Bartellas et al. found that sexual activity decreases during pregnancy, with a contributing factor to this being the belief that sex during pregnancy can harm the baby, despite the fact that only a minority of the women studied had actually discussed this concern with their doctor and had not received their information from a reliable source (Bartellas, Crane, Daley, Bennett, & Hutchens, 2000, pp. 964–968).

More recently, there has been some widespread imagery of the pregnant woman as something other than the virginal stereotype. Kammeyer (2008) acknowledges the influence of Demi Moore appearing naked while pregnant on the cover of *Vanity Fair*, writing: "The magazine's editors were surely aware that, for a small but select audience, the Moore photograph would have more than just shock value: it would also have sexual appeal" (p. 193). Kammeyer's implication here is that the pregnant body is only attractive as a fetish; while Demi Moore is considered to be attractive at any other time in her life, during pregnancy she becomes a fetish object.

Pregnant men, then, take on some of the coding of fetish and/or virgin. Pregnancies in men can then be used to desexualize homosexual relationships and be, as Åström writes, "life-affirming experiences resulting in the joy of fatherhood" (2010, 1.5). However, in the *Merlin* and *Sherlock* fandoms the pregnant man matches the mainstream view of it, which as Åström identifies "tends to treat the pregnant male as monstrous" (*ibid.*). The difference in pornographic mpreg is that rather than the monstrous being abhorrent, it becomes erotic. By retaining the fetishism with which pregnant bodies are viewed and imposing it onto the male body, which rarely experiences this kind of objectification, the pregnant man thus becomes *both* the virgin and whore through taking on a powerful signifier of the wholesome female archetype of the homemaker.

Monstrosity is retained in these fan works through a clear difference from the texts Åström looks at: they are not domestic fictions. In these works, the monstrous pregnancy is described in detail—it is not merely a means into the domestic sphere. Likewise, sex within mpreg texts is not a means to birth and in fact sometimes takes place during the birth. We see this in one of Annabagnell's most explicit works, *Double Your Pleasure*:

> His prick jerked in his hand and come hit the base of his belly, painting his stretch-marked skin. His body shook with orgasm and the force of the contraction, and he hoped that John would finish soon, because god he could feel [the baby] moving down [2013b, p. 6].

This is a particularly explicit example under the "erotic birth" tag, which also includes works which use the birth in an erotic way without sex actually taking place during the birth. In *Double Your Pleasure,* the pregnant body and birth are merged with the orgasm and sex act, described as if they are one. Annabagnell makes sex during pregnancy into something that is purely eroticism; something that Driscoll (2006) differentiates as "porn sex" rather than "plot sex" (p. 86). Instead of birth being something that is a key plot point, it becomes part of a larger erotic scene. The pregnant body, one that usually only fits into the virgin narrative, is therefore inverted into something that is purely about sex. Sherlock's body is fetishized so that birth becomes an erotic experience, with his body described and objectified in meticulous detail.

This objectification is, as Marks (1996) writes, "one possible mode of straight female looking at male bodies [which] comes through masquerade [...] In this case, to look sexually at men I must masquerade as a gay man, i.e., provisionally borrow a gay male gaze" (p. 127–128). Here, Marks identifies that the female gaze cannot be reached purely through subverting the male gaze and by looking at men, and instead poses one possibility of the female gaze as that of "masquerade." The way many mpreg writers construct a female gaze is through this masquerade. Sherlock's body is eroticized through the act of John's—and by extension the reader and the writer's—Looking, and the body is then entrapped within the physicality of pregnancy and this erotic Looking. This erotic birth narrative provides another lens to look at birth through. Rather than the eroticism of the pregnant body just being an extension of the subjugation of the female body, the inscribed sexuality of the pregnant body is exposed through its being repurposed into the context of an mpreg narrative.

This is not to say that the fetishization of birth and pregnancy is a new thing; Kammeyer (2008) outlines that the fetishization of the pregnant female body is something that has been happening for quite some time (p. 192). What then, specifically, about pregnancy is tantalizing to both the fan fiction writer and reader? Kammeyer cites the number of pregnancy fetish websites available as evidence that "pregnant women with large breasts are indeed sexually stimulating for many men" (pp. 192–193), working on the assumption that enlarged breasts—a cliché point of male interest—is what draws people (specifically men) to the pregnant body. However, he goes on to make the distinction that lactating women and the use of breast pumps is found on separate sites to generic pregnancy kink sites, and although Kammeyer himself does not draw this conclusion, his research suggests that what is attractive here is not the breasts but the belly itself (pp. 192–193). A study conducted by Enquist et al. looks specifically at male attraction to pregnant and lactating women, stating early upbringing and the Oedipal Complex as likely causes, especially if the person has seen his mother breastfeeding (Enquist, Aronsson, Ghirlanda, Jansson, & Jannini, 2011, pp. 140–147). It seems that the assumption of men being attracted to breasts more than any other part of a woman skews the inquiry into the attraction to pregnancy. When it comes to the pregnant man in fan fiction, for example, there are usually no breasts or lactation involved. Mpreg fiction instead finds innovative ways to use the pregnant body to its full erotic potential, lingering on visceral descriptions of the pregnant male body and how this body is restricted, feminized and in pain. Within mpreg fiction it can be argued that the attraction comes primarily from a combination of bondage, domination, submission and masochism.

BDSM Pregnancy

As the focal point of attraction, the belly of the pregnant man can become the means for creating BDSM practices within mpreg fan works. The belly is the most prominent restricting and painful element in the sex acts described within mpreg. As Gross (2006) identifies, there is no clear definition of BDSM beyond an enjoyment of pain, and this limited definition focuses on the sadomasochistic elements more than the bondage and domination (p. 57). In many mpreg works the pregnancy is clearly painful and erotic at the same time, but it is more an expression of the reader and writer's masochism than the protagonist's sadism. For example, in *Pressure* (2013c), Annabagnell has Sherlock in pain from his pregnancy, but neither character is inflicting or enjoying the pain:

> "Come on, love, turn around for daddy, won't you?" John crooned, rubbing his hands gently across the expanse of Sherlock's stretched skin. "You can't come out facing that way. Bum first doesn't work."

> "Plus it's fucking uncomfortable," Sherlock added, wincing as an errant punch of defiance hit his spine and sent a shock of pain up his back. "Turn the other bloody way 'round" [pp. 2–3].

While neither character is necessarily portrayed as enjoying the pain, since this is a porn narrative everything within it seeks to enhance the eroticism. The stretched skin and the morphing of the body give a non-immediate pain that is both sacrificial and testing the limits of the body. Wounding comes from within and is imprinted on the body and the pain is described erotically through the voyeurism that the reader has over the tactile experience. This is not just morphing the cisgender male body into a body that can be impregnated, but transforming it into a wounded, sexualized body. Agency and control is given over to the fandom though being able to impose this pain.

This has obvious BDSM elements; the enjoyment of pain, the practice of aftercare, the stretching of the body to almost breaking point and the relative dominance/submission of the partners. There is a clear link between the pregnancy and the dominance; the incurring of pain and the submission of the pregnant partner to the pain inflicted upon him by the other character. This differs from pregnancy kink in mainstream pornographic content in that the breasts are not the focus; in these mpreg fan works, the belly and the stretching of pregnancy (albeit through semi-fictionalized biological functions) take center stage.

Bonding from within, induced through the biological functions of the body, acts as a device to bond the male characters in other ways. *Sherlock* and *Merlin* mpreg works are dotted with the idea of the pregnant male being bound to the dominant partner as part of a societal expectation brought on by their biology, mirroring the societal expectations of pregnancy in a woman. In Annabagnell's *Double Your Pleasure* (2013b) Sherlock is seen to be walking at "almost a stagger, he thought, with his belly so low and full—over to the bed" (p. 5). This can also be seen in gwyllion's *For the Good of the Kingdom* (2012), a story which was specifically written in response to a narrative prompt issued by a curator within the *Merlin* mpreg fest: "Arthur really loves the swell of Merlin's belly, and even more than that he loves knowing that he caused it" (merlinmpreg_mod, 2012):

> Beneath the covers, he stroked Merlin's naked shoulder. His skin was smooth and warm. He traced the curved line of flesh and muscle, blazing a trail down Merlin's back until his fingers fanned out over the swell of Merlin's rump, ample with padding that announced his condition. Even with Merlin's thick ceremonial robes and his favourite tunics cleverly altered to make room for his new girth, the pregnancy was obvious to the citizens of Camelot [gwyllion, 2012, p. 1.].

Both in these texts and in other fan works, the pregnant male is bonded to his partner and his pregnant condition, in a way that is clearly eroticized by the visceral bodily descriptions of the belly which come to represent the bonding through pregnancy. Adhering to the requested themes and conditions specified by the prompt, in *For the Good of the Kingdom* Arthur is seeing his lineage and the expectations of the King within Merlin's pregnant body. The fact that these are gay male relationships (coupled with the additional specific dynamics of king/servant/consort and detective/assistant/lover) makes for an erotic breaking of the taboo of how we are supposed to see birth and the adherence to societal expectations of birth (monogamy, sacrifice, child rearing), yet renders these erotic within slash fiction through the context of homosexual love and the visceral descriptions of the body. This objectification creates specific power dynamics between two men, which use the state of pregnancy as part of the dominance/submission taking place.

Mpreg works can also explore specific power dynamics and bindings by featuring forces external to the rational wishes of the protagonists taking control over their bodies. While *Merlin* is more overt with it, both *Sherlock* and *Merlin* contain elements of destiny—and the ultimate destiny of the two protagonists to be together. In *Merlin*, this connection is explicitly referred to as predestined following a conversation between Merlin and the Great Dragon, whilst in *Sherlock* Mycroft Holmes is the first to allude to this connection, stating that "[John] could be the making of my brother. Or make him worse than ever" (Moffat, Gatiss & McGuigan, 2010). This bound-by-destiny concept is extended in mpreg works through an additional bound-by-one's-own-body paradigm, something which takes a particularly prominent role within the Omegaverse—an alternative universe wherein humans have innate animalistic sexual natures featuring inherent "natural" instincts, imperatives and behaviors.

In the Omegaverse, dominant Alphas claim, breed and impregnate submissive Omegas. As Busse (2013) notes, this is not simply an animal transformation, but a whole other world that draws on terminology around breeding, heat cycles and bonding as well as male pregnancy (p. 317). The Alpha and Omega dynamics explored in some mpreg works play to this, ultimately generating an erotic bondage paradigm which combines being bound by culture, bound by biology and bound by destiny. For example, in *The bond of Alpha and Omega* by fan author kinkmerighthererightnow, John is instinctively drawn to Sherlock: "John tried to breath [*sic*], tried not to focus on Sherlock smelling probably like a ripe 'come-and-breed-me-Alpha'-fruit" (2016, p. 5). This focus on breeding in Alpha/Omega texts suggests an allusion to the concept of the queer/breeder dichotomy and asks the question: what if queers were basely motivated as breeders? (Warner, 1991, p. 9). These animal urges, rather than using reproduction to legitimize queer relationships into the familial structure, are used to sink them deeper into taboo though pregnancy and pregnancy fetish.

Agency and the Belly

The pregnant belly is not only a vessel for symbolic significance; in itself it also provides a means of eroticism, pain and restraint. This duality is integral to mpreg, since in the majority of mpreg texts the pregnant belly is the focal point for the pornographic interest. The belly provides a physical restriction; a deviation from the norm of the male body and a potential for the body to grow—to be stretched and to be swollen. Bonding through pregnancy, therefore, is a form of agency being relinquished by the pregnant partner, and these binding dynamics are then combined with the specific elements of the pregnant belly.

The pregnant belly is rendered kinky because of its semantic and societal significance, but within the belly kink there is also an interest in the physicality of pregnancy—similar to the physicality of being full of food—without there necessarily being a specific interest in the reproductive elements of pregnancy. It is telling that many mpreg texts also have elements of feederism—doubling the ways in which the male body is being manipulated and stretched—and that prominent authors in the mpreg genre also write in the feederism genre; much of Annabagnell's fan fiction and mpreg work, for example, more broadly combines feederism and pregnancy, drawing on the idea of pregnancy cravings as well as the stretching of the belly. *Chocolate and Pickled Gherkins* (2010) by pushkin666 contains nothing but a description of Merlin's pregnancy cravings—there is absolutely no plot, perhaps giving us a clear example of, where Driscoll (2006) identifies porn sex and plot sex, something that can be understood as porn feeding. Giovanelli and Pelusco (2007) and Prohaska (2013) argue that feederism is a culturally constructed fetish which realizes both the Western attitude to fat and to eating, since "in a society that cloaks foods rich in saturated fat and calories in danger, mystery, intrigue, it makes sense that the fetishized food choices of women, as well as the act of consumption itself, become symbolically linked to pleasure, sexual or otherwise" (Giovanelli and Pelusco, 2007, pp. 331–332). Feederism in mpreg draws on these cultural significances of feederism to manipulate a male body in the ways in which female bodies have been manipulated, by both the cultural significances and social ramifications of pregnancy and control over the weight and calorific intake of a body.

It would be tempting for a reader to merely gloss the pregnant partner as the woman in a slash fiction dynamic, and while there are certainly some aspects of feminization of the pregnant partner, feederism in homosexual male relationships draws also on the taboo of not fitting the desired thin aesthetic for gay men. As Pyle and Lowey (2009) identify, in the gay male community fat men are considered a fetish, and a thin or muscled frame is the archetypal gay figure. The gay pregnant man challenges not only what we think of male physiology but also what we think of gay male desirability and aesthetic. Mpreg works are dotted with elaborate descriptions of Sherlock and Merlin's thin, unmuscled, pale bodies, stretching them out into one that creates the erotic through a figure which subverts the idealized male body. Mpreg works use this to dominate the male characters—rendering feederism as something that a fan fiction reader or writer can indulge in through the kind of masquerade Marks poses. Feederism as an erotic taboo therefore plays into the idea of wanting to stretch and grow the gay male body, and as a result, both feederism and the pregnant man (and often a combination of the two) challenge what we know about the male figure. By having figures that are both being fed and being impregnated, the body loses agency in a way that also transforms it, with the belly acting as the focal point for this transformation.

In some cases, the belly can become the *only* eroticized part of the pregnant male body; often, the genitalia of the pregnant partner is left undescribed (which has the side effect of circumnavigating exactly where this baby is going to be birthed from) and the belly is given eroticized attention. When the texts focus on the belly is when the language starts to become the visceral, erotic descriptions we are used to seeing attached to the erogenous zones of the female body. Returning to Annabagnell's *Double Your Pleasure,* she writes, "It seemed to Sherlock that John had spent most of Sherlock's pregnancy at least half-hard [...] From the very beginning, when Sherlock's stomach just barely started to show, John's cock perked right up and greeted the sight" (2013b, p. 1). Here, the focal point for eroticism is clearly the belly: the pregnancy is what makes the partner desirable. Particularly with language like "swollen, glowing, blooming," this is not simply a crude or humorous use of belly kink; it is a visceral erotic depiction with the belly being the focal point for the restricting and kinky elements. What this adds up to is an enlarged belly as a restriction imposed by an outside force—and the larger the belly, the more restricting it becomes.

Behar (2009) uses the notions of the body as a surface and the restriction as a projection to understand how bondage operates: "BDSM's visual culture includes bondage images in which wilful bodily movements must negotiate against or coordinate with restriction or restraint" (p. 2) and the restraint acts to "nullify" the subject's will (p. 3). Behar is approaching this from a fashion perspective, but the way the belly is transposed onto something like a thin cisgender character's body operates in very much the same way; the body is interfaced with and restricted, and the subject's will is suppressed as he learns to co-ordinate with the restriction. For example, in Annabagnell's *(Almost) Sex on The Beach* Sherlock walks with his "right arm cupping his belly as he waddled towards the shoreline" (2013a, p. 2). This combines the eroticized belly with the physical restriction that it projects onto the body;

Sherlock, accustomed to canonically free and flexible movement, now has to negotiate the new physical restriction and work around it. Val_Creative in *Realism* (2014) uses this mechanism of bondage in an explicit sex scene:

> [Merlin] pressed with the side of his face to his own bed, arching his lower half into Arthur's hands steadying him on his knees, huge belly distended. He rocked back with small, uncoordinated thrusts, hardly getting the maneuvering desired [p. 9].

The barrier to movement and by extension, sex, is one that is caused by the belly—by the object of desire. Behar's perspective looks at external forces interfacing with the body and while the pregnancy is a part of the body, it is clearly being used here to interface onto it. The forces that control it are not at the will of the restricted person. As with gwyllion's engagement with the prompt of Arthur adoring the swell of Merlin's belly and taking both pleasure and pride in knowing that he caused it, the agency is given over to the impregnating partner and the voyeur reader/writer, not the impregnated character. The bondage comes directly from the forbidden sex act, rather than something that is imposed onto the body as part of the sex act. This gives mpreg a circularity that is difficult to achieve with other forms of BDSM; the sex act causes the restriction, which in turn heightens the sex act.

Cisgender Bodies and Taboo

Mpreg, then, can operate as a BDSM practice. However, this practice is very specific to online fan cultures and relies upon the specific mechanisms that this space allows. As Hellekson and Busse (2014) write in their introduction to *The Fan Fiction Studies Reader*, "If [the term fandom] requires an actual community of fans who share an interest, then Sherlock Holmes would easily qualify as the first fandom, with fan-written Holmes pastiches serving as the beginnings of fan fiction" (p. 6). Likewise, the legend of King Arthur that *Merlin* draws its canon from forms part of the long history of works which form fan fiction's lineage of retelling stories and reworking the same characters throughout history (Watt, 2004, p. 49). These new versions of *Sherlock* and *Merlin* do not shy away from their canonical texts, referencing them in a way that encourages audiences to both read back into the source texts and to create their own works as the BBC writers have done. *Sherlock* uses episode titles that mirror the original *Sherlock Holmes* texts; for instance, *A Study in Scarlet* becomes *A Study in Pink*, *A Scandal in Belgravia* becomes *A Scandal in Bohemia* and *The Hound of the Baskervilles* becomes *The Hounds of Baskervilles* (Doyle, 2009; Vertue & Cameron, 2014). *Merlin* takes a similar approach, with episode titles such as *Le Mort d'Arthur* which comes directly from Sir Thomas Malory's telling of the Arthurian legend (Malory, 2015).

Sherlock and *Merlin* in their television iterations present an opportunity for fan fiction writers to create works that are as legitimate as their canonical content, thus offering a unique opportunity for an appearance of relative legitimacy in the process of creating queer fan fiction. *Sherlock* and *Merlin* fan fiction presents what Jones (2002) calls an "actualization of latent textual elements" (p. 82). There is an explicit but denied homosexuality within the canon of the television series, so much so that *Sherlock* in particular has been called out for "queerbaiting"—a term which describes a text alluding to and profiting from the suggestion that a heterosexual character is queer, without making this character canonically queer (Fathallah, 2015, p. 491). However, *Sherlock* and *Merlin* fan fiction ultimately creates a specific opportunity to queer a body of work and a source text which has already gone some way to queering itself, through both having a queer fandom and being fan works in themselves. These conditions allow mpreg to take this a step further into the realm of taboo by writing male cisgender bodies as pregnant.

The first of the specific conditions which allow mpreg fan fiction to flourish from a source text is the ability for any mpreg writer to take control of the portrayal of a cisgender body. The erotic restriction presented by mpreg is heightened by the fact the cisgender male bodies which are manipulated in fan works are experiencing a restriction they ultimately cannot experience either in the real world or in the canonical worlds from which they are drawn and developed. What *Sherlock* and *Merlin* slash fiction generally adds to its source texts is an explicit and often pornographic queering of the canon, building on foundations that are already themselves works of fan fiction. However, what is unique here is how through the source texts being open about their fan fiction nature, *Sherlock* and *Merlin* mpreg is allowed to be subversive in its queerness—but not through its status as fan fiction. This allows space to envision and create a cisgender pregnancy narrative that is not so far removed from the canonical content as to be unrecognizable. Where the taboo of the pregnant man becomes particularly subversive is when it is used to codify a queer body through pregnancy onto the bodies of presumably cisgender actors, through an interface with a pregnant, swollen belly. The taboo and forbidden element is therefore generated within the queer and kinky themes in the text, something that is not always as possible with other popular fandoms such as *Supernatural* or *Doctor Who* which are works owned by their respective production companies.

Within mpreg, these specific cisgender bodies and characters are acknowledged, referenced and subsequently impregnated. Steenhuyse (2011) uses transportation theory to examine the specific nuances of fan fiction with regards to scene setting and character generation and identifies that in fan fiction a specific shared landscape and set of characters is already established. For example, drawing on works which reference the set of *House*, Steenhuyse demonstrates how readers "can fill out generic references (for example to a 'small desk in the corner') with specific images from the show (in this case, of a desk with a computer, positioned near a large window)" (p. 3). A large part of the shared language of these narratives is the physicality of actors who portray the characters and many mpreg works draw specific bodily elements of lead actors' appearances in order to explicitly reference the bodies of specific actors. On AO3, the *Sherlock* fandom in particular has specific tags for the BBC's version of the characters, as given the abundance of *Sherlock Holmes* adaptations it is important that the reader and writer are referencing the same body in the process of reading and writing.

In many mpreg texts, the body of an actor is used to create a fetishized description of the pregnant male body of the character. This is particularly evident when the texts make explicit reference to their use of an actor's appearance to inform the depiction of a character in fan texts. For example, in *Oh What Would a Man Not Do for Love?* (2013), Evenlodes_Friend cites images of Benedict Cumberbatch with bleached hair as the inspiration for this mpreg fiction. This is an explicit reference to how the actor Benedict Cumberbatch—not the character Sherlock—appears in *The Fifth Estate,* in role for which Cumberbatch bleached his hair. This is part of the playfulness of fandoms centered around a specific actor, whereby the fandom acts as a conduit through which the actor's body can be queered into and through the taboo sex acts we see in these narratives. Within this, enough is left (or omitted) to allow a reader to fill in the gaps with the shared canonical references, this situating the reader(s) in a shared narrative space. This creates an immersive experience which still provides readers and writers with opportunities to able to engage in mpreg practices which are taboo as both tropes and as discursive interpretive practices.

Specialness and Monstrosity

Mpreg exists in an uncanny valley between forbidden and accepted forms of the queering of its canonical work. In this way, mpreg as a kink operates within a liminal space that can only exist within fan cultures. Part of what makes this operation so effective is the mix of specialness/monstrosity that the pregnant man possesses in these works through using the characters of Sherlock and Merlin as they are presented in the BBC shows.

Given how the pregnant man's body can be culturally read as something special, monstrous or impossible, the erotic focus of this corrupted specialness plays with the virgin/whore dynamic, making a gifted but perverse figure. Both Sherlock and Merlin as characters already possess a canonical specialness which, while useful for overcoming their challenges in the show, is ultimately shunned by their respective wider societies. For Merlin, this means being in possession of magic, something punishable by death. For Sherlock, this means having a scientific, calculating mind but a socially unacceptable identity as a high functioning sociopath. Mpreg is often brought about by either magic or futuristic science, and what makes the protagonists special in mpreg fictions is their ability to get pregnant. Merlin and Sherlock are already coded as gay and already coded as abhorrently special. This means that as a reader, our reference point from the outset therefore allows us a believable world where the cisgender man can become pregnant—where we are able to reclaim the body of the oppressor into an erotic freak.

The very thing that makes this specialness taboo is not only how pregnancy is seen culturally, but also how specifically pregnant men are portrayed. Sparrow (2008) investigates the possibility of future technologies allowing cisgender men to become pregnant and dismisses their right to do so as something which "constitutes a reductio ad absurdum of the idea of reproductive liberty" (p. 275). Likewise, Warner (1991) in *Fear of a Queer Planet* outlines the perceived separation between queer and non-queer people, outlining this as "made practical and enforceable by family ideology—between alternative sexualities and social reproduction. Indeed, in Anglo-American cultures the colloquial term by which many queer people define the enemy is not 'straights' but, bitterly, 'breeders'" (p. 9). Coupled with the sensationalist media attention given to transgender pregnant men, the pregnant man is seen as an abject figure—somewhere between absurd, impossible and freakish. For queer people it can represent a crossing into the world of breeders—for the heterosexual community, an impossibility or an abomination.

The specialness of mpreg often comes from both the specialness of the character and their access to science, magic or both. Anatomy and biological functioning becoming altered by magic or science play a large part in constructing the erotic body in mpreg. Both *Merlin* and *Sherlock* offer opportunities for this, since they have the characters of Gaius and John respectively, both of whom are medical professionals who can pour over the intricacies of the body of the pregnant man. Morwen_Maranwe in *Masterpiece Theatre* (2014) imagines a pill which can enable the male body to become pregnant, and the *Edge of the Unknown* series (elirwen, 2012) features Gaius' medical assessment of Merlin's pregnant anatomy: "The organs are in a bit different positions, but other than that I don't see any problems. There'd never been a male pregnancy so I can't tell for sure, but I think your body is simply adjusting, making space for the foetus to grow" (p. 4). By constructing a world in which a cisgender male body is impacted and examined in the same scientific ways that a female or transgender body would be, the pregnant cisgender body, which even its owner does not see as a sexual body, thus becomes a medical problem to be uncovered and investigated. This in turn allows for pregnant sex later once the body has been medically examined and its differences addressed to enhance the taboo nature of the sex. These are bodies that are both queer *and* breeder, and subsequently abject to both, performing acts which neither are made for.

While all these works play on the construct of a cisgender body through the use of an actor's body, some slash works do make the character explicitly transgender. Halberstam (2010), examining the representations of Thomas Beatie (sensationalized as the first ever pregnant man, although Halberstam rightfully queries this title), notes that "the fault lines between disgust and acceptance are remarkably narrow nowadays, and so while obvious and unresolved gender variance (butchness) still solicits frowns and groans, an outwardly gender-conforming family made up of a transgender man and his 'wife' can be comforting and easily tolerated" (pp. 77–78). While an easy toleration may not be everyone's experience, there is certainly a fine line between the perceptions of abject or conformist queer lives. By putting the pregnant man into a pornographic work, fan fiction writers destabilize this fault line, using an already abject concept (pregnant sex) and tying it in with what Halberstam identifies as a close-to-acceptable form of queerness (although this is still rendered to some extent abject through the pregnancy being within an outwardly conforming gay male relationship). This is then imposed onto the cisgender actor's body, and in works where the character becomes explicitly transgender, such the transgender Sherlock depicted in *GIFT* by kingofthegingerales (2013), a doubling of acceptance and non-acceptance ties these works together. In one act they claim the cisgender body as transgender, imposing it onto a normalized body, and then render this into the realm of erotic taboo by making it into a sex symbol.

In *Merlin,* Arthur is the normalized character, he is the "one of these real rough, tough, save the world kind of men" as Gwen puts it in the show, whereas Merlin is coded as more feminine, and submissive (Jones et al., 2008)—and this is tied in with Merlin's magic; his vulnerability that is also his strength. In some works, however, science and/or magic are utilized again in order to make it possible for the characters to possess something resembling a transgender body; for example, in *The Golden Age* weezlyismyking (2015) uses the magical potentiality inherent within the *Merlin* universe to make both Arthur and Merlin have magic, with Arthur's manifesting as him having a vagina. The transgender body is thus coded as an impossible or magical body; as the characters as they exist in these works are in a state they could never achieve without the use of supernatural powers, the implication is that such impossibility is not the case in reality, but that it is when existing on a cisgender man. By equating this specialness to being transgender, queer identity is recoded as powerful and special, rather than dangerous. What on the surface is a taboo sex act actually relies on a destabilization of the cisgender body through the body of the actor.

Digital Worlds

As the popularity of the Omegaverse shows, there are depictions and explorations of sexuality that have grown exponentially within online fan fiction communities. Busse charts the evolution of the Omegaverse trope as something that has come about through the participatory culture of fan writing, and also cites the nature of online fan fiction whereby someone can search for their specific kinks, rather than an approximation of what they are looking for (Busse, 2013). Given that pregnancy fetish, pregnant men and kink exist outside of cyberspace, it could be argued that mpreg provides a mirror to the outside world, reflecting desires that already exist without cyberspace. In mpreg fiction, we therefore see not only tropes and fetishes that can exist only in cyberspace but also bodies that cannot exist elsewhere.

Andermahr (2005), when talking about Winterson's *The Powerbook*, explains that the body is rendered disembodied through cyberspace; in *The Powerbook* the protagonist/audience can become whatever and whoever they desire and the text purposely avoids description that would embody the protagonist (p. 113). Many mpreg texts take up this same technique for tackling impossible bodies, with the bodily changes associated with male pregnancy often including brief mentions of characters developing genital structures through which to give birth. In many others, the body morphs unseen—meaning we can have a body that references a real life cisgender body but that has a phallus *and* a birth scene in the same erotic work, without the transformation being described within the text. Due to the participatory nature of the work, other fans are not out looking for the blooper of the transformation not being addressed or described, and the body is allowed to take on a more fluid form; since all that exists of the erotic mpreg body is what is described within the text alongside what is referenced of the body of the actor, this shared, constructed body becomes accessible and malleable.

Conclusion

What the majority of definitions of BDSM share is that there is an element of control—where one body hands over agency to another, and in mpreg, the agency of both the body of the actor and the body of work is handed over to the collective fan community. A transformative act of BDSM, one which relies heavily on the body of the cisgender actor and uses the creating and breaking of taboo to enact pornographic works, mpreg is collaborative and counter-public work which queers the cisgender bodies of very prominent mainstream actors. While the descriptions of the bodily transformations are often absent, descriptions of sex acts, biology and genitalia are intrinsic to the pornographic nature of mpreg fan works. This allows readers to open up and control a BDSM pornographic world which would otherwise be inaccessible to them—i.e., porn actors can become celebrities and can cross over into non-pornographic works, but non-erotic actors rarely cross over into pornographic content. Mpreg porn therefore gives the writer and reader full agency over the actor's body; in mpreg fan works, a celebrity can be seen to be both engaging in explicit sex acts while his body is manipulated into being pregnant, another thing that it would be not only unlikely but impossible to achieve.

In mpreg, it is not only the sex acts that are an act of BDSM. In the case of *Merlin* and *Sherlock*, mpreg slash fiction exists in keeping with the queer fan cultures that the shows nurture and encourage, and the act of reading and writing mpreg becomes a collective act of dominating the cisgender body. Mpreg transposes the cisgender body into a media form in which mainstream discourse would have it never belonging, but one which conversely relies on its presence and participation to exist at all. Mpreg in the form it exists in fan fiction can therefore only exist within fan fiction, but through this it uses BDSM practices to reclaim bodies otherwise inaccessible to audiences. What mpreg does best, then, is to give us power; it creates a world in which immovable, untouchable bodies become malleable and accessible.

References

Andermahr, S. (2005). Cyberspace and the Body: Jeanette Winterson's *The Powerbook*. In N. Bentley (Ed.), *British Fiction of the 1990's* (pp. 108–122). London: Routledge.
Annabagnell. (2013a). *(Almost) Sex on the Beach*. Archive of Our Own.
Annabagnell. (2013b). *Double Your Pleasure*. Archive of Our Own.
Annabagnell. (2013c). *Pressure*. Archive of Our Own.
Åström, B. (2010). "Let's Get Those Winchesters Pregnant": Male Pregnancy in *Supernatural* Fan Fiction. *Transformative Works and Cultures, 4*. http://dx.doi.org/10.3983/twc.2010.0135.
Bartellas, E., Crane, J.M., Daley, M., Bennett, K.A., and Hutchens, D. (2000). Sexuality and Sexual Activity in Pregnancy. *BJOG: An International Journal of Obstetrics & Gynaecology, 107*(8), 964–968.
Behar, K. (2009, December). Command and Control: Cybernetics and BDSM. Paper presented at the *Digital Arts and Culture Conference*.
Busse, K. (2013). Pon Farr, Mpreg, Bonds and the Rise of the Omegaverse. In A.F. Jamison (Ed.), *Fic: Why Fanfiction Is Taking Over the World* (pp. 316–323). Dallas: Smart Pop.
Conan Doyle, A. (2009). *The Penguin Complete Sherlock Holmes*. London: Penguin.
Condon, B. (Director). (2013). *The Fifth Estate* [Motion Picture]. United Kingdom: Entertainment One.
de Beauvoir, S. (2010). *The Second Sex* (C. Borde and S. Malovany-Chevallier, Trans.). London: Random House. (Original work published 1949).
Derecho, A. (2006). Archontic Literature: A Definition, a History, and Several Theories of Fan Fiction. In K. Hellekson and K. Busse (Eds.), *Fan Fiction and Fan Communities in The Age of the Internet: New Essays* (pp. 61–78). Jefferson, NC: McFarland.
Driscoll, C. (2006). One True Pairing: The Romance of Pornography and the Pornography of Romance. In K. Hellekson and K. Busse (Eds.), *Fan Fiction and Fan Communities in the Age of the Internet: New Essays* (pp. 79–96). Jefferson, NC: McFarland.
elirwen. (2012). *Edge of the Unknown*. Archive of Our Own.
Enquist, M., Aronsson, H., Ghirlanda, S., Jansson, L., and Jannini, E.A. (2011). Exposure to

Mother's Pregnancy and Lactation in Infancy Is Associated with Sexual Attraction to Pregnancy and Lactation in Adulthood. *The Journal of Sexual Medicine*, *8*(1), 140–147.
Evenlodes_Friend. (2013). *Oh What Would a Man Not Do for Love?* Archive of Our Own.
Fathallah, J. (2014). Moriarty's Ghost: Or the Queer Disruption of the BBC's Sherlock. *Television & New Media*, *16*(5), 1–11.
Gardener, J., and Jones, B. (Producers). (2008). *Merlin—The Complete Collection: Series 1–5* [DVD]. London: BBC/FremantleMedia International.
Gardner, J., and Jones, B. (Producers). (2008–2012). *Merlin* [Television series]. London: Shine Limited.
Giovanelli, D., and Pelusco, N.M. (2007). Feederism, a New Sexual Pleasure and Subculture. In S. Seidman, N. Fischer, and C. Meeks (Eds.), *Handbook of the New Sexuality Studies* (pp. 331–336). London: Routledge.
Gross, B. (2006). The Pleasure of Pain. *Forensic Examiner*, *15*(1), 56–61.
gwyllion. (2012). *For the Good of the Kingdom*. Archive of Our Own.
Halberstam, J. (2010). The Pregnant Man. *The Velvet Light Trap*, *65*(1). 77–78.
Hellekson, K., and Busse K. (Eds.). (2014). *The Fan Fiction Studies Reader*. Iowa City: University of Iowa Press.
Jones, J., Michie, J., Capps, J., and Murphy, J. (Writers), and Hawes, J. (Director). (2008). The Dragon's Call [Television series episode]. In J. Gardner and B. Jones (Producers), *Merlin*. London: Shine Limited.
Jones, S.G. (2002).The Sex Lives of Cult Television Characters. *Screen*, *43*(1), 79–90.
Kammeyer, K.C. (2008). *A Hypersexual Society*. New York: Palgrave Macmillan.
kingofthegingerales. (2013). *GIFT*. Archive of Our Own.
kinkmerighthererightnow. (2016). *The Bond of Alpha and Omega*. Archive of Our Own.
Kripke, E. (Producer). (2005–). *Supernatural* [Television series]. Burbank, CA: Warner Bros. Television.
Malory, T. (2015). *Le Morte d'Arthur*. New York: Canterbury Classics.
Marks, L.U. (1996). Straight Women, Gay Porn, and the Scene of Erotic Looking. *Jump Cut*, *40*, 127–136.
Merlinmpreg_mod. (2012, November 12). Fest Round Up [Blog Post]. LiveJournal.
Moffat, S. and Gatiss, M. (Writers), and McGuigan, P. (Director). (2010). A Study in Pink [Television series episode]. In M. Gatiss and S. Moffat (Producers), *Sherlock*. London: Hartswood Films & BBC Wales.http://www.bbc.co.uk/programmes/articles/4yTrVL4srk48mKs8bhK4TvM/other-sherlock-related-websites.
Morwen_Maranwe. (2014). *Masterpiece Theater*. Archive of Our Own.
Prohaska, A. (2013). Feederism: Transgressive Behavior or Same Old Patriarchal Sex? *International Journal of Social Science Studies*, *1*(2), 104–112.
pushkin666. (2010). *Chocolate and Pickled Gherkins*. Archive of Our Own.
Pyle, N., and Loewy, M. (2009). Double Stigma: Fat Men and Their Male Admirers. In E.D. Rothblum and S. Solovay (Eds.), *The Fat Studies Reader* (pp. 143–151). New York: New York University Press.
Rubin, M. (2009). *Mother of God: A History of the Virgin Mary*. New Haven: Yale University Press.
Sparrow, R. (2008). Is it "every man's right to have babies if he wants them"? Male Pregnancy and the Limits of Reproductive Liberty. *Kennedy Inst Ethics Journal*, *18*(3), 275–299.
Val_Creative. (2014). *Realism*. Archive of Our Own.
Van Steenhuyse, V. (2011). The Writing and Reading of Fan Fiction and Transformation Theory. *CLCWeb: Comparative Literature and Culture*, *13*(4). http://dx.doi.org/10.7771/1481-4374.1691.
Vertue, S., and Cameron, E. (Producers). (2014). *Sherlock Series 1–3* [DVD]. London: 2entertain/BBC.
Warner, M. (1991). Introduction: Fear of a Queer Planet. *Social Text*, *29*, 3–17.
Watt, C. (2004). Familiarity Breeds Content in Online Fiction Creation and Consumption. *Indiana Libraries*, *23*(2), 49–50.
weezlyismyking. (2015). *The Golden Age*. Archive of Our Own.
Winterson, J. (2001). *The Powerbook*. London: Vintage.

Erotic Imaginaries of Power in Fan Fiction Tropes

SAMANTHA CLOSE *and* CYNTHIA WANG

Introduction

The origins of this study began with the frustration of one of the authors who had just finished reading a slash fan fiction story: how could there be no actual sex in a story rated E for Explicit? Her girlfriend snickered. "You should just ctrl-f for 'cock' when you start a story," she suggested. "That way you'll know."

One of the central questions in the early scholarship of slash fandom was why straight women would be so invested in writing and reading stories about gay male sex. As fandom and fan studies research has expanded, it's now clearer than ever that slash fans identify with a wide variety of sexual orientations and, for some, engaging with fan fiction is part of their process for coming to understand their own desires and needs—even in their unfulfillment! Slash has been revealed to have expanded beyond gay men to include, among others, F/F pairings or femslash—which portray romantic and sexual relationships between female characters. However, while the typically fannish stance of "your kink is okay, my kink is okay," is often good ethics, it can be lazy theory. This study grew and developed through conversations between the authors; both queer women, one who reads almost exclusively male slash fiction and one who reads almost exclusively female slash fiction. We, like destinationtoast (the fandom statistician and meta-commentator), wanted to better understand the relationship between certain parts of the male anatomy and female, queer erotic imaginations. Ctrl-F for "cock," indeed.

Fan fiction isn't always necessarily about sex, and fandom's rapid expansion via the Internet has accelerated the development and spread of pan-fannish textual tropes. Slash provides a space to explore difference in social organization, in gender, in biology, in politics, and beyond. This essay focuses on futanari, a trope specific to pairings of female characters in which bodies sexed as female also have penises. If that exploration more often than not swings in way that is enticingly explicit, who are we to complain? However, a focus on difference within slash fan fiction can obscure what stays the same. Even though futanari switches the traditional focus of slash to female bodies, sex continues to be defined by the presence of the penis-phallus. Problematic power dynamics, including the heteronormativity fan fiction so often opposes, continue to come up. In this essay, we argue that while bodies in futanari slash fiction are being queered, sexuality and social power dynamics largely are not.

Theorizing Identities Within Fandom

Fan fiction has traditionally made a space for queer narratives within heteronormative canonical worlds. Queering up is not just about representation, however, such as casting Kirk and Spock as gay or pansexual rather than as straight. It is also about queering bodies. Even as far back as *Star Trek: The Original Series* (1966–1969), fans took off from Spock's canonical half-alien biology to imagine differently embodied sex acts—at the very least, his dick was clearly green (Penley, 1992).

Much early work in fandom studies drew on feminist media and cultural studies scholarship to move away from the trend of conceptualizing fandom via "the marginalization and stigmatization of women's cultural tastes and interests[,] towards an emphasis on fandom as an alternative space for identity formation and collective expression" (Jenkins, 2014, p. 93). As such, and given the continuing legal battles to preserve fandom's right to exist within a copyright regime, fan creation was often cast in a positive light (Tushnet, 2014). Slash fan fiction does, after all, bring queerness to heteronormative canons, provide space for women to be creators, audiences, and friends, and it often powerfully imagines egalitarian relationships outside of patriarchal societal structures. However, as fans themselves were discussing at that time and as later scholarly work pointed out, this positive light could overly idealize the genre and ignore issues such as homophobia, misogyny, racism, and consent (Green, Jenkins, & Jenkins, 1998; Mizoguchi, 2008; Zubernis & Larsen, 2012). Fans assume that slash fiction subverts and resists heterormative narratives. Indeed, fan studies has too long been content to stop looking for challenges to heteronormativity beyond slash, and has been prone to under-theorizing the relationship between slash and heteronormativity. For example, a straight interracial couple is a challenge to heteronormativity, even though it is not slash. It may seem counter-intuitive for slash to also possibly express homophobic sentiments. However, particularly in early slash, it was quite common for writers to cast their male leads not as gay, but as heterosexual men who happened to fall in love with each other—a clear erasure of, and aversion to, queer identities even while writing and reading about men having sex with each other (Green, Jenkins, & Jenkins, 1998).

The argument that slash can reinforce homophobia was raised particularly forcefully in Japan around the mostly female fandom for *yaoi*, now institutionalized as Boys' Love, based in *doujinshi*, or fan-made manga. *Yaoi* fandom and Boys' Love include the textual tropes of penetrator as dominant and receiver as submissive in terms of power, which do not reflect actual gay male sexual identities. *Yaoi* fandom emerged into the media spotlight in Japan in the 1990s, at roughly the same time as did rising queer activism, including the first court cases challenging anti-gay discrimination (Hori, 2013). In 1992, a self-identified gay male activist critiqued *yaoi* in a feminist zine as "a genre in which men belonging to the homosexual minority were being depicted in a purely fantastical way by and for women belonging to the heterosexual majority" (Hori, 2013, para. 4). Readers, both *yaoi* fans and not, took both sides in what became a fierce debate, with participants often reflecting deeply on the problems of reconciling affective feelings with political commitments (Hori, 2010 & 2013; Vincent, 2007). Particularly as mainstream media finally does begin to integrate more representations of gay, lesbian, and queer characters, the foundational assumption that slash is resistant to heteronormativity and patriarchy must be revised. As Hunting (2012, para. 6.7) argues in her analysis of *Queer as Folk* fan fiction written after the end of the series, "that most fan writers choose an ending that is more heteronormative than the canon's ending demonstrates the extent to which fans can produce work that is more normative than the canon they write within."

In many ways this should not truly be a surprise. If the unofficial motto of Western fandom is "Infinite Diversity in Infinite Combinations" (IDIC), then not all of those combinations are likely to be progressive ones. However, when looked at through other lenses, diversity within fan fiction is remarkably finite. The general absence of female characters in both slash and *yaoi* has long been a topic of internal and external discussion in both Japan and the West. One prominent strand of theoretical reasoning suggests that female slash and *yaoi* fans identify with one or both of the male characters, who are generally much more psychologically fleshed out and less stereotyped than the canonical female characters, and also desire to experience a relationship outside the bounds of heterosexuality under patriarchy—which must thereby be with another man (Penley, 1992; Green, Jenkins, & Jenkins, 1998; Suzuki, 1998; Aoyama, 2009). Others posit that female writers and readers, as a marginalized gender group, enjoy their control over male characters and their bodies (Green, Jenkins, & Jenkins, 1998; Zubernis & Larsen, 2012; Nagaike, 2003). There is unlikely to be either a single or a simple explanation, and the inertia of existing community practice and tradition[1] is also important to consider. Beyond the focus on men, however, misogyny surfaces in slash fandom as female characters in both canon and fan works often draw an immense amount of hate. As Blair (2010) points out in her study of the LiveJournal community Yaoi Daily, it does not follow that focusing on relationships between male characters requires hostility towards female characters.

Some fans have taken on both of these questions by reflecting on why, in a space with such diverse representations of sexuality, there is a huge disparity between male/male slash (M/M) and female/female slash (F/F). One statistical analysis of the Archive of Our Own found that only 9 percent of the total works were identified by the authors as containing a female pairing, versus the 50 percent of the archive that contained a male pairing (toastystats, 2016). Even calling F/F "femslash," rather than assuming its inclusion under the slash umbrella, indicates its felt difference (toastystats, 2016). Studies of F/F, and of female characters in slash more generally, add an important corollary to the theories above. They point out that most F/F creation happens in fandoms for media properties with numerous prominent female characters, a still unfortunately limited source (toastystats, 2014; Blair, 2010). That being said, there is likely something more going on than simple lack of canonical material when fans can generate a detailed, trans-fandom alternative universe with different biological rules, such as the Omegaverse, but not see their way to expanding on secondary female characters.

This argument parallels and intersects with those made by scholars and fans concerned about another notable absence in the infinite diversity in infinite combinations paradigm of fan fiction: the absence of characters of diverse races and ethnicities. Discussions which point to F/F as marginalized often fail to note that F/F is still a very white space. While it is certainly true that popular media depicting more than one central character of color is still very limited, fans' well-known propensity to build on minor (white) characters makes this a thin argument. Similarly, as canonical media begins to include more and more characters of color, fandom's overwhelming focus on white pairings in fandoms for series such as *Teen Wolf* and *Star Wars: The Force Awakens* points to an investment in whiteness, rather than queerness, as a structuring force (Pande & Nadkarni, 2013; Klink et al., 2016).

Wanzo (2015, para. 1.6) goes further in pointing out that "despite their invisibility in fan studies, African Americans are often hypervisible examples of fandom and demonstrate affective relationships to fandom that complicate existing studies of fans." When fan studies focuses on women, the emphasis is often on their "resistance to being normative women through their consumption," since women's marginalization often takes the form of strictly defined behaviors, attitudes, appearances, interests, and social roles (Wanzo, 2015, para. 2.5). However, women of color face a different ideological terrain altogether; their identities as women are non-normative simply by their existence. Being a fan, then, can be a choice towards sameness as well as towards otherness (Wanzo, 2015). The complexity of this movement is clear in the words of an African American fan of Japanese rock music, who recalls, "I have been called 'white girl' and 'weirdo' because I like things that do not fit into the black 'norm'" (Imaoka, 2007, pp. 96–96). Such experiences fit the common critique of American fans of Japanese popular culture loving it for its Otherness, rather than for its own sake or with knowledge of Japan's cultural context, but it inflects it very differently (Napier, 2007; Imaoka, 2007 & 2010).

What should by now be clear is that even as F/F and people of color feature significantly less frequently in fan creations and fan studies, they are certainly there. So too, sometimes, are homophobia, misogyny, and racism—and it is to the detriment of scholarship to continue to gloss over the questions this presents. Raced, gendered, and queer identities (for a start) impact heavily on the way that fans' erotic imaginations intersect with power. This is not to invite a regressive move into shame. One of fandom's greatest cultural strengths is its ability to imagine things differently, which also requires noticing when imagination is re-treading disquietingly familiar ground. We must understand the social role of fantasy in its nuance, rather than dichotomize it between "an optimistic outlook on life (difference as utopia, where rape is actually a really good romp in the sheets) versus a pessimistic outlook (difference as dystopia, where rape is rape and clearly unethical)" (Williams, 2010, p. 223). Indeed, the nuances we found in our exploration of futanari characters go beyond this binary of difference as dystopia or difference as utopia. The stories negotiate normative social dynamics via the difference of queer bodies, thereby rejecting the rigid understandings of the utopic/dystopic binary. This allows us to understand the deep complexity of the appeal of this particular trope in the erotic imagination of readers. Hence, in this essay we focus on the fannish imagination as evidenced through the pan-fandom trope of futanari, seeking to understand its textual construction of bodies and of sexualities, as well as the ways in which these interplay with erotic power dynamics and identity politics.

What the F--- Is Futanari?

While slash and *yaoi* (along with the F/F equivalent of *yuri*) are both practices in which largely female readers and writers re-imagine canonically straight characters in queer ways, they are not the same practice, nor is one derivative of the other. Modern slash largely developed within Western science-fiction and media fandom, and remained underground as much because of its freewheeling appropriation of copyrighted characters as its sexual content (Jenkins, 1992; Coppa, 2006). Modern *yaoi* actually traces its history back to a critically acclaimed novel, Mari Mori's homoerotic *The Lovers' Forest* (1961/2012). Both *yaoi* and *yuri* grew through the intersections of commercially published *shoujo*, or girls' manga with fan appropriations of canonical characters from both *shoujo* and *shonen* (boys') manga (Mizoguchi, 2003; Vincent, 2007). Fans from Japan as well as from the United States have long had an interest in each other's popular culture, although American media is much more mainstream in Japan than the other way around. Particularly as both nations embraced network communications, vibrant contact zones grew up wherein fans could more swiftly and directly communicate with each other. This has led to a flourishing increase in production in the intersections between slash, *yaoi*, and *yuri*.[2] One of these intersections is the pan-fandom trope of futanari.

Futanari is the Japanese word for hermaphroditism or androgyny. As a trope, it originally became popular in pornographic anime and manga before filtering into Japanese and English fannish practice (Maser, 2013; Nagayama, 2006). A futanari character combines a biologically male apparatus, the penis, with an otherwise biologically female body, often including a vagina. Balls are optional. The trope is also commonly known and tagged as "g!p," "girl penis," or "girl peen." Pande and Nadkarni (2013) call for fans to engage with race and cultural specificity thoughtfully, rather than reproducing the structures of power evident in canonical media and the societies that produced it. The F/F futanari trope is arguably a case where that has occurred. Japanese gender practices and social structures contradict an implicit assumption in much Western Fan and Gender studies "that an understanding of gender as socially constructed necessitates a rejection of gendered social roles and gendered power hierarchies" (LeBlanc, 2011). Futanari builds on this Japanese outlook wherein "sexual acts are more often viewed as *asobi* (play) and not an identity-determining factor" (Hall, 2010, p. 219). Scholars question whether a "gay identity" exists in Japan as it does in the West, critiquing the idea that Japanese homosexuals "lack" such an identity and should develop one (McLelland, 2000).

As Western scholars writing about this trope in the context of its emergence in English-language fan works, however, it is important to consider how our viewpoint requires "adopting, negotiating, or rejecting American discourses of sexuality and identity" and thus bringing new meaning to the trope (Hall, 2010, p. 219). Ethnicity and national origin impacts strongly on negotiations of gender and sexuality. Despite futanari's status as an F/F trope, some communities dedicated to female slash explicitly disallow it, unless the character is trans in the canon. These communities often also outlaw genderswap, a trope in which canonically male characters are imagined in female bodies. These actions can be read as striving to preserve focus on "normal" female bodies, but in doing so they can inadvertently place potentially transphobic boundaries around gender expressions. On the other hand, futanari's status as a fictional trope also raises concerns about "the use of transgendered and trans-sexual bodies as tropes in the exploration of cisgendered identities when the quotidian realities of translives are given little consideration" (Busse & Lothian, 2009). Trans* fans frustrated with fetishistic and even transphobic depictions of trans-seeming bodies and experiences in genderswap created the specific subgenre of transfic, "fan fiction about transgender characters, usually characters who are not transgender/transsexual in canon" (Beazley, 2016; Transfic, 2016).

Part of our initial interest in futanari was the possible relationship between the trope's imagined bodies and trans* identities. Futanari's fusion of a male sexual organ and a female body recall American terms like "girlfag" and "transfag," which were "coined during the late 1990s in the U.S. to describe persons who were female-assigned at birth and who feel an intense fascination for and identification with gay men," wanting to have sex "like a boy" even while anatomically female (Meyer, 2010, p. 244). However, what our analysis suggests is that futanari is a biological and a meta-textual trope, rather than an identity. This trope overlaps with the similarly pan-fandom trope of the Omegaverse, but where Lexa of *The 100* might say "I'm an alpha," a term which, like futanari, signifies a body with a penis-like organ and otherwise female biology, she would never say "I'm a futanari." Similarly, one's story "has" a g!p tag rather than a character within it "being" a g!p. The distinction between identity and trope is key in analyzing the relationship of futanari to trans* bodies and imaginaries. Erotica author Kella Z. Driel (2016) puts it simply, arguing "the word 'futanari' shouldn't be synonymous with an actual M2F transgender, since magical futanari bodies have nothing to do with genuine transgender experience." Japanese trans* people are much more likely to identify themselves via the term *newhalf* (Driel, 2016; McLelland, 2002). Similarly, trans* scholarship suggests that gendered appearance and social recognition of gender is often more important than the sexual biology on which futanari focuses (Schilt and Windsor, 2014). Thus, our focus is not on the trans dimension of futanari but rather, as much as this distinction is possible, on the relationships between female bodies, sexualities, and social power.

Futanari in many ways reverses both the biological and symbolic implications of the fannish trope of male pregnancy, or mpreg. While "mpreg allows a female writer to play out themes of female bodies, concerns of gender in relationships, and issues of reproduction [at] a certain emotional distance by divorcing the pregnancy from the female body," futanari takes the theories that female fans enjoy identifying with or controlling male bodies to the next level, physically attaching a penis to a female body (Busse, 2013, p. 320). As it does so, however, it also re-affirms an ingrained cultural notion in both Japan and the United States that sexuality and sexual pleasure is reduced to and dependent on the penis/phallus (Schilt and Windsor, 2014). It is notable that *yuri* fandom has much less intersection with futanari than F/F slash fiction does—*yuri* focuses on homosexual desire as a desire between and for similar bodies, which does not accord with futanari's emphasis on biological difference (Maser, 2013). Like mpreg, futanari's condensation of the biological and the cultural—particularly the culturally stereotypical—are potentially politically alarming and can veer into the explicitly transphobic (Busse & Lothian, 2009; Busse, 2013). Futanari as a trope creates a space in which the queering of bodies allows for a wider scope of female homoerotic imaginations at the same time as it reinforces a heteronormative paradigm of power, as articulated through the privileging of the penis in sexual actions. Futanari simultaneously queers the body and resists queering symbolic power.

Fan fiction is a playful, metaphorical, exploratory space. It would be a grave misreading to suggest that fans desire the real life enactment of problematic tropes, such as the biological need for sex that removes characters' abilities to consent to sex in the Omegaverse. And yet, stories set in the Omegaverse which make use of this trope are still very popular, which points to the emotional resonance that these narratives elicit. Futanari is a worrying trope not in the biologies it depicts but in its emphasis on male sexual organs even in sexual relations between women, as well as the collapse of stereotypical gendered traits onto sexual biologies.

To better understand the textual constructions inspiring futanari's emotional appeal, we performed a content analysis of the most visible and popular futanari stories on the Archive of Our Own (AO3). Part of the Organization for Transformative Works, AO3 is one of the largest archives of fan works in existence, currently boasting over two million fan works. We chose AO3 as our site of inquiry because of its high popularity amongst fan fiction readers and writers alike, as well as its easily searchable tag system.[3] We searched for the tag "Futanari," then picked the three pairings with the most number of works from these search results: Rachel Berry/Quinn Fabray or "Faberry" (*Glee*, 2009–2015), Clarke Griffin/Lexa or "Clexa" (*The 100*, 2014–present), and Krista Lenz [Historia Reiss]/Ymir or "Yumikuri" (*Attack on Titan*, 2009–present). For each pairing, we took the top three works with the most kudos (AO3's version of "like") and the top three works with the most views, many of which overlapped. This resulted in a sample of twelve stories: four Faberry, four for Yumikuri, and four for Clexa. We used only stories that depicted the target pairings as the main pairing, as one of the challenges in statistical analyses of fan fiction is that many stories tagged both F/F and M/M contain only brief appearances by the female characters.[4] Interpretations of futanari varied widely within these stories, from one in which the character possessing the g!p switched from chapter to chapter, to narratives which blended futanari and the Omegaverse, to those which explicitly used futanari to explore politics of difference. By focusing in on the most beloved (greatest number of "kudos") and commonly read (greatest number of views) stories in the most popular futanari pairings on AO3, this small archive gives a reasonable sense of what fans like reading within the collective futanari imaginary.

Queer (Lesbian?) Bodies

In futanari works, fans re-imagine the bodies of canonically female characters and their relationships with each other. This re-imagination ruptures the canonical narrative and makes a space for queer readings within that text: two of the three most popular futanari pairings, Faberry and Krista/Ymir, are non-canonical. While Clexa is canonical, all of the stories selected by our analysis procedure took futanari even further, into the alternative universe of the Omegaverse. Here we explore how bodies are queered via their textual construction in futanari narratives and the gender non-binary ethos that permeates the portrayals of the bodies within this alternate universe, notwithstanding what are at times highly patriarchal and heteronormative portrayals of masculinity. The ethos is non-binary in the fluidity of its unlikely combinations: she/her pronouns, the erasure of female biological attributes, an all-woman narrative space, and extreme hegemonic masculine behavior.

Some stories acknowledge the additional male apparatus in their narrative and incorporate that recognition (and often expressed undesirability of such apparatus) into the story, and others do not. This acknowledgment of the normal and abnormal is a mechanism by which the queering of the female body is articulated. In CherishMimi's Faberry story, *Cherished Affliction* (2013), Quinn Fabray is portrayed as having a penis and acknowledges it as "abnormal female genitalia." Similarly, in Kendarrr's *Better Remember* (2013a), Rachel not only acknowledges her penis, but is ashamed of it, which results in a pivotal plot point where Quinn is put into a position of comforting Rachel, further deepening their emotional connection. Finally, in Atma's Yumikuri fic *Hormonal Issues* (2013), Ymir quite accidentally, through the eminently well-thought out course of breaking into her comrade's lab and stealing and drinking an unidentified potion, grows a penis that later causes her much embarrassment and humorous distress. In each of these cases, the abnormality of a penis on a female body is overtly acknowledged.

Such a move arguably makes non-normative queer bodies visible, at least within the imagined worlds of these stories, while also distinguishing them from trans* bodies whose changes are not "abnormal," unexpected, or embarrassing but deeply desired and acquired through significant effort. This approach to futanari recalls a foundational *shoujo* manga trope of fathers raising their daughters as boys so as to have male heirs and preserve their lines of succession (Meyer, 2010). Although classic *shoujo*, such as Riyoko Ikeda's manga, *The Rose of Versailles* (1972–1973), and their fannish *yuri* interpretations tended to shy away from the explicit realities of anatomy, preserving a line of succession logically necessitates a dick somewhere along the way.

Explicit use of female pronouns for characters with male anatomies also serves to queer these characters. The erasure of female attributes is quite prevalent in a number of futanari works. For example, Lexa, who is always the Alpha (and hence the one with the penis), rarely (if ever) has her female bits mentioned. The only thing that alerts the reader to the fact that she is female is the use of female pronouns and her name. Such ambiguity within the story allows both for the imagined potential of transgenderism on one hand, whereby a biologically male Lexa is understood through her felt female gender, and a denying of the F/F sexual queerness through the imposed invisibility of the female body on the other. The use of female pronouns without descriptions of female anatomy makes a queer space for fluid bodies. The erasure of feminine attributes could also be read as a resistance to the objectification of the female body—subverting the reader's "gaze," so to speak, from an imagined visual perspective. However, it also allows the reader to imagine any love scene as a heterosexual one. By this reading, the erasure of the female form is a form of trauma that denies the full extent of the lesbian imaginary.

While many of the works we looked at seemed to erase the female biological aspects of their futanari characters, Kendarrr's *Better Remember* (2013a) does not. Rachel's penis and breasts are both clearly and continually "visible" in the text. In this story, however, Rachel is portrayed as the submissive partner. In this way, the female attributes of Rachel are still subject to domination—she is in the position of possessing a penis but not the powerful phallus. This demotion of the g!p, however, represents a queering of the dominant relationship trope within futanari. While we emphasize common interpretations of tropes here, it is essential to also note such instances where works diverge—fandom is anything but monolithic.

Switching

One of the notable differences between futa and male slash, even the more biologically transgressive tropes such as Omegaverse, is the prevalence of switching. Quite famously, *yaoi* and, to a lesser extent, Western male slash designates one member of a pairing as the more dominant and/or penetrating top (or *seme*) and the other as the more submissive and/or receiving bottom (or *uke*). Meyer (2010) found, for example, that the penetrator/receiver, perpetrator/victim trope was an important trope for German *yaoi* fans. They appropriated the English word "rape" to use in their stories instead of the German word, which would have been, for them, immediately associated with the actual act of rape. This move demonstrates their concern to differentiate between the tropes of fannish imagination and the reality of sexual assault.

The sexual practice of switching (changing which character has the g!p from chapter to chapter) resists built-in sexual hierarchies of power and non-egalitarian relationships. Switching subverts the notion that one character within a story or a pairing holds all the power. As the penis jumps between two characters, so does the penetrative power. As such, neither character settles into a normative dynamic structure, even within the story itself, which compels a reader to forego their pre-existing assumptions about the power dynamic between the characters.

A good example of this switching can be found in Kendarrr's *Faberry Smut G!P Compilation* (2013b), which features Rachel Berry and Quinn Fabray. This is a series of short stories featuring Rachel and Quinn, who trade off having a penis from chapter to chapter. Because this is not a canonical pairing, the sexual acts and relationship of this female on female pairing represent a fairly typical fannish queering of the narrative within the *Glee* universe as well as the explicit queering of bodies. Moreover, the trading off of the penis results in few dominance dynamics. There is little continuity to the story—each chapter seems more or less discrete. There is no explanation for how the penis got where it is in the first place—it is presented more or less as natural. In reading this compilation, the reader is also kept off-balance and on their toes, having to read rather carefully to ascertain which character has a penis in that specific chapter.

The idea of disclosure through switching is also embedded within the work itself. One chapter has Quinn pretending to be Rachel's boyfriend to Rachel's family—the author plays with heteronormativity here, but in a winking "I know something you don't know" way. Diana Fisher discusses this in the context of Russian gay and lesbian immigrants' "tactical use of closet space" (2008, p. 174). Sexuality is often not an immediately visible aspect of an individual, and in her research, Fisher explains that lesbians often use the assumption of their heteronormativity to their advantage. Both in real life and in these stories, the ability to "hide" one's sexuality and disclose (or to not disclose) "unseen" information about one's sexuality becomes an act of empowerment and subversive glee (no pun intended) on the part of the queer individual.

The Magical Penis

The focus of futanari characters is always on the presence of the g!p. The penis is the object that is "different" to the female body; the object that quite literally stands out in most cases. Pornography studies argue that the experience and depiction of sexual pleasure is centered in the penis (Williams, 2010). In futanari, sexual pleasure is not the exclusive domain of the penis, but it is often derived from the phallus, with the penetrative act depicted as the ultimate culmination of sexual pleasure. Moreover, the dynamics of power within the social worlds presented within these stories often posit that the possessor of the penis is also the possessor of social power. This reinforces notions of patriarchal society and its privileging of the phallus as a fulcrum of power.

While the penis does not necessarily always connote domination in the sense of BDSM, the phallus holds both power over sexual pleasure and others within society. In the Clexa fan works, which take place predominantly in the Omegaverse, there are variations, complexities, and nuances of actual sexual performance—but less of social role. Sometimes the Omega is dominant in the bedroom, or takes control in a few scenes, but the rigid hierarchal structure of ABO dictates that power lies with the penis, no matter what the private behavior of the characters happens to be. In these Omegaverse futanari stories, power appears biologically (rather than socially or culturally) constructed, through the penis-phallus. The Clexa story, *as you are mine, i am yours* (popper, 2016) discusses how, when Lexa is frustrated and Clarke touches her arm in an attempt to calm her down (and is subsequently able to), Clarke's "inner Omega practically dances in joy." This simple statement implies Clarke's identity as Omega is not only social or cultural, but innate and compulsory, with certain physical relationships formed around a rigid social hierarchy.

In a similar way, *Cherished Affliction* (2013) by CherishMimi depicts a futanari G!P (Quinn) within a BDSM relationship with the normative-bodied Rachel Berry. The G!P is explained as an "abnormal female genitalia" that developed as Quinn reached puberty, suggesting this apparatus is biologically natural. Unlike in Kendarrr's *Better Remember* (2013a) where there is an emotional recognition of the abnormality of such an appendage, *Cherished Affliction*'s Quinn mentions it but displays no shame. Indeed, she uses the penis as a phallic signal of her power and domination over Rachel, particularly Rachel's physical body. While, as discussed earlier, there is a gesture toward the queering of the body with this, the seeming naturalness of the penis as phallus, a symbol for power and as a vehicle for pleasure, pervades these works. The social power that Quinn enjoys even outside the bedroom signals the reinforcement of patriarchal masculinity, despite the queering of the narrative by depicting an explicit relationship between the female characters of Rachel and Quinn.

The penis (and by extension, the possessor of the penis) is consistently the vehicle for sexual pleasure and power throughout the stories we reviewed, even when it is not altogether desired. In Atma's *Hormonal Issues* (2013), Ymir acquires a penis accidentally. It is not altogether clear whether or not the penis is temporary. Ymir seems downright disgusted at this newly found apparatus and its functions. In one scene, she masturbates to orgasm, then smears the semen on a piece of bread and takes a bite. She is then overcome with a sense of disgust and wonderment that people would willingly ingest such vileness. In another scene, Ymir asks Krista to stop staring at the penis and to "let [her] put it away before anyone else finds out" (Ch. 1, para. 66). As we can see here, there is an element of shame associated with both possessing the penis and having people find out. However, later in the story Ymir and Krista have sex, and the penis is still the source of pleasure—both oral and vaginal—as Ymir says that the sex was "[r]eally good. Really, really fucking good. You?" and Krista responds, "S-same" (Ch. 1, para. 165–166). Such a scene serves to reinforce the notion that the penis, while perhaps not necessary for sexual pleasure within this particular work, is still the source of immense pleasure beyond what women would otherwise experience. Even given the social undesirability of a g!p within this deliberately queered world, the erotic imagination persistently desires a phallus as the fulcrum of pleasure.

With the penis comes the potential for production and offspring, which is often imagined as a desired familial structure in these narratives. Impregnation is often a result of the depicted futanari/female sexual acts. The author of *Little Omega* (2015), short_stack_100, continually teases the readers by hinting at Clexa babies in the author notes—for instance, asking for input as to what their names might be. In this way, the imagined desired family, while still queer, is only made possible by the presence of the penis. Similarly, *Totally Worth It* (2014) by CanaanAlphardForever is a fluffy story that nevertheless includes familial issues with a homosexual relationship. Throughout the story, Krista's mother wishes that her daughter would have a more "normal" relationship, especially one that can bear her grandchildren. Krista and Ymir are secretly smug that Krista's mother does not know that Ymir has a penis and can impregnate her. So while problematic discrimination is articulated through the mother's desire for Krista to be with a man for the purpose of grandbabies, the biology (penis) is gleefully hidden as a sort of Shakespearean thumb-bite to those who would discriminate and acts as a way to negate the implications of that discrimination. The act of impregnation, if we were to follow Diana Fisher's argument about the tactical use of closets as a form of subversive empowerment, places empowerment firmly in the realm of a heterosexual potential for reproduction and offspring. While a queer reading is certainly still possible, the emphasis on heterosexual mechanisms as the pathway to a desired family structure undermines the queer potential by once again placing power in the phallus's biological embodiment as the penis.

Biologically Determined Power Structures—Animal Metaphors and Omegaverse

In roughly half of the works, the imagined biological aspect of futanari also works through animalistic ethos. All four of the Clarke/Lexa stories that we reviewed are based in the Omegaverse (also known as "A/B/O"). A Yumikuri fic called *She-Wolf* (Atma, 2014) portrays Ymir as a she-wolf, including the associated sweat and animalistic stench. Ymir plays the dominant role, getting rough with Krista (called "Christa" within this work). While Ymir's penis in this story seems to be present and not present in cycles, other people notice. Ymir, due to her "manliness" and her "hots for the ladies," grows balls. In other words, her gender representation and sexuality *determined* her biological anatomy. Because of her balls, Ymir endures a hint of ostracization, and as such, there is a distinct recognition of Ymir's difference from the other characters in the story. Girls would "back up and away from her, calling her a devil and she-wolf and other names that only spurred the freckled wonder on harder until she turned [to] face the girls and bark at them like a beast" (Ch. 1, para. 29). Interestingly, though, Ymir is accepted into a group of men because, as a "[dick-haver], figuring if it's going to function as fully as any man's dick would, they may as well let her in the group as a sign of camaraderie" (Ch. 1, para. 13). In this way, camaraderie is defined through shared anatomical parts rather than gender, behavior, or any other personal attribute. Ymir's social position, and thus social power, is directly correlated with how her beast-like manifestation is presented and read in a rather heteronormative way by other characters. The presence of her penis accords Ymir phallic power—men accept her into their circles while women see her as someone to be feared.

The prevalence of the Omegaverse, a world which functions with strict hierarchies based on biology, within Clexa narratives seems to suggest that because Clexa is already a canonical couple, there needs to be another level of queering, or of fantasy, in order to please the erotic imagination of the reader. However, the Omegaverse functions under the assumption that there is a biological basis for the power dynamics displayed, including dominance and submission, within a community. Moreover, with the fantastical and inherent queering of bodies in the Omegaverse, we also see an almost hyper-heteronormative mentality within some of these narratives. In the Clexa works which emerged as most popular given our analysis procedure, Lexa is depicted as an Alpha; the dominant social group whose members all have penises, regardless of gender. Clarke is depicted as an Omega; the submissive social group. Such a power dynamic fits well into the plots of the canonical storyline, where Clarke tends to be the "softer" of the pair at first, with Lexa the more ruthless one with guarded emotions and less vulnerability. Hence, there is already an apparent heteronormative dynamic in the canonical source that is intensified, rather than transformed, via the Alpha/Omega designations in the subsequent fan fictions. Moreover, the depiction of the mating process was prevalent in this pairing. All of the Clexa works in this study depict Clarke in some form of heat, which Lexa is helplessly attracted to and aroused by. Tension builds toward the act of penetration within a virginal defloration narrative structure. For example, N1ghtWr1ter's *Strange Love* (2015), which is a first-time "knotting" story, follows a typical heterosexual defloration process, where tension builds continually through four chapters to culminate in only one incident of knotting.

Although we have focused mainly on textual construction and, by extension, the work of authors, readers have explicit expectations for troped stories. The Clexa story *You're never prepared for how it feels...* (2015) by clexaqueen seems to be a contentious story in the community. The content had some issues with consent, including imprisonment of the Omega Clarke by the Alpha Lexa. The story continued to progress beyond simple possessive control into what a number of commenters perceived as unnecessary violence, especially when Lexa indiscriminately murders another character in an irrational jealous rage. One commenter states:

> [T]here are definitely some serious consent issues. Even if there was a much smaller degree of communication than would be realistic, for the purposes of fitting canon or this story or whatever, Clarke just goes from unwillingly complying with lexas [sic] orders and trying to sneak off and such to having sex with her and forming a mating bond. There needs to be explicit consent given with full presence of mind, or you need to tag dubious consent if the consent is not given with full presence of mind, of which heat is an example. Even if a character says yes while in heat, they still need to say it without the influence of any chemicals, substances, hormones, or anything else like that. And if there is a total lack of explicit consent of any kind, wherein one character says out loud that they want and will allow the character to which they are speaking to have sex with them, then you need to tag rape/non-con and use the archive warning as well [clexaqueen, 2015].

Another commenter responds:

> Yeah I noticed this as well. The switch happened way too quickly. But! It's not rape/non-con it's more Dubious Consent as Clarke didn't say she didn't want it. I've seen a rape ABO and it was weird as fuck. The transition was too quick and the communication too little between the two [*ibid.*].

The comments themselves reveal an interesting normative framing of the Omegaverse which despite its queer potentiality and flexibility was still supposed to fall within certain boundaries and adhere to certain expectations. Readers became slightly upset when the story did not conform to the expected standards. One commenter argued that although they liked the story overall, there were a few elements they did not like: "How Lexa slapped Clarke [...] if [they] were mates, Lexa wouldn't be able to harm her [...] and also how Lexa is just too controlling" (*ibid.*). Other readers, as we have seen, took issue with the dubious consent aspects of some of the Clexa stories, outlining the expected framework for such a trope and calling the author out on not adhering to those standards. Lexa seemed, to some readers of this work, to be "overly Alpha"—overly violent, overly possessive, quick to kill when jealous and with problems in communicating when it comes to consent, making some readers uncomfortable and hence breaking the pleasure of the erotic imagination.

The Omegaverse, however, seems to be used as an excuse to depict and enjoy these problematic dynamics. In one scene in popper's Clexa fic, *as you are mine, i am yours* (2016), Clarke (Omega) performs oral sex on Lexa (Alpha): "Lexa groans above her and grabs the back of Clarke's head, pushing her forward, forcing her to take more of her cock inside her mouth" (Ch. 1, para. 74). A commenter on this work states: "I liked this. The roughness surprised me but then again it is ABO and she did apologise in the aftercare" (popper, 2016). Here, the reader reacts to the roughness of the scene, arguably with some discomfort initially, struggling with their own comfort level for non-normative narratives and the "rough" depiction of fellatio. However, their concerns are assuaged by invoking expectations about the Omegaverse and BDSM frameworks of aftercare following sexual encounters. In this way, the fannishly normative Omegaverse acts as a sort of safety net when the story veers into dubious territory. This fictionalization can give the distance needed for recuperation after traumatic events, particularly sexual assault (Zubernis & Larsen 2012). However, it is somewhat difficult to square that reasoning with authors' and readers' framing of stories around their erotic potential.

Conclusion

Within fan fiction, the futanari trope can allow space for queer re-imaginings of stories and, particularly, women's bodies. In political and social climates where the rejection of non-binary gender expressions is becoming a sadly common reality, having an outlet for non-heteronormative imaginaries is essential for a great number of individuals who do not conform to society's standards. As we have seen in this essay, futanari slash fan works in practice are a vehicle by which this queering can happen, pushing and resisting the normative boundaries that are seen in canonical storylines and expanding possibilities for sexual desires, bodies, and relationships.

However, while futanari allows for queering, it has also created a subculture where the erotic imagination takes great pleasure in the extreme heteronormative, pushing back against the "queer normal" within fan fiction. The community-based nature of fan fiction argues that this pushback is a force within, as well as outside of, fandom. There are complex *desires* for these heteronormative, patriarchal power dynamics, which are played out with what sometimes comes to be only superficial hybridization and transformation. Particularly, there is a consistent reinforcement of pleasure framed through a phallic patriarchal perspective in the stories we studied here.

The dynamics of futanari within slash fan fiction are complex and nuanced. These works straddle both a space for queering and for the reinforcement of heteronormative sexual pleasure and patriarchal dynamics of power. We see this as a reason not to condemn fans and fandom but to recognize and strive to understand the *additional* counternarratives working in conjunction with fan fiction's familiar transgressive queer counternarratives. These collective non-normative counternarratives subvert mainstream heteronormative narratives; they continually interrogate the frameworks of gender, sexuality, and identity dynamics that are still seen as "normal" within broader society, while simultaneously highlighting the diversity and complexity in negotiating non-normative desires. After all, if we do not understand how growing within a patriarchal and heteronormative society impacts on our imaginations, we cannot free them.

Notes

1. The fan fiction archive we studied, for example, was originally founded by people active in slash fandom, which subsequently impacts who came to know about and populate the archive (toastystats, 2014).

2. For example, essays by Donovan, Malone, and Abraham in the *Boys' Love Manga* anthology respectively explore *yaoi* in the United States, Germany, and Indonesia. Pande and Nadkarni (2013) narrate their reflections on fandom as seen from India, including the authors bonding over slash based on Japanese anime *Weiss Kreuz*. Meyer (2010) suggests that the massive Japanese fandom for *Harry Potter* stems at least in part from the series' similar setting to that of many early *yaoi* manga.

3. As opposed to Fanfiction.net, a central fan fiction archive site which does not allow for tag-based searches.

4. We originally found five stories for Clexa, but because one of these did not depict Clexa as the main pairing, we dropped it from our analysis. This issue of identifying primary versus secondary pairings occurs regularly in analyses of femslash, prompting F/F fans to come up with directed search tactics to avoid wading through stories with primary M/M or F/M relationships (toastystats, 2016).

References

Aoyama, T. (2009). Male Homosexuality as Treated by Japanese Women Writers. In G. McCormack and Y. Sugimoto (Eds.), *The Japanese Trajectory: Modernization and Beyond* (pp. 186–204). Cambridge: Cambridge University Press.

Atma. (2013). *Hormonal Issues*. Archive of Our Own.

Atma. (2014). *She-Wolf*. Archive of Our Own.

Beazley, M. (2016, February 23). Transfic: A History. *FAN/FIC Magazine*. Retrieved from https://fanslashfic.com/2016/02/23/transfic-a-history.

Blair, M.M. (2010). "She Should Just Die in a Ditch": Fan Reactions to Female Characters in Boys' Love Manga. In A. Levi, M. McHarry, and D. Pagliassotti (Eds.), *Boys' Love Manga: Essays on the Sexual Ambiguity and Cross-Cultural Fandom of the Genre* (pp. 110–125). Jefferson, NC: McFarland.

Busse, K., and Lothian, A. (2009). Bending Gender: Feminist and (Trans)Gender Discourses in the Changing Bodies of Slash Fanfiction. In I. Hotz-Davies, A. Kirchhofer, and S. Leppänen (Eds.), *Internet Fiction(s)* (pp. 105–127). Newcastle upon Tyne: Cambridge Scholars.

Busse, K. (2013). Pon Farr, Mpreg, Bonds, and the Rise of the Omegaverse. In A.E. Jamison (Ed.), *Fic: Why Fanfiction Is Taking Over the World* (pp. 316–322). Dallas: Smart Pop.

CanaanAlphardForever. (2014). *Totally Worth It*. Archive of Our Own.

CherishMimi. (2013). *Cherished Affliction*. Archive of Our Own.

clexaqueen. (2015–2016). *You're Never Prepared for How It Feels*... Archive of Our Own.

Coon, G.L., Lucas, J.M., and Frieberger, F. (Producers). (2007). *Star Trek, the Original Series: Seasons One, Two and Three* [DVD]. Hollywood: CBS Home Entertainment.

Coppa, F. (2006). A Brief History of Media Fandom. In K. Hellekson and K. Busse (Eds.), *Fan Fiction and Fan Communities in the Age of the Internet: New Essays* (pp. 41–59). Jefferson, NC: McFarland.

Driel, K.A. (2016, March 25). "What's a Futanari and Why Should You Care?" [Blog post]. *Transgressive Erotica for a Kinky World*. Retrieved from https://kellazdriel.wordpress.com/2016/03/25/whats-a-futanari-and-why-do-i-care/.

Fisher, D. (2008). Immigrant Closets. *Journal of Homosexuality, 45*(2–4), 171–192.

Green, S., Jenkins, C., and Jenkins, H. (1998). Normal Female Interest in Men Bonking: Selections from the Terra Nostra Underground and Strange Bedfellows. In C. Harris and A. Alexander (Eds.), *Theorizing Fandom: Fans, Subculture, and Identity* (pp. 9–38). Caskill, NJ: Hampton Press.

Hall, A. (2010). Gay or Gei? Reading "Realness" in Japanese Yaoi Manga. In A. Levi, M. McHarry, and D. Pagliassotti (Eds.), *Boys' Love Manga: Essays on the Sexual Ambiguity and Cross-Cultural Fandom of the Genre* (pp. 211–220). Jefferson, NC: McFarland.

Hori, A. (2010). Yaoi wa gei sabetsu ka? Manga hyōgen to tashaka [Does Yaoi Discriminate Against Gay Men? Manga Portrayals and the Creation of Others]. In Y. Hiroaki (Ed.), *Sabetsu to haijo no ima 6: Sekushuariti no tayōsei to haijo* (pp. 21–54). Tokyo: Akashi Shoten.

Hori, A. (2013). On the Response (or Lack Thereof) of Japanese Fans to Criticism That "Yaoi" Is Antigay Discrimination. *Transformative Works and Cultures, 12*. doi:10.3983/twc.2013.0463.

Hunting, K. (2012). *Queer as Folk* and the Trouble with Slash. *Transformative Works and Cultures, 11*. http://dx.doi.org/10.3983/twc.2012.0415.

Ikeda, R. (1972–1973). *The Rose of Versailles*. Richmond Hill: Udon Entertainment.

Imaoka, L.B. (2007). *Consuming & Creating Difference: The Underground Anime and Jrock Movement Among American Youth* [M.A. Dissertation]. California State University—Northridge.

Imaoka, L.B. (2010). Consuming and Maintaining Difference: American Fans Resisting the Globalization of Japanese Pop Culture. *disClosure: A Journal of Social Theory, 19*(1), 73–84.

Isayama, H. (2009). *Shingeki no Kyojin* [Attack on Titan]. New York: Kodansha USA Publishing.

Jenkins, H. (1992). *Textual Poachers: Television Fans and Participatory Culture*. New York: Routledge.
Jenkins, H. (2014). Fandom Studies as I See It. *Journal of Fandom Studies*, *2*(2), 89–109. https://doi.org/10.1386/jfs.2.2.89_1.
Kendarrr. (2013a). *Better Remember*. Archive of Our Own.
Kendarrr. (2013b). *Faberry Smut G!P Compilation*. Archive of Our Own.
Klink, F., Minkel, E., Quinn, H., Pande, R., Shadowkeeper, C., and Punla, P. (2016, May 23). Transcript: Episode 22A: Race and Fandom Part 1 [Podcast]. Retrieved February 1, 2017, from http://fansplaining.com/post/144813752418/transcript-episode-22a-race-and-fandom-part-1.
LeBlanc, R.M. (2011). "The Politics of Gender in Japan." In V. Bestor, T.C. Bestor, and A. Yamagata (Eds.), *Routledge Handbook of Japanese Culture and Society* (pp. 116–28). Abingdon: Taylor & Francis.
Maser, V. (2013). *Beautiful and Innocent: Female Same-Sex Intimacy in the Japanese Yuri Genre* [Doctoral Thesis]. University of Trier, Trier, Germany. Retrieved from http://ubt.opus.hbz-nrw.de/volltexte/2015/944/pdf/Maser_Beautiful_and_Innocent.pdf.
McLelland, M. (2000). Is There a Japanese "Gay Identity?" *Culture, Health & Sexuality*, *2*(4), 459–72. doi:10.1080/13691050050174459.
McLelland, M. (2002). The Newhalf Net: Japan's "Intermediate Sex" On-Line. *International Journal of Sexuality and Gender Studies*, *7*(2–3), 163–75. doi:10.1023/A:1015897117075.
Meyer, U. (2010). Hidden in Straight Sight: Trans*gressing Gender and Sexuality Via BL. In A. Levi, M. McHarry, and D. Pagliassotti (Eds.), *Boys' Love Manga: Essays on the Sexual Ambiguity and Cross-Cultural Fandom of the Genre* (pp. 232–256). Jefferson, NC: McFarland.
Mizoguchi, A. (2003). Male-Male Romance by and for Women in Japan: A History and the Subgenres of "Yaoi" Fictions. *U.S.-Japan Women's Journal*, *25*, 49–75.
Mizoguchi, A. (2008). *Reading and Living Yaoi: Male-Male Fantasy Narratives as Women's Sexual Subculture in Japan* [Doctoral Thesis]. University of Rochester. Retrieved from https://urresearch.rochester.edu/institutionalPublicationPublicView.action?institutionalItemVersionId=5822.
Mori, M. (2012). The Lover's Forest. In K. Nagaike (Ed.), *Fantasies of Cross-Dressing: Japanese Women Write Male-Male Erotica* (pp. 135–185). (n.p): Brill. (Original work published 1961).
Murphy, R., and Falchuck, B. (Producers). (2009–2015). *Glee* [Television series]. United States: 20th Century Fox Television.
Nagaike, K. (2003). Perverse Sexualities, Perversive Desires: Representations of Female Fantasies and Yaoi Manga as Pornography Directed at Women. *U.S.-Japan Women's Journal, English Supplement*, *25*, 76–103.
Nagayama, K. (2006). *Ero manga sutadīzu: Kairaku sōchi toshite no manga nyūmon*. Tokyo: East Press.
Napier, S.J. (2007). *From Impressionism to Anime: Japan as Fantasy and Fan Cult in the Mind of the West* (1st ed.). New York: Palgrave Macmillan.
N1ghtWr1ter. (2015). *Strange Love*. Archive of Our Own.
Pande, R., and Nadkarni, S. (2013). From a Land Where "Other" People Live: Perspectives from an Indian Fannish Experience. In A.E. Jamison (Ed.), *Fic: Why Fanfiction Is Taking Over the World* (pp. 344–354). Dallas: Smart Pop.
Penley, C. (1992). Feminism, Psychoanalysis, and the Study of Popular Culture. In L. Grossberg, C. Nelson, and P.A. Treichler (Eds.), *Cultural Studies* (pp. 479–500). New York: Routledge.
popper. (2016). *As You Are Mine, I Am Yours*. Archive of Our Own.
porluciernagas. (2014, January 18). Sexualized Saturdays: Femslash and Fandom [Blog post]. Retrieved from https://ladygeekgirl.wordpress.com/2014/01/18/sexualized-saturdays-femslash-and-fandom/.
Roddenberry, G. (Creator). (1966–1969). *Star Trek: The Original Series*. United States: Paramount Television.
Rothenberg, J. (Producer). (2014). *The 100* [Television series]. United States: Warner Bros. Television.

Schilt, K., and Windsor, E. (2014). The Sexual Habitus of Transgender Men: Negotiating Sexuality Through Gender. *Journal of Homosexuality, 61*(5), 732–48. doi:10.1080/00918369.2014.870444.

short_stack_100. (2015). *The Little Omega*. Archive of Our Own.

Suzuki, K. (1998). Pornography or Therapy? Japanese Girls Creating the Yaoi Phenomenon. In S.A. Inness (Ed.), *Millennium Girls: Today's Girls Around the World* (pp. 243–267). Lanham, MD: Rowman & Littlefield.

toastystats. (2014, May 28). Femslash: Where Is It? [Archive post]. Retrieved from http://archiveofourown.org/works/1704926/chapters/3629783.

toastystats. (2016, February 15). F/F stats: Femslash February 2016 [Blog post]. Retrieved from http://destinationtoast.tumblr.com/post/139410106784/toastystats-ff-stats-femslash-february-2016.

Transfic. (2016). In *Fanlore*. Retrieved from http://fanlore.org/wiki/Transfic.

Tushnet, R. (2014). "I'm a Lawyer, Not an Ethnographer, Jim": Textual Poachers and Fair Use. *Journal of Fandom Studies, 2*(1), 21–30. https://doi.org/10.1386/jfs.2.1.21_1.

Vincent, K. (2007). A Japanese Electra and Her Queer Progeny. *Mechademia, 2*(1), 64–79. https://doi.org/10.1353/mec.0.0000.

Wanzo, R. (2015). African American Acafandom and Other Strangers: New Genealogies of Fan Studies. *Transformative Works and Cultures, 20*. http://dx.doi.org/10.3983/twc.2015.0699.

Williams, A. (2010). Raping Apollo: Sexual Difference and the Yaoi Phenomenon. In A. Levi, M. McHarry, and D. Pagliassotti (Eds.), *Boys' Love Manga: Essays on the Sexual Ambiguity and Cross-Cultural Fandom of the Genre* (pp. 221–231). Jefferson, NC: McFarland.

Zubernis, L., and Larsen, K. (2012). *Fandom at the Crossroads: Celebration, Shame and Fan/Producer Relationships*. Newcastle upon Tyne: Cambridge Scholars.

A Bad Bromance

Betrayal, Violence and Dark Delight in Subverting the Romance Narrative

CHARITY A. FOWLER

Introduction

Fan fiction in general, and slash in particular, has been both lauded as an inherently feminist project (see Jenkins, 2013) and decried as misogynistic (Scodari, 2003). This discussion has reverberated in popular media as well. Blogger Ally Boguhn (2015) at *Everyday Feminism* agrees with Henry Jenkins that fan fiction can be a feminist pursuit if done right. However, linking fan fiction to the recent upswing in "calling-out" problematic elements in media texts, she warns that transformative possibilities do not automatically make fan fiction political or progressive; rather, many works are just as problematic as traditional media. This is undoubtedly true in some respects, but it also centers being a "feminist pursuit" on being a certain type of feminist, fails to take into account the possibility of subversion in "problematic" art, and elides nuanced discussion.

In fan fiction, fans "rework and rewrite [the text], repairing or dismissing unsatisfying aspects" in the source text (Jenkins, 2013, p. 162). This work takes many forms, including changing the endings, fixing character deaths or broken relationships, eroticizing the text, or shifting its genre. Slash usually arises from a combination of the last two: non-romantic relationships in the source text are eroticized and the genre shifts to combine romance and pornography (Driscoll, 2006; Penley, 1992). Some slash ships arise from rivals or antagonists (Cabell Hankinson Gathman, 2005), but a significant number grow out of close friendships; in fact, the "friends to lovers" trope is one of the most popular in fan fiction (Klink, 2016). Henry Jenkins' utopian conception of slash offering a glimpse of what a "new kind of male friendship might look like" (Green, Jenkins & Jenkins, 1998, p. 20) certainly fits this mold. A third type of pairing combines these two: characters who were once close, but whose relationship is now broken. To arrive at the happy ending dictated by the romance narrative, many slash works "fix" these relationships, restoring intimacy and trust between the partners. However, others choose a darker path.

Rather than examining fan fiction which "repairs" the source text and relationships within it, this essay explores narratives which not only refuse to fix anything, but sometimes break them further. My analysis begins with the claim that slash functions to rewrite the romance narrative in a more egalitarian fashion, resisting the impetus of heteronormativity and hegemonic masculinity (Bacon-Smith, 1992; Jenkins, 2013; Penley, 1992 and Russ, 1985). This essay examines how and where these broken relationships fit in to slash's paradigm and asks whether they offer the same subversive potential, and explores related questions about slash, romance and the subversiveness of transgression. I ultimately argue that just as utopian slash does, these bad bromance works offer resistance to heteronormativity in three main ways, some of which align with utopian slash and some which do not. First, bad bromance slash operates on a personal and communal level to challenge restrictions upon and the shaming of expressions of unruly female desire. Second, by its refusal to follow many of the conventions of slash, bad bromance slash criticizes heteronormative, hegemonic masculinity and its violent strictures as a counterpart to utopian slash. Finally, bad bromance slash challenges the structural and thematic conventions of the romance narrative, destabilizing reader expectations and opening greater space for queered pleasures while also offering a critique on the normative function of romance itself.

As exemplars, I analyze fan fiction centered on three of these "bad bromances": Miles/Bass from *Revolution* (2012); Raylan/Boyd from FX's *Justified* (2012); and Spike/Angel from *Buffy the Vampire Slayer* (1997) and *Angel* (1999). These characters function as each others' friends, mirrors and antagonists through their source texts; all of them had a close bond with their partners at one time which has been damaged by betrayal—the bromance gone wrong. As a result of this canonical antagonism, many of the works contain emotional and physical violence. For some time now, disagreements over how to handle elements such as these in fan fiction have fractured certain fandom spaces, leading to instances of aggressive policing, bullying and calls for censorship. These debates are not new—to fandom or feminism—but neither are they settled, and they offer a foundation from which to launch the argument about bad bromance slash and female desire.

"Your fave is problematic"

The question of whether one can enjoy complex and problematic media and still be a good person, a feminist, and a "good social activist" (Rachael, 2011, para. 2, lines 2–3) has gotten a lot of blogging traction, and the answers vary. The common response from third-wave feminists tends to be a cautious "yes," but one which comes with suggested guidelines[1] for doing so: acknowledge it is problematic; don't apologize for or defend it; acknowledge the feelings of other people; and, if you're concerned, look for less problematic things to enjoy (Robyn, 2014). Others, however, disagree; not just about professional media, but fan fiction as well. On Tumblr, some fans (known as "antis") not only find fan fiction or ships containing elements such as violence, abuse, incest and non-consensual or dubiously-consensual sex problematic as texts, but also conflate textual depiction with the author's endorsement and accuse fans of these ships of promoting incest, romanticizing abuse and being pedophiles and rapists or, at least, apologists for the same (uniwolfwerecorn, 2016). Beyond posting these beliefs on their own blogs, they also engage in cyberbullying authors and fans to the point, sometimes, of suicide baiting. Taking on a moral position of protecting victims, antis also take up the mantle of shaming and silencing women's expression of unruly, or impure, desire.

This debate traces back to the sex wars that split second-wave feminism in the 1970s and 1980s, which also coalesced around "problematic" media (namely, pornography) and fantasies. Resting at the heart of issue are conflicting ideas about reality and representation. Like today's antis, some anti-pornography feminists argued that the representation of misogynistic and violent images in pornography perpetuated the domination of and violence against women in the real world. This included both pornographic images and literature: Andrea Dworkin (1974), a leader of the movement, did not consider literature to be artistic representation, but narratives that "penetrate into the psyche as reality" (p. 32). Further, she argued that our culture "predetermines who we are, how we behave, what we are willing to know, what we are able to feel" (p. 34) and that murder, suicide and genocide all arose "as a direct consequence of the imperatives" of sex roles (*ibid.*). Therefore, if Dworkin is right and texts teach us how to be who we are and how to behave via imitation, without mediation, then censoring texts that depict violent violations and abject states of being makes sense. This is certainly the position antis take, claiming that fan fiction which deals with dark topics not only eroticizes abuse, but causes measurable harm to potential and actual victims, in a straight line from representation to reality (mcclaln, 2016; tobermoriansass, 2016). Sex-negative feminists link media like pornography directly to male oppression of women, and argue that only in their eradication can women find liberation from patriarchal oppression.

Not everyone agrees, however. Even those who reach a different conclusion than Dworkin do acknowledge that culture shapes even what we consider our innermost desires. Gayle Rubin (2007), a strong proponent of sex-positive feminism, still acknowledged that sexual desire is a social product, and Michel Foucault (1978) argued that our desires are not pre-existing and inherent, but arise out of specific social and historical practices. However, sex-positive feminists argue that a fundamental difference exists between fantasy and reality, and that fantasy is an important site in the battle against patriarchal oppression. Studies in multiple disciplines have demonstrated how patriarchy alienates women from their own desire (Diamond, 2011, p. 43). Thirty years after the sexual revolution, that has not changed very much. Sex education curricula, the media, and general cultural discourse still send heteronormative messages privileging male desire, portraying "good girls" as sexually passive gatekeepers of male desire, and shaming women who step out of line. Adrienne Rich once said that women are "hiding in a closet within patriarchy" (in Payne, 2010, p. 320), "lying about who they are, lying about their own sexual desires to both themselves and others, lying about their hopes and dreams." This constant lying leaves women "semiconscious" and complicit in subjugating their own sexuality (*ibid.*). Thus, pro-sex feminists believe that exploring your own pleasure, especially within a community of support, even if involving "problematic" things, can be a profoundly liberating goal. This tends to be the position of the pro-dark fan fiction shippers opposing the "antis" on Tumblr (tobermoriansass, 2016).

Thus, the debate encompasses the importance of feminine desire and issues surrounding women's sexual liberation or exploitation, their agency or lack thereof, and their capacity to give meaningful consent. Anti-pornography feminists were also quite often anti-heterosexual sex, anti–BDSM, and anti-butch/femme dynamics in lesbian relationships (Echols, 2016), something that has seen little change. Examining E. L. James' *Fifty Shades of Grey* (2011) at RadFemHub, blogger Smash (2012) argues that BDSM is culturally analogous to domestic abuse and that women only engage in it due to cultural conditioning and eroticizing male domination in order to survive it (Smash, 2012, para. 11). Careful to say she is not "blaming these women for attempting to carve out a space for female agency" (para. 15, line 1) in a male-dominated society, Smash nevertheless puts quotation marks around "choose" when writing about what she clearly sees as a lack of agency. Conversely, Rubin and other queer theorists argue that denigrating a woman's ability to freely consent, as Smash does, is an "implicit system of ideological condescension" (2007, p. 167). Underlying this denial of women's ability to consent is a belief Rubin calls the "brainwash theory," which is the belief that anyone who engages in sexual acts "so disgusting that no one would willingly perform them" (pp. 168–169) must have been tricked or coerced into doing so. The logical outcome of this condescension requires devaluing forms of feminine desire that do not look like one thinks they should look. Ironically, this outcome means sex-negative feminists sound a great deal like those espousing patriarchy.

In policing other women's desires and fantasies and infantilizing them by denying them sexual agency, sex-negative feminists' goals of a structural critique get lost in their replication of patriarchal power which condones only ideologically "pure" sexuality (Glick, 2000 and Rubin, 2007). Sex-positive feminists, on the other hand, resist any form of feminism that claims to "liberate" them from patriarchy only to then shame them in the same way it has for centuries. This shaming leads to anxiety regarding the enjoyment of "problematic" fiction—it's the same shame women have been made to feel for enjoying "problematic" sex. We've replaced being a "good girl" with being a "good feminist," and traded one cage for another. Being aware of potential harm is important, but policing *desire* replicates the harmful effects of patriarchy far more than any "problematic" media objects. This does not mean that certain "practices, fantasies, orgasms, etc., are either 'good' or 'bad'" (Downing, 2013, p. 95). However, it does mean that shaming people for their fantasies is not progressive, but regressive, and that women being willing to share their fantasies—especially "problematic" ones—to reach out and form a community around them, is the very opposite of problematic.

When Pauline Réage's *The Story of O* (1965) was published, critics discussed the connections of submission and female desire, but another inquiry arose about Réage's identity and true gender.[2] The question was important, Amber Musser (2015) asserts, because while O's "submissive posture does not challenge gender norms that assume a naturalized feminine submission, Réage's act of authorship does" (p. 122). While male slash writers certainly do exist, the genre is one substantially penned by women, and the works they produce reflect some exploration of their own desire. This act of authorship by slash writers, then, of reclaiming their own desire, expressing it and sharing it, can offer the same challenge to gender norms and heteronormativity as Pauline Réage did. This, as much as any rewriting of masculinity, was a large part of the excitement over slash's subversive potential among early fan scholars: women were writing about their desires, exercising their voices in expressing their fantasies and their existence as sexual beings (Penley, 1992 and Russ, 1985). They were refusing to lie and subjugate their desires. That early excitement, however, was also surrounding the type of slash that depicted loving, supportive relationships—slash which rewrote the romance novel into a more egalitarian narrative. While this has relevance for discussing the tropes in the works themselves and the functions they perform, it has less relevance in relation to female desire. Slash was heavily reviled in the early days of fandom, which made women carving out a place for their narratives and a community around them all the more subversive. The same holds true today. While some people still deride slash writers, for most fans, enjoying slash is not the site of danger and risk it once was. However, with the cyberbullying perpetuated against those who write darker fan fiction, being willing to still post and circulate such fiction with all its "problematic" elements, being willing to say, "I think this is hot, and that does not make me a bad person," is the same rebellion against coercive sexual purity and functions as a reclamation of female desire and a refusal to be shamed.

Antagonistic Courtship: Interplay of Sex and Violence

Writing a story centering on a broken couple one refuses to fix often involves violence, both emotional and physical. A lesser form of that violence appears in what has been deemed a necessary component for any pairing—platonic or erotic—to be intriguing: antagonism (Cabell Hankinson Gathman, 2005, pp. 14–15). The connection between antagonism and attraction is not new: if two characters meet and hate each other right away, the audience knows they will most likely fall in love or become best friends. Similarly, antagonism escalating to violence is not, in and of itself, unexpected in fan fiction, slash or otherwise. In many ways, it crystallizes Freud's contention that all love is ambivalent, made up of both love and hate. In choosing these pairings as examples, my overarching criteria was the emotional significance of the relationship to the characters involved and the presence of betrayal or serious antagonism in some form. What I found was that the pairings had significant similarities in other areas as well, such as the way they the characters largely define themselves against one another, though along no clear moral lines. None of the six are heroes. At best, Miles, Angel and Raylan are anti-heroes, but both Bass and Spike arguably develop into anti-heroes themselves by the end of their canons. Meanwhile, Boyd operates as more of an anti-villain than antagonist. Further, all six characters consistently slide along the light/dark spectrum at varying stages in their source texts—for instance, Bass starts out as the voice of reason holding Miles back from his darker impulses, until he suffers one too many tragedies and visibly shatters. Meanwhile, Miles still does questionably moral things until near the end of the series, when he finally says to Bass, "We're the good guys now. It's time we start acting like it" (Kripke, Callaway, Parrott & Boyd, 2014).

Like love and hate, sex and violence often go together, especially in popular narratives, which often eroticize aggressive sexuality (Shepherd, 2013, p. 31). However, rather than being merely problematic, violence can serve a liberatory purpose for the characters; in slash, it often sets up a hurt/comfort scene. Violence in a healthy slash pairing, as in romance, usually comes from outside the relationship (Radway, 1984, p. 75, and Russ, 1985, p. 87). Following its enactment on one character's body, the other partner provides nurturance. The touching involved often then becomes a pretext for sexual touching and a device to get the characters into bed and toward intimacy they might usually resist. This is the payoff utopian slash often offers. However, in bad bromance pairings, the violence comes from *within* the relationship and can range from a fist fight to torture or rape. MissJeeves' *No Afterglow in Harlan* (2013), flurblewig's *Nothing That I Understand* (2010) and ElDiablito_SF's *M Is for Mine* (2013) all deal with varying levels of violence within this scope, including dubious consent and a fist fight between Boyd and Raylan, incredibly violent sex between Spike and Angel, and a non-negotiated BDSM encounter between Bass and Miles.

In *Justified*, Raylan (the lawman) and Boyd (the outlaw) grew up together in Eastern Kentucky and worked in the coal mines together as young men, where Boyd once saved Raylan's life after a cave-in—a critical point, as "we dug coal together" becomes a shorthand for the complexity of their relationship throughout the series. They went their separate ways, but twenty years later ended up back in Harlan on opposite sides of the law, which is the source of most of their antagonism. However, that antagonism grows throughout the series as Raylan consistently acts as if he has the moral high ground, which Boyd finds hypocritical given that some of Raylan's actions are as morally suspect as Boyd's. Verbal antagonism is the status quo for Raylan and Boyd in canon, even when they are getting along. That is where MissJeeves' *No Afterglow in Harlan* (2013) starts, before escalating. Most of the story consists of them fighting, physically: Boyd is determined to have sex, and Raylan's feelings on the matter are distinctly unclear, even though he is the narrator. The work opens with Raylan already quite drunk in Boyd's bar by the time Boyd joins him. Raylan makes a comment to the effect that he never misses when shooting at a suspect. Boyd, referring to when Raylan shot him just one inch shy of his heart, leans in close, breath "hot on Raylan's neck," (p. 2) and reminds him that he missed, once. Raylan turns to look at Boyd with "a comeback forming on his lips that might also be a death threat" (*ibid.*). He doesn't say anything, however, caught by eye contact with Boyd and an "emotion Raylan doesn't care to identify" (*ibid.*). This moment is ultimately fleeting, but it establishes that Raylan is not neutral when it comes to the sexual tension underlying his and Boyd's acrimony. It is physical violence, however, that marks the tone of their sexual encounter later in the evening.

Issues of consent abound—Raylan is drunk, says "no" more than once, and actively tries to get away from Boyd to the point of breaking furniture. He eventually does consent, though not terribly enthusiastically. However, whether his lack of enthusiasm is genuine or him behaving like a U.S. Marshall *should* behave when being solicited by a criminal is unclear. The use of the tag "mildly dubious consent" complicates the question further, especially when contrasted with the fact that when Raylan objects to Boyd leaving hickies on his skin, he does so because they are where his coworkers can see—not because Boyd is leaving them in the first place. His verbal consent could be either capitulation or eager demand—the text offers no tone beyond Raylan's impatience. Once they're naked, Raylan expects violence and even tries to provoke more of it, yet Boyd gentles and makes sure that Raylan is ready and willing to continue. That brings the true level of Raylan's resistance into question, again, as he could put an end to it at that point, but as Boyd gentles, so does he. Most of the work is getting the two to this point; the sex itself happens in two sentences, and once it's over the hostility is back on Raylan's part, at least:

> "I heartily endorse resolving our differences in this manner, in the future," Boyd says, fully dressed and immediately infuriating. "You just give a whistle when you're filled to the brim with the need for my dick."
>
> "I should have brought my gun," Raylan says, instead chucking the lube dispenser at Boyd's head. It's chunky and solid, and best of all it connects with Boyd's cheek [MissJeeves, 2013, p. 6].

The short exchange is all they really say about what has just happened. However, it raises the question of Raylan's consent again—Boyd is "immediately infuriating" once he's dressed, suggesting maybe he wasn't infuriating while naked despite Raylan's reservations. However, rather than providing any more clarity, the narrative ends with Boyd leaving, uttering the eponymous line, "Oh, well, no afterglow in Harlan" (p. 7).

Nothing That I Understand (2010) by flurblewig and *M Is for Mine* (2013) by ElDiablito_SF are also both violent texts—both physically violent in the damage they inflict on the characters and emotionally violent in addressing the darkness inherent within each party through violent words as much as touch. Despite all the pain they have caused each other, partners in bad bromance pairings are also the archetypical couple who cannot quit one another, even when their relationship becomes toxic for them and those around them. These relationships border on obsession, and often include strong elements of jealousy or possessiveness where the characters wind up taking out on each others' bodies the words that they cannot say.

Angel and Spike met when Spike was first turned into a vampire in the late 19th century and forged their bond by spending twenty years traveling the world, indulging in murder, mayhem and erotic play together. In his "mentorship," Angel breaks down the man Spike was before he became a vampire and remakes him in his own image, to the point that when they reunite, Spike tells him, "You were my Yoda," (Whedon, Greenwalt & Kretchner, 1997). Their relationship breaks when Angel is cursed with regaining his human soul. However, many of his cruelties toward Spike came both before and after that, as their vacillating ensouled states keep them at odds through most of both *Buffy the Vampire Slayer* and *Angel*.

Nothing That I Understand by flurblewig (2010) is set during Season 5 of *Angel*, when the two vampires are working together in Los Angeles. In the story, Spike goads Angel, the narrator, into sex by reminding him of their time as monsters and insisting that he is the only one who can give Angel what he needs and accept what he is. The language and tone is taunting, almost cruel in places, and always crude: Spike *wants* Angel to vividly remember the violence he inflicted on Spike (of which Angel is not proud), reminding Angel of how he has always loved "making me bleed, making me come, making me yours," how he used to get off on beating Spike "half to death" then "fuck[ing] what was left" (p. 7). Spike taunts Angel that the violence, pain and blood are what gets Angel off, just as they do Spike—the "just like me" point is one Spike drives home. Afterward, Angel swears there won't be a next time, but there always is, and they end up having "brutal, punishing sex" with both men "screaming in pain, denial and pleasure" (p. 8). That the sex is "punishing" and they both scream in "denial" suggests that the violence each character is inflicting on the other is intended as a measure of atonement. When their friends do not understand, however, and intervene, Angel takes their chastisement about the unhealthiness of his and Spike's relationship to heart, and sends Spike away. That this constitutes an unhappy ending for them, where the violence might have helped their guilt, complicates the reading of the violence as "good" or "bad."

In *Revolution's* canon, Miles and Bass grew up together, joined the Marines, went to war, survived an apocalypse and founded a country. They call each other "brother" and are so entwined that Miles asks Bass at one point, "What the hell would I be without you?" (Kripke, Owusu-Breen, Pitts & Toye, 2012). Miles' betrayal, when it comes, is clear, deliberate and severe: eleven years after the Blackout that caused the apocalypse, he tries to kill Bass and abandons him when he can't go through with it. When they see each other again four years later, Miles disavows their three decades together, lying and telling Bass he means nothing to him (*ibid.*). Set mere days after Miles tells Bass he means nothing to him in the canon, ElDiablito_SF's *M Is for Mine* (2013) has him sneaking back into town and into Bass' bedroom to seemingly disavow that denial by re-staking a claim on Bass, while engaging him in an un-negotiated, rule-free BDSM game. Bass narrates the story, but, unlike Angel, he does not become an actor in Miles' mysterious motivations; instead, he is acted upon, silenced first by Miles' command, and then by a gag. The reader accompanies Bass on an emotional roller coaster from hurt and anger to desperation and terror as he spills out how much he loves Miles, but only in his head. Unlike Spike and Angel, who hurt each other in a mutual way for fully understood motivations, Miles all but immobilizes Bass. When Miles speaks, he alternates between telling Bass how much he needs and loves him and calling him a whore for sleeping with other people in the four years Miles has been gone. The possessiveness here resonates with the tropes of obsession and drowning desire characteristic of darker romances, but when Miles abandons Bass again in the aftermath, the narrative strips away the expected conclusion and emotional payoff of reconciliation.

Despite being the arguably more injured parties—the ones abandoned and reviled—Bass and Spike both appear to eagerly welcome their partners back into their lives. When Miles insists that Bass needs a reminder about who he belongs to, Bass laughs, because "he knew whom he belonged to—he wasn't the one who walked out, the traitor" (ElDiablito_SF, 2013, p. 6). Angel, too, gets possessive with Spike after trying to push him away, growling "mine" as he tears off Spike's clothes and "drags his own fangs in a jagged, bloody line from throat to groin. Marking. Claiming" (flurblewig, 2010, p. 6). Like Bass, Spike merely chuckles and agrees, "Think we established that a while ago, pet" (*ibid.*). However, Angel and Miles are not able to fully take that step back into Spike and Bass' lives: Angel, because he thinks he's hurting Spike and Miles, most likely because of his own self-loathing mingled with his desire to not abandon the niece who depends on him. Still, before leaving, each character asserts his claim on his partner through physical violence; Miles, by carving his initial in Bass's ass, and Angel, by leaving his mark on Spike. But when Miles leaves and Angel sends Spike away, what does that say about the authenticity or future of these claims? All three of these stories use violence as the way to communicate deep emotions and needs within their hegemonically masculine characters, and none of them do so very effectively. In bad bromances, Angel and Miles, two of the most in-control characters in their respective canons, become those who lose themselves to the violence of the emotions they have been repressing. For all six characters, violence serves as a catharsis, leaving them drained in its wake, but, ultimately, the violence solves nothing. It carves out a moment in time, but when it passes, the men are all alone again. The violence in bad bromance may act as catharsis, but it does not expiate their sins.

This is a sharp departure from the idealized, egalitarian romance narrative. In *Reading the Romance,* Janice Radway (1984) surveyed her sample of romance readers about things which should never be in a romance novel; rape and torture were in the top five (p. 74). Similarly, a survey of over 7,600 fans revealed that "non-con" is a widely reviled trope in fan fiction (Klink, 2016). "Dubious consent," however, has nearly the same number of fans who love it as who hate it. This corresponds to Radway's readers' cautious approval of the use of "a little forceful persuasion" (1984, p. 75), so long as the hero is overcome with his love and desire for the heroine, rather than maliciously perpetrating a "true rape" (p. 75). Given the cultural conversation regarding rape and affirmative consent, some people have found this inexplicable, in the same way that many find women writing slash inexplicable, but this ties directly into the earlier discussion of female desire, representation, reality and fantasy. Fantasy and desire are not reality, and violence and rape in fantasy cannot be translated literally, but always map onto something else—like, perhaps, the desire to experience an unconstrained sexuality for which you cannot be held responsible or made to feel bad for indulging in (Russ, 1985, pp. 90–91, and Shulman & Horne, 2006). The way these fantasies are misconstrued may well place another layer of silence and shame over women's willingness to share their fantasies. Thus, when they are actively shamed for them, but still share them, that can be a radical reclamation of their sexual selves.

The violence in bad bromance slash complicates the paradigm seen in utopian and hurt/comfort slash which makes a sequential transitional from violence, to rough sex, to emotional purging, to satisfaction. While some narratives may allow a few moments of peace for their characters following acts of violence, they explicitly remind the reader how fleeting it is by the end, echoing in substance what Boyd and Raylan agree to: there is no afterglow in Harlan. This refusal to follow the romantic paradigm of violence operating as a space for emotional development lends credibility to the claim that violence may be eroticized in these works. However, it is certainly not romanticized or presented as healthy; on the contrary, this unstable, unhappy conduct clearly operates within dysfunctional relationships. The narratives capitalize on the juncture of sex and violence, but ultimately illustrate that violence solves nothing. If unhealthy relationships are presented and acknowledged as clearly unhealthy, are they still problematic? Is problematic media regressive, as we are so often told—or can it serve, instead, progressive and maybe even subversive purposes? When it comes to female desire, I would argue that it is progressive in the sense of an individual liberation, but it also offers another point of resistance to heteronormativity.

One of the most insidious things about heteronormativity is how it makes gender relations, power imbalances, and gendered roles and behaviors seem inherent, leading to statements being taken as fact that men are more aggressive and violent, while women are peaceful and passive, for example. Given the traditional hierarchy of the binary codes of male-gendered attributes as superior, a critique of those attributes as negative subverts the essentialized norms. Claims about the subversive, resistant nature of slash often circle around just this. Joanna Russ (1985), for instance, delights in Kirk/Spock slash because of its "attempt to establish a very radical androgyny in its characters" (p. 94) where "questions about who is the man and who is the woman, who's active and who's passive, even who's who, *cannot even be asked*" (p. 95).

Bad bromance slash does this, too, though differently. Rather than engaging in utopian fantasy and idealizing the bond between these men, bad bromance slash shows the harm inherent in structures of hegemonic masculinity. Women explaining the harm this can do to them or their frustration in heterosexual relationships can almost be background noise, but by removing women from the equation, bad bromance slash illustrates how it harms men, as well, without a treatise. With no adventures, no crises to solve, just a relationship in front of them that means *something*, the characters resort to violence instead of discussion, emotional elision rather than expression: they do what they are "supposed" to do, as men, and they are left miserable by it. Miles can only admit his love while violently dominating Bass; Raylan refuses to admit he wants Boyd at all, forcing their encounter toward violence instead of anything with an emotional connection; Angel and Spike rip each other apart and still find no peace or redemption. Their bodies may be satisfied, but *they* are not—and, in that, the emptiness of culturally valorized masculinity is laid as bare as utopian slash reveals it, by forcing the men to break it. The two function here as two sides of the same coin, like the men themselves. This refusal to allow a "fix" or to let them off the hook also leads to the final ways in which bad bromance challenges traditional conceptions of the work of slash: its disregard for the conventions of romance and narrative.

Romance, Pornography and Happy Endings

The link between romance, female desire, and fan fiction has long been recognized in fan studies. Constance Penley (1992) contends that romance creates the field in which fan fiction writers write, but their narratives work toward a "better romance formula" (p. 489) that fulfills their fantasies. Anne Kustritz (2003) reiterates Jenkins' argument about fans "repairing" the source text and applies it specifically to male protagonists, to whom slash allows a level of emotional honesty and intimacy with each other which is denied by hegemonic masculinity in the source text. Similarly, in romance novels, the hero generally starts off performing hegemonic masculinity, but the narrative turns on his ability to express tenderness and emotion to the heroine after his earlier distance or cruelty (Toscano, 2012).

Surveys show that what fans and romance readers want most from their narratives is escalating intimacy; a slow build to a deep relationship between the partners and a happy ending (Klink, 2016, and Radway, 1984). To change the nature of a story "signals dissent from social norms as well as narrative forms" (DuPlessis, 1985, p. 20), which makes people uncomfortable: they prefer it when stories and their endings are recognizable (DuPlessis, 1985; Miller, 1981, and Roof, 1996). With their refusal to fix the broken narrative, works of bad bromance slash almost always break these codes, and their endings defy the expectations of readers and conventions of a happy ending. They accomplish this either by crafting an explicitly unhappy ending or refusing to give the characters or the reader any real sense of closure at all.

Nothing That I Understand (2010) opens with Spike waiting for Angel to come home from what he thinks is a date. Their interaction quickly escalates from bickering, to a fight, to very violent sex. After the initial encounter, they fall into an addictive pattern of violence and sex which the rest of their friends grow worried about. Eventually, concerned about Spike, several characters stage an intervention for Angel, telling him he needs to stop the relationship he has with Spike because it isn't right or healthy. When they try to compare Angel and Spike's relationship to the unhealthy one that Spike had previously had with Buffy, Angel differentiates the two but keeps the real reason to himself, thinking silently: "You didn't love him" (flurblewig, 2010, p. 10). In a romance, the moment when the hero recognizes his feelings and gives them a name should lead to his confession of love and a happy ending. Here, though, Angel *doesn't* share. In fact, despite Spike giving him every chance to ask him to stay, Angel ultimately sends the other vampire away with a cold, "Are you still here?" (p. 12). Spike snaps and leaves with a parting shot: "I suppose that's about what I expected. Love you too, asshole" (*ibid.*). Angel waits until he's gone to whisper his own acknowledgment of that love, and the narrative ends on a hollow, heartbroken note.

Refusing to fix a broken pairing can often mean breaking it more. Sometimes this may be in new directions, while other times the narrative is set at a point where the fan reader knows what is to come in the source text and the devastation it will wreak. JaqofSpades' *The inescapable truth* (2014), a *Revolution* fan story, is one such instance. The story takes place before the start of the series, depicting the last encounter between Miles and Bass before Miles' canonical attempt to assassinate Bass. However, rather than the in-depth plan Miles had in canon, his decision to assassinate Bass in JaqofSpades' story is not final yet, and he is looking for a way out of it. However, instead of sympathetic, Bass is cold and implacable and at least partly to blame for the relationship's problems. The *Revolution* fandom often judges Miles' betrayal of his best friend more harshly than Bass's despotic acts toward largely secondary or nameless characters, the worst of which comes after Miles tells him he's nothing to him. Ergo, the fandom generally concludes that Bass is clearly acting out, and most works shift their gaze backward: if Miles had not betrayed Bass in the first place, none of the terrible things of Season 1 would have happened; if Miles had not lied to Bass about their relationship's meaning, the worst of the damage could still have been avoided.

By showing a colder Bass, *The inescapable truth* makes it easier to empathize with Miles, who comes across as a sympathetic character, understandably frustrated with Bass' creation and ruling of the Republic and his growing cruelties. Still, the conflict in the narrative truly sparks when even this colder Bass follows an established hurt/comfort trope: seeing Miles is wounded, Bass rushes to his side, indicating he still cares as he attempts to treat Miles' wounds, but Miles rejects the overture:

> "Fuck off," he reacts, slapping those too-familiar hands away. He's not quick enough, though, and it hits him the same way it always does, a swelling symphony of Bass, Bass, Bass. Rough-gentle hands, and the concern flaring in too-blue eyes. The smell of him.
>
> It breaks over him like a wave, and they're 18 again [JaqofSpades, 2014, p. 2].

The narrative is sensually lush and grounded in sense memory that pulls Miles back to the first time they had sex, while Bass stays close, "rough-gentle hands moving with a very different purpose now" (*ibid.*). Miles is tempted to give in, but pushes Bass away, because he "doesn't want to see Bass in the President's cold, blue eyes" (*ibid.*). While this suggests that the "Bass" constructed by Miles' memory is still in there, not just the "General. President. Madman," Miles actively chooses to reaffirm the absence of Bass, calling him "[a] fucking megalomaniac" (*ibid.*). Bass snaps away and gets a drink with shaking hands, which hints to the reader that Bass may not be as cold as he seems; that he might still be "Bass" somewhere inside the man he's become. However, the rest of the encounter devolves into threats, insults and Bass mocking their past as lovers, which convinces Miles of the inescapable truth: "This isn't him. He wouldn't. The knowledge drops like a noose around his neck" (p. 3). The narrative ends by twisting the idea of having "one more time" into Miles' sensualized pleasure in Bass' upcoming death: "[The] next time they meet? It will be the smell of gunpowder that gets him hard" (*ibid.*). Small pieces of the narrative indicate different causes of the estrangement than in the source text, and the inability to depend on knowledge of canon leaves the reader with no idea whether Miles will be able to go through with the assassination.

In both of these works, the narrative conventions of slash—the sexualization of the relationship that opens the men up to a greater intimacy—fail to appear, and the works negate the claims often made about slash offering an ideal union which is egalitarian and emotionally honest. Bad bromance works often end unhappily for just this reason—a failure to communicate and an unwillingness to be vulnerable. Through violence, in flurblewig's *Nothing That I Understand* (2010) Angel maintains his hegemonic masculinity and instead condemns himself to loneliness out of stubborn pride, and his very unhappiness in doing so serves as a critique on that same masculine essentialism. Similarly, in JaqofSpades' *The inescapable truth* (2014), Miles suffers through the disconnect between memories of the boy he loved and anger at the man Bass has become. He *wants* Bass to still be there, but won't truly look to see if he is because that could change his mind, so he pushes Bass away when the other man does reach out. In Bass's reaction to the rejection—the trembling hands—JaqofSpades offers us a hint of his vulnerability, a sense that, like Miles, he too is holding something in, but neither of them can embrace the intimacy a utopian slash narrative offers. Instead, they stay locked in their own heads, and sex and love are not enough to bridge the gaps generated by stereotypically masculine stoicism and pride.

Thus, the narrative denies the reader the purported benefit of slash: it fails to re-appropriate either male protagonist into someone who can satisfy the emotional needs of slash readers and writers in ways which hegemonic masculinity prohibits. The feeling lingers that the tragedies could have been averted if the men had just been willing to communicate with one another. Their failure to do so induces both sadness and anger, in much the way Radway's (1984) readers spoke about their emotional responses to "failed" romance novels. While the readers wanted their men to be men (1984, p. 74), they also wanted them to be men who could bend—and the absence of the hero's satisfying emotional capacity to pursue his heroine is evident in these works. However, this failure to follow the map of the traditional romance narrative sequence, with its roots deep in heteronormativity, is not a failure of the bad bromance slash story. While some people might prefer a happy ending, the fact that these works are being created and shared suggests that writers are pushing back against the unrealistic goal of "happily ever after" and choosing to consider the narrative options beyond that border.

Narrative Closure and Ideology

The other way that bad bromances subvert the happy ending convention is by complicating narrative closure itself. In *Come as You Are: Sexuality as Narrative* (1996), Judith Roof argues that narrative is the primary mode through which we organize and understand the world, including sex and sexuality. Indeed, the logics of narrative are closely linked to sexuality—a beginning, a conflict through the middle, a triumph/climax and completion. Freud located the drive in the reproductive demand, thus normalizing heterosexuality; the conflict was the aberrations in the middle that might steer one off course from that normal sexuality, i.e., queerness (Roof, 1996, pp. xix–xxi). Eroticism, Roof argues, comes from those places of queerness—the "dynamic produced by a concatenation of edges, gaps, loss, and desire [which is] structurally unfixed except as it coexists with and is produced and enjoyed despite cultural imperative" (p. xxiii). However, that reproductive end always looms—and like a sexual climax, the end of a narrative must carry with it an element of satisfaction; it must make sense of what came before (p. 6). In *Narrative and Its Discontents*, D.A. Miller (1981) likewise finds the power of narrative itself within these middle segments—as narrative is, by its nature, suspense and indecision, instability and disequilibrium, and rife with possibility. *Something* must happen to cut off that possibility, to give closure, and it must be something we can see as an end if we are to be satisfied and not caught in the discomfort of suspense and indecision. Endings come from non-narratable elements—for instance, marriage or death in a romance. Endings give release, but the disturbing middles have more power—so much so that endings cannot ever truly defeat them, just signal the story is over to give the audience peace.

Rachel DuPlessis (1985) argues that narrative, especially romance, is its own expression of ideology, and agrees with Roof that it is necessary for imposing heteronormativity. Romance itself is a form of ideology, one which defines expected gender roles and teaches women what to expect from life by cutting off their possibilities—the ending for female characters is always marriage or death. She advocates for "writing beyond the ending," which she defines as "strategies that sever the narrative from formerly conventional structures of fiction" (1985, p. x). Roof, too, hints at this possibility in her expansion of Miller and DuPlessis' possible endings to include "orgasm [...] victory, salvation, the production of something (insight, a child, *another story*, the story itself, knowledge, identity)" (Roof, 1996, p. 6, emphasis mine).

This concept of ongoing potential, happening elsewhere, maps well onto the narratives of fan fiction, with their own inherent instability; the narrative elements in the middle are what Jenkins (2013) calls the "unrealized possibilities of the text" (p. 23) from which fan fiction is generated. The continuation of fan fiction keeps the narrative middle (and thus, the enticing emotional stakes) of a text alive, yet, at the same time, individual works of fan fiction generally impose narrative closure on their own stories. However, in the following works, the characters and readers are stuck in dilemmas and possibilities for which the narrative provides no closure. This is particularly common for slash fiction written in liminal spaces where the characters are separated for long lengths of time, with their relationships held in stasis—even as the narrative in the source text moves forward. *Revolution's* source text provides long stretches of time in and between episodes to insert missing scenes, but the very nature of the ongoing narrative in the larger text requires that unless one imposes a non-canonical ending the characters in fan fiction return to their lives as antagonists with the possibility of their meeting again left uncertain.

ElDiablito_SF's *M Is for Mine* (2013) offers one such ambiguous ending for Miles and Bass. Given Bass is the narrator, and Miles offers no explanations, we can only speculate as to Miles' intentions and reasoning for being there, which makes the tone of the encounter and the work itself even more ambiguous. Miles never explicitly apologizes for, or takes back, telling Bass he meant nothing to him. Instead, he overwhelms Bass and takes him on an emotionally and physically exhausting roller coaster ride—then, despite claiming to love him and telling him how much he needs him and ordering him to remember who he belongs to, Miles just leaves. Given his possessive comments, the carving of his initials in Bass's skin, does Miles expect Bass to be celibate, waiting for him to show up in the middle of the night, while during the day they lead armies against each other? Are Miles' declarations of love a promise that he is going to find a way out of this and come back and claim what's his for good? Neither the reader nor Bass have any way of knowing—Miles leaves and the story ends.

As Roof (1996) describes, the lovers' mutual orgasms provide one sort of ending and the sense that another story may have just begun, but the ambiguity remains. With its detailed descriptions and explicit sex scene, *M is for Mine* offers an excellent example of what Catherine Driscoll (2006) calls "porn sex," where sex is lingered over and the timing of the narrative "mimic[s] the representative structures of pornography" (p. 86). Further, in many ways the work reads as PWP ("Plot? What plot?"), a subgenre of fan fiction where sex happens with little to no narrative context, and which often ends following the lovers' orgasms. On the other hand, the intense emotional context of the setting in relation to the most emotionally devastating episode in the series thus far makes the sex feel like it *should* be the kind that moves the plot forward (Driscoll, 2006, p. 85). As such, not only is the ending ambiguous, but the work itself exists in a liminal space; the deliberate failure of this story and others like it to provide more emotive closure leaves both the narrative and its readers trapped in the middle where all possibilities still writhe.

Raylan and Boyd works which fall in the bad bromance category often demonstrate these ambiguous endings identified by Roof (1996), just as *No Afterglow in Harlan* (2013) did. This seems appropriate due to the canonical personalities and interpersonal dynamics of the characters; both men are far more difficult to pin down and shift their moralities with a fluidity the other four characters do not have, rendering readings of the characters themselves ambiguous from the outset. *Loose Ends by the Score* by Sandrine Shaw (2017) offers a slightly more hopeful interpretive space than the other works in this essay, but one which is still rife with ambiguity. Unlike the previous works, it is set post-series, so no canon knowledge on the part of the reader can explicate the ambiguity. The work does not begin on a very auspicious note and, told from Raylan's point of view, the air of suspicion that it begins with flows throughout:

> Boyd shows up at Raylan's doorstep a month after his release. Raylan goes for his gun the second he opens the door, and Boyd already has his hands up. It's a beautifully choreographed, well-practiced dance they've been doing for too long now to miss a step [Sandrine Shaw, 2017, p. 1].

The source of his unease is unclear; it could be their level of animosity before Boyd went to prison, but Raylan visited him there and the series ended on a moment that read as reconciliation, both acknowledging their fire-forged bond: "we dug coal together" (Yost, Golan, Andron, Cavell & Arkin, 2015). Despite this, Raylan lets him in. Boyd sleeps on the couch and Raylan leaves for work the next morning, hoping Boyd will be gone when he gets home. Boyd is still there when Raylan comes home wounded, which leads to a hurt/comfort scene layered over the usual snark and banter they continue to exchange. Boyd keeps talking as he patches Raylan up until Raylan remembers that "there's only ever been two ways to make Boyd stop talking, and one of those is to shoot him" (Sandrine Shaw, 2017, p. 4). Even though it has been "time measured in decades rather than years" since Raylan kissed Boyd (p. 5), Raylan falls into it, letting the first spark of non-annoyed emotion come through as he thinks how Boyd tastes "devastatingly familiar" and the kiss "almost gets to be too much" (*ibid.*). A few more verbal barbs later, and the two wind up in bed.

Here, too, the narrative follows the traditional arc of utopian slash, allowing both men to show vulnerability and connection, albeit with banter and playful antagonism reminiscent of early seasons of *Justified.* Raylan even finds himself verbalizing the thought that perhaps this is where they were always meant to end up. Still, when Boyd declares the next morning that he's going to stay, Raylan's first urge is to go for his gun. He resists, but their sexual encounter has not suddenly made him trust Boyd, a criminal. He characterizes the smile Boyd gives him as "that shark smile of his," and doubts Boyd's declarations that he can go straight this time:

> It could be a joke, or maybe not. It's hard to tell with Boyd sometimes. It doesn't matter either. Boyd's gonna do whatever the fuck Boyd's gonna do, and somewhere down the line he and Raylan are gonna clash and find themselves on opposite ends of a gun [Sandrine Shaw, 2017, p. 7].

Still, the narrative ends on a slightly more hopeful note: "Or maybe not—maybe this time, the story will have a different ending. Raylan allows himself a small, wistful smile. Wouldn't that be something" (*ibid.*). Like its title suggests, *Loose Ends by the Score* does not just indicate the characters' loose ends with each other and their pasts, but the narrative's loose ends as well. While less disruptively ambiguous than ElDiablito_SF's *M Is for Mine* (2013), the narrative here still refuses clear closure. Is Boyd lying? If not, will he be able to follow through? Will Raylan ever let himself trust him? If not, can they have a functional relationship? The ending may not be explicitly unsettling, but in refusing to tie up those loose ends, it leaves open a space of possibility for readers to play. The hopeful ending nods at a happy ending without over-promising; it remains grounded in the histories and shifting presents of characters unmoored from their narrative setting, who are not yet certain if they are equally unmoored from their pasts.

Roof's (1996) option to validate an ending that comprises the beginning of a new story can apply here. More than the unhappy ending, then, the ambiguous endings of these works push back at narrative closure and romantic conventions. In doing so, these narratives open more space for the slide and pleasure of continued play. The very nature of fan fiction means refusing to close a text; fans return to it again and again. In this way, individual works can be read more as pauses that willfully remain in the middle. Through playing in "the pleasure in the middle" (Roof, 1996, pp. 37–38), we resist the strictures of a sexuality bound in the reproductive imperative of heteronormativity, a resistance which allows extended to continually subvert the narrative conventions and structures of romance. Fan fiction other than bad bromances and dark slash can offer these options, of course, but breaking out of one imperative makes it easier to see the others. Refusing the clear, happy ending for readers who will follow the works down that road leads us to ask *why* we expect a happy ending and what possibilities not getting one opens for us to explore as creators and consumers of popular media texts.

Conclusion

Pat Califa was most likely right in his belief that we cannot "fuck our way to freedom" (in Shepherd, 2013, p. 30). A focus on individual liberation, sexual or otherwise, is not going to address the systemic inequalities in the world. However, by being part of transgressive sexual performances, we begin to see the "contradictions and tensions in the organizing logics of the competing discourses which support heteronormative politics of sexuality. Exposing those contradictions facilitates thinking—and enacting—sexuality and sex/gender in radically divergent ways" (*ibid.*). Bad bromance can serve as a site for this thinking.

The first space it offers is in the transgressive sexual performance of the writing itself. If the act of writing utopian, egalitarian slash resists heteronormativity (either because of its queer content or because women are writing sexually explicit fantasies and sharing them with one another), then the act of composing and sharing these darker works does so even more. In many ways, writing utopian slash no longer carries the same subversive charge; it's no longer an underground, secretive practice. Likewise, while still constrained in some ways, women are more vocal about their fantasies than they were thirty years ago. *Fifty Shades of Grey* (James, 2011) has even opened up space for women to talk about kink and to vocalize those desires (Downing, 2013 and Dymock, 2013), and the refrain of "safe, sane and consensual" remains in that arena, as well as with sex-positive feminists (Glick, 2000). But what about sex that is not safe, not sane, perhaps not consensual? What about fantasies that some consider anti-feminist? What about things that offend others? What about sharing those fantasies in a climate where those who conflate your fantasy with your actual, real-world desires are quick to try and shame you for them? Writing and sharing these darker works challenges the restrictions which both patriarchal and only nominally liberating perspectives attempt to enforce. Like publishing *The Story of O*, posting these works in and of itself can be a challenge to heteronormative expectations.

These works resist the dictates of heteronormativity by serving as the mirror to utopian slash. Where utopian slash frees men from the bonds of hegemonic masculinity to find a love and a bond denied them in the source texts, bad bromance slash binds them back into it to point out the shadows and how the men in these works are the architects of their own misery. Whether through enacting violence or maintaining emotional distance, these characters fail to connect with one another, thus also "failing" the promise inherent in utopian slash and its attendant theories, and in the expected romance narrative as well. However, this failure merely points out the flaws in utopia. It acknowledges the messy realities of the world, pulls them into fantasy, takes pleasure in them—because messiness is part of life, part of being human—even while acknowledging that no matter how cathartic, any release of this kind will only be temporary without meaningful change. This possibility of change is where bad bromance slash challenges both heteronormativity and utopian slash. The data available shows that fans and romance readers alike want their happy endings, but bad bromance consistently refuses to deliver. It will not gloss over darker aspects to tie them up with a pretty bow. It will not wave a wand and tidy up the mess.

DuPlessis (1985) argues that truly non-heteronormative texts must resist the constraints of convention and many of the narratives in this type of fan fiction do achieve this. The ideology of romance is the ideology of heteronormativity, even when the lovers are not a heterosexual pair. While we can never break out of narrative completely, disrupting it and making ourselves and our readers uncomfortable makes the artificiality of the romance clear: no one lives happily ever after in real life, nothing is so neat and simple. By intentionally subverting the prevailing discourses of romance by refusing its narrative compulsions towards generating neat, happy endings, and allowing for the mess of unproductive, dissatisfying violence and overwhelming emotion that does not get resolved, bad bromance (along with other dark slash fiction) destabilizes the presumed normality of the heteronormative.

Do these works and others like them have elements that some might deem "problematic"? Undoubtedly. Among just the works I examined here, for instance, the lack of clarity around the issue of Raylan's consent in *No Afterglow in Harlan* certainly has no easy answer. Likewise, Miles' treatment of Bass is troubling, particularly the potential for further harm he could do with the mixed messages he relays and his possessive seizure of the control of Bass's person after throwing him away. However, returning to Califa, reading and writing these works can serve as a transgressive sexual performance, and facilitate further inquiry. Sex and love are messy. Life is messy. Our literature and desires both reflect that. Bad bromance is a small thing, but by breaking the utopian vision we have of slash and of romance, it offers us the chance to examine more about ourselves and desires, and the ways we find ourselves confined within them. Maybe we can't "fuck our way to freedom," but opening the conventional boxes which we regulate our imaginations to is a good start.

Notes

1. For discussions on how to enjoy problematic media whilst maintaining a more critical reading position, see Allnatt (2016), Edell (2015), Rachael (2011) and Robyn (2014).

2. Forty years after the publication of the *Story of O*, Pauline Réage was eventually revealed as one of the writing pseudonyms of French journalist and novelist Anne Cécile Desclos.

References

Abrams, J.J., and Kripke, E. (Producers). (2012). *Revolution* [Television series]. Burbank, CA: Warner Bros. Television.

Allnatt, L. (2016, November 28). It's OK to Like Problematic Things. *The State Press*. Retrieved from http://www.statepress.com/article/2016/11/spopinion-liking-problematic-things-boyband-misogyny-one-direction.

Bacon-Smith, C. (1992). *Enterprising Women: Television Fandom and the Creation of Popular Myth*. Philadelphia: University of Pennsylvania Press.

Boguhn, A. (2015, February 14). Flipping the Script: 4 Reasons Fan Fiction Is a Feminist Pursuit. *Everyday Feminism*. Retrieved from http://everydayfeminism.com/2015/02/fan-fiction-feminist-pursuit.

Cabell Hankinson Gathman, E. (2005). *"So he saved my life and then he kicked me in the nuts": Maintaining Non-hierarchical Relationships Through Masculine Rivalry in Slash Fan Fiction*. Presented at the WisCon 29, Madison, WI. Retrieved from www.ssc.wisc.edu/~cgathman/papers/mrslash.doc.

Diamond, F. (2011). Beauty and the Beautiful Beast: Stephenie Meyer's Twilight Saga and the Quest for a Transgressive Female Desire. *Australian Feminist Studies, 26*(67), 41–55. doi:10.1080/08164649.2010.546327.

Downing, L. (2013). Safewording! Kinkphobia and Gender Normativity in *Fifty Shades of Grey*. *Psychology & Sexuality, 4*(1), 92–102. doi:10.1080/19419899.2012.740067.

Driscoll, C. (2006). One True Pairing: The Romance of Pornography and the Pornography of Romance. In K. Hellekson and K. Busse (Eds.), *Fan Fiction and Fan Communities in the Age of the Internet* (pp. 79–96). Jefferson, NC: McFarland.

DuPlessis, R.B. (1985). *Writing Beyond the Ending: Narrative Strategies of Twentieth-Century Women Writers*. Bloomington: Indiana University Press.

Dworkin, A. (1974). *Woman Hating*. New York: Dutton.

Dymock, A. (2013). Flogging Sexual Transgression: Interrogating the Costs of the "Fifty Shades Effect." *Sexualities, 16*(8), 880–895. doi:10.1177/1363460713508884.

Echols, A. (2016). Retrospective: Tangled Up in Pleasure and Danger. *Signs: Journal of Women in Culture & Society, 42*(1), 11–22. doi:10.1086/686751.

Edell, C. (2015, April 30). Your Favorite Media Is Problematic—Here's How to Deal (And What Not to Do). *Everyday Feminism*. Retrieved from http://everydayfeminism.com/2015/04/liking-problematic-media/.

ElDiablito_SF. (2013). *M Is for Mine*. Archive of Our Own.

flurblewig. (2010). *Nothing That I Understand*. Archive of Our Own.

Foucault, M. (1978). *The History of Sexuality. Volume 1: An Introduction*. (R. Hurley, Trans.). New York: Random House.

Glick, E. (2000). Sex Positive: Feminism, Queer Theory, and the Politics of Transgression. *Feminist Review, 64*(19), 19–45.

Green, S., Jenkins, C., and Jenkins, H. (1998). Normal Female Interest in Men Bonking: Selections from the Terra Nostra Underground and Strange Bedfellows. In C. Harris and A. Alexander (Eds.), *Theorizing Fandom: Fans, Subculture and Identity* (pp. 9–38). Cresskill, NJ: Hampton Press.

James, E.L. (2011). *Fifty Shades of Grey*. New York: Random House.

JaqofSpades. (2014). *The Inescapable Truth*. Archive of Our Own.

Jenkins, H. (2013). *Textual Poachers: Television Fans and Participatory Culture* (Twentieth Anniversary Edition). New York: Taylor & Francis.

Klink, F. (2016, October 27). Five Tropes Fanfic Readers Love (And One They Hate). *Fansplaining*. Retrieved from https://medium.com/fansplaining/five-tropes-fanfic-readers-love-and-one-they-hate-73843372408c.

Kripke, E., Callaway, T., and Parrott, R. (Writers), and Boyd, D. (Director). (2014, May 7). Tomorrowland [Television series episode]. In J.J. Abrams and E. Kripke (Producers), *Revolution*. Burbank, CA: Warner Bros. Television.

Kripke, E., Owusu-Breen, M., and, Pitts, M. (Writers), and Toye, F.E.O. (Director). (2012, November 26). Nobody's Fault but Mine [Television series episode]. In J.J Abrams and E. Kripke (Producers), *Revolution*. Burbank, CA: Warner Bros. Television.

Kustritz, A. (2003). Slashing the Romance Narrative. *Journal of American Culture, 26*(3), 371–384. doi:10.1111/1542-734X.00098.

mcclaln. (2016, November 30). Hello, Adults in the Voltron Fandom [Blog post]. Tumblr.

Miller, D.A. (1981). *Narrative and Its Discontents: Problems of Closure in the Traditional Novel*. Princeton: Princeton University Press.

MissJeeves. (2013). *No Afterglow in Harlan*. Archive of Our Own.

Musser, A.J. (2015). BDSM and the Boundaries of Criticism: Feminism and Neoliberalism in *Fifty Shades of Grey* and *The Story of O*. *Feminist Theory, 16*(2), 121–136.

Payne, E. (2010). Sluts: Heteronormative Policing in the Stories of Lesbian Youth. *Educational Studies, 46*, 317–336.

Penley, C. (1992). Feminism, Psychoanalysis, and The Study of Popular Culture. In L. Grossberg, C. Nelson, and P.A. Treichler (Eds.), *Cultural Studies* (pp. 479–500). New York: Routledge.

Rachael. (2011, September 18). *How to Be a Fan of Problematic Things*. Retrieved from http://www.socialjusticeleague.net/2011/09/how-to-be-a-fan-of-problematic-things/.

Radway, J.A. (1984). *Reading the Romance: Women, Patriarchy, and Popular Literature*. Chapel Hill: University of North Carolina Press.

Réage, P. (1965). *The Story of O*. New York: Grove Press.

Robyn. (2014, November 11). It's Okay to Like Problematic Things. *Unite For Reproductive & Gender Equity (URGE)*. Retrieved from http://urge.org/its-okay-to-like-problematic-things/.

Roof, J. (1996). *Come as You Are: Sexuality & Narrative*. New York: Columbia University Press.

Rubin, G.S. (2007). Thinking Sex: Notes for a Radical Theory of the Politics of Sexuality. In R.G. Parker and P. Aggleton (Eds.), *Culture, Society and Sexuality: A Reader* (2nd ed.) (pp. 143–178). Abingdon: Routledge.

Russ, J. (1985). *Magic Mommas, Trembling Sisters, Puritans and Perverts: Essays on Sex and Pornography*. Trumansburg, NY: The Crossing Press.

Sandrine Shaw. (2017, February 14). *Loose Ends by the Score*. Archive of Our Own.

Scodari, C. (2003). Resistance Re-Examined: Gender, Fan Practices, and Science Fiction Television. *Popular Communication, 1*(2), 111–130. doi:10.1207/S15405710PC0102_3.

Shepherd, L.J. (2013). *Gender, Violence and Popular Culture: Telling Stories*. New York: Routledge.

Shulman, J.L., and Horne, S.G. (2006). Guilty or Not? A Path Model of Women's Sexual Force Fantasies. *The Journal of Sex Research, 43*(4), 368–377.

Smash. (2012, April 2). On 50 Shades of Grey and the Erotization of Male Domination [Blog post]. *Radfem HUB*. Retrieved from https://radicalhubarchives.wordpress.com/2012/04/02/on-50-shades-of-grey-and-the-erotization-of-male-domination/.

Social Justice League. (2011, September 18). *How to Be a Fan of Problematic Things*. Retrieved April 24, 2017, from http://www.socialjusticeleague.net/2011/09/how-to-be-a-fan-of-problematic-things/.

tobermoriansass. (2016). A Cat of a Different Coat [Blog post]. Tumblr.

Toscano, A.R. (2012). A Parody of Love: The Narrative Uses of Rape in Popular Romance. *Journal of Popular Romance Studies, 2*(2).

uniwolfwerecorn. (2016). SHIP WARS: A Simple Guide for Fandom [Blog post]. Tumblr.

Whedon, J. (Producer). (1997). *Buffy the Vampire Slayer* [Television series]. Los Angeles: Mutant Enemy Productions.

Whedon, J., and Greenwalt, D. (Producers). (1999). *Angel* [Televisoin series]. Los Angeles: Mutant Enemy Productions.

Whedon, J., and Greenwalt, D. (Writers), and Kretchner, J.T. (Director). (1997, September 29). School Hard [Television series episode]. In J. Whedon (Producer), *Buffy the Vampire Slayer*. Burbank, CA: Warner Bros. Television.

Yost, G. (Producer). (2012). *Justified* [Television Series]. Los Angeles: FX Network.

Yost, G., Golan, F., Andron, D., and Cavell, B. (Writers), and Arkin, A. (Director). (2015, April 14). The Promise [Television Series Episode]. In G. Yost (Producer), *Justified*. Los Angeles: FX Network.

Dubious Consent

The Revival of Ravishment

Ashton Spacey

Introduction—What Is Dub-Con?

In its simplest form, the phrase *dubious consent* (contracted to dub-con) refers to a situational context in which the consent of one, both, or all parties involved is uncertain, and/or a situation where some degree of coercion is used to facilitate an encounter. This is usually a sexual encounter, but not always. Beyond this, dub-con is also a label commonly applied to denote instances where someone's *capacity* to give full consent is ambiguous:

> Dub-con is also used to indicate a relationship (or incident) that precludes the ability to give meaningful consent, such as student/teacher, prisoner/guard, patient/doctor, or child/adult. In these situations, the character with less authority, even if an intelligent adult, is presumed incapable of giving informed consent to a sexual relationship, because the power imbalance is too prone to abuse [Dub-con, 2016, para. 4].

Dub-con fan fiction appears across the vast majority of fandoms and fan work platforms, but while content varies widely, the underlying theme of dub-con narratives is the erotics of consent. As is the case with many subgenres within slash, femslash and fan fiction as a whole, pinpointing the exact origin of dub-con as a term is difficult. Some of the earliest records of its usage suggest that the phrase "dubious consent" (along with the similar tag of "ambiguous consent") was first used in regard to fan fiction in late 2003 in the *Harry Potter* and *Star Wars: The Phantom Menace* fandoms (Dub-con, 2016, para. 7–11). By 2005, both the phrase and the contraction of the phrase began to appear more commonly, and by 2006 a corresponding entry for the term had been added to *Urban Dictionary* (*ibid.*). As with other tags and tropes that are ubiquitous in modern slash, it is important to acknowledge that dub-con as a concept and a trope within the collective fannish imagination is likely to predate these records. As the *Fanlore* entry on dub-con (*ibid.*) notes, many early fandom mailing lists and forums were subscription only, and many authors may have elected to backdate the warnings on their earlier stories with more contemporary tags. As a general literary trope, however, it has permeated the erotic imagination for a significantly longer period and exerted a tremendous and not always positive impact on the rhetoric of desire.

In the 2016 *Fansplaining* Fic Preferences Survey, 7,610 respondents were asked about their preferred tropes and themes in fan fiction. When exploring which fan fiction tropes were the most controversial, the number of people who reported that they loved dub-con and the number of people who reported that they hated dub-con were very close; a "Yay:Nay ratio" close to 1 (Klink, 2016, image 6). Klink writes that such a result, along with similar findings for the Omegaverse and love potion tropes, was unsurprising; all of these themes "pose some of the same problems in the murky realm of consent in the fanfiction world" (para 16, lines 4–5). The "murky realm" that frames these problems are ongoing debates about personal agency, bodily autonomy and the link between sexuality, morality and cultural normativity.

This essay charts the evolution of dub-con as a literary trope in slash fiction and in romance fiction and explores its position within the wider genre of popular literature, given that popular fiction is both a product of and a response to constantly evolving social imperatives and concerns. There are as many configurations of dub-con as the erotic imaginary can conceive, all of which pose difficult and necessary questions about how we understand our place in society, how we interact with other people, how we perceive and articulate our identities and assert our rights to bodily autonomy, and how we are all subject to power structures every day of our lives. However, in this essay I argue that dub-con does something that other forms of popular literature do not: it self-identifies. The very nature of naming and tagging the genre with the specific label of Dubious Consent is, from the outset, an important step in alerting readers to the fact that the erotic scenario(s) contained within the narrative is not an ideal that we should valorize or unquestioningly accept.

From the outset, I must make explicit that dub-con, slash and romance fiction are vast and incredibly nuanced genres. While generalizations have been necessary for the scope of this discussion, to describe any of these complex genres as single, unified and unchanging objects is to miss what makes them powerful cultural agents. This essay explores dub-con where the tone of the depicted scenario tends towards pleasurable submission, but there are significantly more elements to it than this. For example, there are many works which repeatedly and deliberately transition between dub-con and non-con (non-consensual), or works in which the perspectives of the characters involved are rendered unclear and thus readers cannot actively decode the scene as pleasurable or wanted. However, to begin to explore why dub-con as a genre is so prevalent and why it provokes such passionate debate, this essay will explore how dub-con may be a product of, and a response to, the situational contexts and arguments which surround it, and then investigate the literary history from which it has developed.

Dub-Con(troversy)

There is a cloud of controversy surrounding dub-con. Arising from feminist discourse around autonomous personhood and the impacts of rape culture,[1] there is a not unfounded accusation that dub-con can be perceived as being regressive and antifeminist. Dub-con as a trope is criticized as being one which valorizes and glorifies sexual violence, perpetuating harmful cultural ideologies by eroticizing scenarios where consent is not assured. To understand why dub-con continues to generate such debate and why its popularity is so culturally significant, it is necessary to examine these discussions and cultural ideologies in greater detail before we start to explore dub-con's literary history.

In current legal perspectives, consent is generally understood as a *lack of active resistance*—a definition of the term which not only normalizes sexual aggression in erotic encounters, but also victim-blames those who do not resist loudly or strongly enough (Egbert, 2014). However, what is it that a person is expected to "resist" in this definition? Generally, it is understood that when attempting to engage someone in a sexual encounter, using direct physical coercion and/or intimidation is unacceptable. However, when it comes to exerting emotional coercion ("if you loved me, you would"), social coercion ("everyone else is doing it, don't be weird about it") and economic coercion ("if you don't do this for me, I'll withdraw my financial support/I won't let you live here"), the lines of acceptability are rendered less clear in the law. A definition like this, which construes consent as a lack of resistance, renders the question of whether somebody actually *wants* to submit to sexual encounters largely irrelevant—particularly when the coerced party agrees to engage in sexual activity to avoid negative consequences such as a loss of their partner's affection or support, or to avoid social prejudice. Within the operations of rape culture, in real life "dubiously" obtained consent such as this is often used as a defense to justify sexual encounters which would otherwise be understood as non-consensual.

The contexts of our experiences of interpersonal interactions, our self-conceptions and our position within social environments all shape who we are and what we do. Egbert (2014) quotes the concept that in relationships where there is dependency or a power imbalance between the parties involved, the capacity of the more subordinate party to give full consent is damaged because he or she does not have the option to withdraw their consent or to confront their partner's behavior. Egbert posits that this inherent and inescapable inequality means that in any given instance where power is imbalanced, there can be no such thing as full consent and uses this concept to decry BDSM[2] practices and relationships in particular as inherently abusive. Essentialist perspectives therefore posit that the concept of "dubious consent" is ultimately a redundant one. In any real or fictional situation where there is no clear and conscious consent—if there is no "yes"—then the default answer is and must be understood as a "no." From this perspective, to use the label of "dubious consent" is meaningless; it is used instead of acknowledging that coerced consent is often non-consent, making the term dub-con a euphemistic way to downplay instances where coerced consent acts as a form of harm reduction against the threat of violence, sexual aggression, abuse (emotional, mental and physical) and even death. It is a reinforcement of the same dangerous ideologies which the trope claims to resist and explore; the idea that no doesn't always mean no, particularly if you don't offer "enough" resistance or if you "secretly wanted it."

Egbert's suggestion has been fiercely contested by BDSM practitioners and advocates, who argue that an ethos of consent, desire and personal agency underpins every activity and relationship in which they are engaged. This ethos is often reiterated through mantras such as "Safe, Sane and Consensual (SCC)" (Black, 2011) and "Risk Aware Consensual Kink (RACK)[3]" (Mr. Michael, 2010). They and others favor a more flexible and affirmative perspective towards consent, advocating a model where "yes means yes." Looking to expand on the restrictive existing definitions, this perspective defines consent not only as getting permission but also about ensuring that sexual encounters are based on mutual desire and enthusiasm. From a perspective of affirmative consent, a person (or character) has the power to retain and exercise their agency and bodily autonomy when it comes to sexual situations. However, while this is a positive and progressive way to reframe consent—particularly for marginalized groups—the reality is that people (and characters) can and do give consent out of fear, without fully understanding what they are agreeing to, or because they have been coerced. The debate is not a simple one and it is bound by strong ideological positions on all sides.

As explored by Rubin (2006) and Foucault (1976/1978)[4] sexuality has always been cast as dangerous and thus requiring control through any number of cultural restrictions—particularly in the case of female sexuality. Thus, much of our understanding of how consent, interpersonal relationships, and sexual behaviors and identities "should" be operating comes from the ways in which these elements have been socially constructed. Society still mostly operates under a heteronormative paradigm: a system where people (allegedly) fall neatly into distinct "male" or "female" modes of being and behaviors. Anyone can be heteronormative—including people who are not heterosexual—but in reality many people are not actually living completely heteronormative lives. Within this paradigm, "normal" and "natural" male sexuality is construed as being active, domineering and aggressive, and "normal" female sexuality is construed as being passive, submissive and subordinate. This system controls and restricts the behaviors and identities of every individual within it.

According to this system, "masculinity is predicated on overcoming [another's] bodily desire and control" (Pascoe, 2007, p. 100). Men who do not perform (or are not interested in performing) typically "masculine" behaviors and displays of power are rejected by heteronormativity. For example, "real" men are not allowed to reveal too much sentimentality or emotion (such as feeling anxious about their bodies or identities) or to seek feminine roles such as carers, nurses or homemakers. If they fail to express their sexuality in domineering ways (for example, if they have vivid, thrilling fantasies about being dominated by women or other men) they are labeled unmasculine and presented as failures, broken or deviants. When any male desire which does not align with the masculine norm cannot be safely vocalized without being mocked or judged, this can result in a fractured sense of both social and sexual identity with limited ways to articulate, explore or resolve it. Heteronormative constructions of "normal" feminine sexuality dictate that women must be both sexually appealing and chaste. In contrast to men, women are not allowed to actively *desire*—only to passively *want* and to wait for another party's desire to be enacted upon them; to actively assert their own sexual desires may draw their chastity (and thus, their moral character in the eyes of society) into doubt. To fail to subscribe to the pattern set out by heteronormativity is to condemn oneself to being perceived as any number of negative identities, to be shamed, and to be ultimately rejected by society. This subsequently opens one up to the myriad punishments and social exclusions inflicted on failed men and women, such as the Othering of "weird" men and women who enjoy non-normative sex acts and relationships, the slut-shaming of promiscuous or sexually dominant women, and the victim-blaming of women and men who are sexually assaulted for the perceived errors in their judgment or behavior that "resulted" in the attack.

This system has conditioned us to believe that there is one ideal form of relationship and a handful of permissible, "good" ways to have sex. Anything else couldn't possibly be safe, enjoyable, wanted or normal—a social taboo that Gayle Rubin refers to as Sex Negativity (2011). Within this paradigm, it is clear that there are only a handful of acceptable ways to say yes and yet so many ways in which even one's *capacity* to give a no or a yes is ignored, mocked or rendered redundant. When every no means no, but not every yes means yes, where does that leave us? With this as our sexual framework, is there any wonder why there is so much anxiety about sexuality, identity and behavior and how all of these elements interlink? There is much debate and confusion, but open dialogue is only now really beginning to establish itself in the face of moral panics and identity politics. In the interpretive communities of fandom where discourse, dialogue and the erotic imaginary has the space to develop, it is not surprising to find that conversation and narratives which explore consent and desire are flourishing.

Is Dub-Con a Rape Fantasy?

Dub-con as a trope is as complicated and paradoxical as the cultural frameworks from which it has developed; something which forms part of its appeal—but what is it that makes it appealing? It has been suggested in metadiscussion that since rape culture is so deeply integrated into reading positions, dub-con is a result of attempts to negotiate its influence. As such, there is a suggestion that dub-con may primarily operate as a rape fantasy; an imagined scenario where a person is dominated by someone (to whom they give a varying degree of resistance) either through the threat and/or use of physical force, or incapacitation—such as sleep or intoxication. While it may seem paradoxical that someone (who in a slash fiction context is highly likely to be female or a non-binary individual) would fantasize about being forced into sexual activity when they could just as easily fantasize about consensual submission, this type of fantasy has a definite resonance with the erotic imaginary. For example, in a study conducted by Critelli and Bivona (2008), which explores the research literature surrounding women's rape fantasies, approximately 31 percent to 51 percent of the women surveyed had fantasies in which they were forced into sex against their will, with 9 percent to 17 percent reporting these as frequent or favorite fantasies (Abstract, lines 2–4). As Bergman highlights, this would suggest that at least 1 in 10 women were (and perhaps still are) fantasizing at least once per month in a pleasurable way about forced sexual activity (2009, para 45, lines 8–9).

However, the term "rape fantasy" carries with it a considerable amount of baggage—something which often obfuscates investigations into the real psychosexual resonance of these fantasies in both slash fiction and in real life. The suggestion that having erotic rape fantasies indicates an actual subconscious desire to experience the real brutalities of a rape is a damaging misunderstanding of the complexities involved in this type of imagined scenario.[5] Additionally, the argument that these fantasies are a product of natural female masochism—an allegedly instinctual desire within women to obliterate their identities by being dominated and nurtured—is also widely contested (see Felski, 2005). The counter-assertion to these claims is that these fantasies, regardless of one's gender identity, may simply be the products of a desire to realize one's autonomy in relation to another person and to experience the disintegration of boundaries. This section therefore explores how dub-con as a trope appeals to our erotic imaginaries and allows us to reframe and explore the cultural issues and ideologies which surround the genre.

Common understandings of why these fantasies exist in and what purpose(s) they serve tend to boil down into three main frameworks: sexual desirability, sexual blame avoidance and openness to sexual experience. Castleman (2015) explains these terms:

> **Sexual Desirability** is a common fantasy in romance fiction, where a powerful and dangerous man becomes so enthralled by the protagonist that he strives to have her, even if this is against her will. This explanation implies that women have rape fantasies to bolster feelings of seductiveness and desirability.
>
> **Sexual Blame Avoidance** is the most popular explanation behind the prevalence of female rape and submission fantasies, which recognizes that erotic desires may trigger feelings of anxiety, guilt, and shame. By fantasizing about being forced into sexual encounters, the victim is not responsible for the sex and is therefore not responsible for any arousal they feel as a consequence.
>
> **Openness to Sexual Experience** refers to enjoying sex and accepting that enjoyment without anxiety, guilt or shame. People who are open to sexual experience feel sufficiently free to play with erotic scenarios beyond the boundaries of what they'd want to experience in real life.

In a survey conducted with 355 college-aged women, Bivona, Critelli and Clark (2012) tested the veracity of these common explanations behind rape fantasies. Curiously counterpoint to commonly held beliefs about the possible function(s) of rape fantasies, they reported that sexual blame avoidance theory was not supported, sexual desirability theory was moderately supported, and an openness to sexual experience theory received the strongest support. They discovered that the women who had the highest self-esteem and more frequent consensual and desirability sexual fantasies had more frequent rape fantasies—and reported a greater degree of sexual arousal to these.

Arousal and desire operate in two distinct systems and it is important to acknowledge that arousal alone is not consent—it is a physiological reaction in response to stimuli. Additionally, 15 percent of the respondents to Bivona, Critelli and Clark's study identified themselves as survivors of sexual assault. These fantasies may therefore serve another purpose; if we imagine a scenario like this—an assault which may be a widespread occurrence that cannot be predicted or even prevented, or one that has already occurred—we may also be able to fantasize about ways we might react, in order to lessen the fear of the situation or to mitigate the anxiety, guilt and fear of a remembered experience. The crucial erotic element which underpins these fantasies is where and how control is used. When a scenario like this occurs in reality, it removes the control of a victim. In the fantasy, it is manipulated solely by the self—thus rendering these not so much fantasies about rape as fantasies about *submission*.

In a submission fantasy, however aggressive the depicted scenario may be, the fantasist is able to control the imagined scenario from start to finish. They are able to escalate or mitigate any sense of threat, they are able to control how much pleasure they take from the actions that occur, and most importantly they are free to withdraw from the fantasy at any time. Within the space of the erotic imaginary, we are always in control; even when the imagined scenario is violent, destructive and morally objectionable—and certainly not something we would want to encounter in real life. In truth, regardless of the circumstances of the individual fantasist there is no one particular "reason" or motivation behind the enjoyment of these fantasies. The reality is that the appeal of enforced submission scenarios most likely combines all of the elements discussed so far and many others not specified here.

If we argue that a submission fantasy is a safe way to imagine a loss of one's sexual control while also retaining all of one's personal control, the imagined scenario retains its excitement with very little representation of the violences incurred in real rapes. With this in mind, it seems very unlikely that someone who has submission fantasies is actually inclined to actually want to be forced into unwanted sexual activity. Indeed, given that many readers and writers of dub-con report a strong aversion to non-con sexual scenarios in fan fiction, with Klink reporting non-con as being the second most widely reviled trope identified by respondents (2016, image 5), this would imply that the appeal of dub-con is not violence or a painful, lasting loss of control. Dub-con ultimately relies heavily on dramatic irony; regardless of the plot context, in dub-con narratives the erotic focus of the trope is on the submission of one or more parties in the face of an applied power—a submission which is almost always assured. The thrill is in not knowing how, when and why that submission is going to occur as a result. What may be at the heart of dub-con's appeal is the conflict between the erotics and anxieties of uncertainty.

In the turbulent waters of the erotic imagination, these multiple reasons and desires combine with the cultural and historical frameworks that have dictated how sexuality should be "correctly" experienced and subsequently regulated. Under the rubric established by heternormativity, that which does not fit becomes taboo. As a result, that which is taboo is socially construed as being simultaneously monstrous and exciting. If, as Bataille writes, "the main function of all taboos is to combat violence" (2001/1962, p. 41) perhaps we can argue that these fantasies might serve a purpose as a means to consciously or subconsciously negotiate reading positions within historically inflexible gender and power structures. By envisioning enjoyable scenarios in which we engage in enforced submission but remain fully in control, we are able to reframe the restrictions that our cultural position places on our bodily agency and our capacity to give consent—not just to what we actively desire, but to the ways we passively experience other, non-sexual forms of enforced submission every day.

Consent, Power and Desire in Popular Fiction

We have established that in many cases, dub-con operates as a submission fantasy which allows a space to explore how identities and desires are in conflict with, and yet subject to, power and gender structures. This conflicted subjectivity extends far back from current reading positions and has permeated the erotic imagination in other forms of popular literature for centuries—and while fandom itself remains quite unique, fan fiction remains a product of a rich literary history. Fans and academics[6] have often drawn compelling parallels between slash fiction and romance fiction as both genres tend to deliberately foreground notions of sexuality, power and gender identity. Additionally, erotic scenes in both slash and romance fiction are rarely totally divorced from these themes, even if these are not the primary focus of the narrative. Like other forms of popular literature, slash fiction ultimately allows us to articulate and explore social concerns and ideologies within a creative, interpretive space.

Slash has thus been positioned both in relation to and in opposition of romance fiction's heteronormative structures and content. Janice Radway's *Reading the Romance* (1984/1991) has become a seminal text for many people looking to explore how slash fits into the wider literary landscape, and how it both correlates to and differs from romance fiction—another form of popular literature primarily generated by and for women and marginalized groups. Woledge (2006), for example, proposes that slash fiction ultimately retains romance fiction's preoccupation with establishing equality and intimacy and does not so much rebel against existing romantic tropes as *emulate* them. However, she notes that slash builds on "some of culture's less salient ideologies" (such as the operation and confines of the heteronormative paradigm) to highlight images of love and intimacy that are not associated with interpersonal male relationships (2006, p. 100). In this way, slash has been held up as a genre which correlates to, but is not simply an extension of, romantic conventions; one which valorizes a more egalitarian paradigm of power, desire and mutual pleasure within relationships of any configuration—even when slash stories feature acts of violence, sexual aggression and dominance.

In her book, Radway explored how reading romance fiction is valued for the way it makes readers feel. Readers seek a "general sense of emotional well-being and visceral contentment" (1984/1991, p. 70) from stories about mutual love, where a hero's gently expressed devotion soothes a sense of deprivation in the reader caused by the dissatisfying frameworks and emotional behavior paradigms mandated by heteronormativity. While the readers sought narratives that provided nurturance, protection, passion and love, romance fiction only offered very limited frameworks to help them negotiate and interpret the inflexible forms of masculinity they were likely to encounter in their real lives: "In learning how to read male behavior from the romance, a woman insulates herself from the need to demand that such behavior change" (p. 151). However, given that readers of popular literature are not uncritical passive consumers, while the romances reiterated heteronormativity's strict behavioral mandates Radway argued that such works do act as a cultural release valve. This allowed women to "express proscribed emotions and feelings of outrage and self righteous anger, and to express repressed fears in the free realm of the imaginary" (p. 158)—albeit with limited scope to challenge or to reconcile heteronormativity's opposing binary interests.

In both romance and slash fiction, an aversion to "bad romances" has often been reported. These stories portray behaviors and events which are legitimized by the harmful and oppressive ideologies that forms of popular fiction often attempt to negotiate and/or resist, and subsequently usually provoke strong emotions—particularly stories where sexual scenarios or instances of conflict appear detached from any overarching emotional signifiers. For example, when asked to identify which tropes were the most objectionable to encounter in a story, Radway's readers "generally agree[d] that bed-hopping or promiscuous sex, a sad ending, rape, physical torture, and weak heroes have no place in romance" (p. 73). These are findings which coincide with some of the results of the *Fansplaining* Fic Preferences Survey, which suggest that rape, death and bullying are among some of the tropes readers find most objectionable in fan works, and that "corruption" of favorite characters is one of the most controversial (Klink, 2016, images 5 & 6). Whatever the topic, a "good" romance must therefore convincingly address and assuage a reader's fears and reservations, but a "bad" romance only serves to reveal and highlight these fears.

Given that some of the themes involved in bad romances may be too close to reality, instances of domineering sexual behavior in romance and slash fiction therefore tend to be encoded in the theme of desire overwhelming control and "are not constructed to glorify or eroticize violence but to use it just as all the structures [of slash and romance fiction] are used: to engender intimacy" (Woledge, 2006, p. 108). Curiously, though, both the romance readers consulted by Radway (and to some extent, the fan readers who responded to the *Fic Preferences Survey*) have relayed that what they do not find as objectionable as outright sexual assault is "a little forceful persuasion" (Radway, 1984/1991, p. 75). This is a phrase which refers to instances in which a hero employs some degree of coercion—usually physical, but sometimes emotional or economic—to exert sexual sway over a heroine; scenarios which sound incredibly similar to those which regularly fall within the remit of modern dub-con. This distinction on the surface seems artificial, given that coercion is employed to negotiate a lack of clear consent. In the next section, this essay will explore the subtle but vital dividing line between what is encoded and interpreted as an assault and what has historically been referred to in popular literature as *ravishment*.

The Revival of Ravishment

In Margaret Mitchell's *Gone with the Wind* (1936), notorious scoundrel Rhett Butler carries fiercely independent Scarlett O'Hara kicking and screaming up the stairs to the bedroom—a scene that has captivated the erotic imaginations of millions of readers for decades and drawn passionate debate from all sides. For some, the scene depicts a marital rape; while Scarlett does appear to give some form of consent eventually, she openly reports experiencing pain and fear, and feeling that he has "humbled her, hurt her, used her brutally through a wild mad night" (p. 800)—emotions which would suggest that her consent was, if not completely absent, then obtained dubiously rather than given freely despite how she reports in the same sentence that she "had gloried in it" (*ibid.*). While others do not dispute Scarlett's relayed experiences, they point to the vivid sense of thrill she also reports feeling

> [...] a wild thrill such as she had never known; joy, fear, madness, excitement, surrender to arms that were too strong, lips too bruising, fate that moved too fast. For the first time in her life she had met someone, something stronger than she, someone she could neither bully nor break, someone who was bullying and breaking her [p. 800].

The next morning, Scarlett reflects on the night before—feeling a mixture of shame, delight and embarrassment at her own reckless submission:

> Oh, she should be ashamed, should shrink from the very memory of the hot swirling darkness! A lady, a real lady, could never hold up her head after such a night. But, stronger than shame, was the memory of rapture, of the ecstasy of surrender. For the first time in her life she had felt alive, felt passion as sweeping and primitive as the

> fear she had known the night she fled Atlanta [...] For one night, he had had her at his mercy but now she knew the weakness of his armor. From now on she had him where she wanted him. She had smarted under his jeers for a long time, but now she had him where she could make him jump through any hoops she cared to hold.
>
> When she thought of meeting him again, face to face in the sober light of day, a nervous tingling embarrassment that carried with it an exciting pleasure enveloped her.
>
> "I'm nervous as a bride," she thought. "And about Rhett!" And, at the idea she fell to giggling foolishly [pp. 800–801].

It is interesting to note that Scarlett's shame is primarily experienced in advance of what she believes would be an outcry from wider society at her unfeminine sexual rapture. A "real" lady—a lady who behaves in accordance with the appropriate behavioral stipulations set out by the heteronormative paradigm—could not openly take pleasure from such passion as she has experienced. Her embarrassment stems from this conflict of personal and social identities and the lingering fear of social rejection by external others who deem her behavior inappropriate, while the giddy pleasure she reports is a product of her personal response to her actions and arousal.

When characters like Scarlett O'Hara report experiencing arousal—a response to stimuli—have they really consented? Returning to the understanding that arousal is a response to stimulus, it is crucial to understand that many rape victims report feelings of immense shame for having experienced any form of arousal or sexual pleasure during their attack (see Morber, 2013). In reality, having experienced Rhett's brutality, it is wholly possible Scarlett would have been likely to find this conflict significantly less pleasurable than she does in fiction. Additionally, when characters like Rhett Butler are so domineering and hold more physical power than their partners (and given that Rhett has repeatedly made threatening remarks to Scarlett both in the scene and throughout their relationship), what would have happened if Scarlett had not consented? With these questions in mind, the reader must approach and interpret the situation armed with at two sets of frameworks; their own and Scarlett's.

In the case of *Gone with the Wind*, the reader's interpretive framework is informed by their own subjective understanding and an awareness that it is important to read these excerpts within the context of the whole book *and* the wider context in which the novel was set. Not only the American Civil War and Reconstruction Era in which the story itself occurs, but also the cultural climate of 1930s America where it was written, published and received. A reading must also therefore be informed by Scarlett's perception of the encounter as pleasurable and a new source of power for her—particularly given the pervasive culture of female infantilization and fetishization in which the book was not only set but also written. Scarlett relays that she is fully aware of the assault on her personhood and agency which has transpired, yet she finds herself conflicted with how she expected to feel, and furthermore, how she *is* expected to feel.

Is it misogynistic for us to deny the agency of Scarlett and other characters like her—either by ignoring and belittling her fears and concerns in favor of reading a happy ending, or by implying she is antifeminist because of the way she chose to interpret what happened to her and took pleasure from her submission? The staircase scene and dozens of other scenarios like it have generated a significant amount of literary and cultural criticism, on top of explorations of the wider problematic themes of racism, classism, colonialism, slavery and violently sexist attitudes which all feature prevalently within *Gone with the Wind* and other classic literature. How, then, are such problematic themes both presented, discussed and eroticized in popular literature—a genre which we are aware is both a product of and a response to social and cultural systems and events?

If one begins to chart changing attitudes towards autonomy, rape and authorial intention when stories of sexual violence are narrated in literature, it becomes apparent that there is an old term, dating as far back as the Middle Ages, which has been previously used to describe an experience like the one Scarlett O'Hara reports. The trope of *ravishment* has persisted in the erotic imaginary for centuries. Jocelyn Catty offers the following definition of the term:

> Derived from the Latin *raptus*, meaning "violently seized or carried away," ravishment described an experience in which a person was so carried away by sensual pleasure that he temporarily lost the ability to exert conscious control—ravishment subverted the will. Literary works were accused of using this technique to instil vice[...] Beautiful women were also described as "ravishing," or able to infuse men with an uncontrollable desire [1999, in Greenstadt, 2009, p. 9].

Wilkins (2016), quoting Kathryn Gravdal, relays how the use of the original term *ravissement* has always represented a semantic transition from violent abduction to sexual pleasure: it at first described a process of physically abducting a woman and "carrying her away," then later "carrying a soul to heaven," then the "secular, affective meaning of being 'carried away emotionally'" and then to a definition referring to sexual desire (p. 2). Evelyn Burge Vitz proposes that this is in line with medieval attitudes towards love, which was often likened to "a violent experience which happened to you—entered or penetrated you, took possession of you, corrupted your reason and imprisoned you, male and female—against your will" (in Wilkins, 2016, p. 2).

Wilkins notes that both the medieval romance and the chivalrous romance as we understand it from a modern perspective share structures of desire, wherein one encounters an object of desire and obstacles to that object which ultimately need to be circumvented. Where the chivalrous romance features the courtly love of an unobtainable object, the medieval romance concerns itself more with the visceral (and almost supernatural) effects of realizing one's desire (Wilkins, 2016). However, all stories that fall within the scope of ravishment feature the same popular tropes of submission and domination; the same paradigms of power and desire which are played out and reframed to varying degrees within differing contexts. This acts as a means to reconcile difficult, complex and deeply erotic concepts with the cultural understandings of bodily autonomy in which they are produced. For example, modern narratives would now rightfully frame unwanted sexual advances as an unacceptable act against one's personhood, whereas medieval and early modern romances (generated within the cultural contexts of the forms of patriarchy and the heteronormative binary which were then in operation and informing medieval and early modern legal and theological frameworks) would more commonly position acts of sexual violence as being defined largely in opposition to the ideal state of chastity. Catty (1999) notes:

> From medieval times, statutes were passed prohibiting "ravishment"—a crime that did not clearly distinguish forced copulation from abduction, or the "taking away of women." Thus ravishment was envisioned as a form of theft in which the primary victims were not the women themselves, but their fathers or husbands. The most influential of these statutes stipulated that it was a crime for a man to ravish a woman *whether she consented or not*—a perspective that only made sense in a legal context where she was regarded as an object of property subject to misappropriation [in Greenstadt, 2009, pp. 12–13].

Given the cultural shifts that have occurred over the last century in terms of understandings of bodily autonomy, relationship structures and cultural attitudes towards sex and sexuality, the medieval definition of ravishment would not be likely to sit well with modern audiences. So, the more modern reinvention of ravishment as a term to describe a sense of erotic abandon and the ecstasy of surrender may be a conscious way for an author to avoid invoking the rightfully negative implications of the word "rape"—the most commonly used word to describe sexual activity without one's consent—by instead offering a different term. Newer definitions of ravishment, such as those we can see attached to the modern label of dub-con, emphasize "the possibility of being swept away by pleasure, even in the experience of being threatened by sexual aggression and violation" (Wilkins, 2016, p. 3).

However, ravishment still carries with it an unpleasant tone of false morality; one which still presents the notion that someone can be "asking for it" or be partially responsible for their own violation. This definition merely repeats the existing frameworks of the heteronormative paradigm in which one side of the binary is weak, submissive, passive and in need of protection and the other is aggressive, domineering, active and predisposed towards violent consumption—and nobody is somewhere between these two states or can move fluidly between them. Catty (1999) notes that one is both ravishing and open to ravishment, particularly in the case of women:

> Whether others look at her or she herself does the looking, the result is the same: she jeopardizes her chastity and is "spotted" with lust. In the end what matters is that, by venturing into the public gaze, a woman enters a regime of ravishment ruled by the uncontrollable forces of desire. The only way to avoid being morally tainted is to stay home [in Greenstadt, 2009, p. 10].

This damaging conflation of moral purity and chastity still continues to underpin modern forms of the heteronormative binary, such as Scarlett's musing that a "real lady" could never actively seek sexual rapture of her own accord. However, if a "real" masculine sexuality overcomes a "real" feminine one (regardless of the genders or sexual identities of the parties involved), and pleasure is the result of such a union, then the moral disgrace of the encounter is traditionally reduced.

Angela Toscano (2012) provides a compelling insight into how forced seduction in literature functions as a discursive act. The idea that one can "force" a seduction implies that there are seductions where no force is necessary; seduction in this framework is presented as being akin to temptation, and therefore a form of persuasion which requires the complicity of the person who is being seduced (p. 9). Toscano posits that a forced seduction, therefore, is presented not as a simple rape but as an attempt to compel interaction and persuasion in order to make one party complicit with their own violation. If identity is at the root of desire, a ravisher wants their victim to respond to them, either positively or negatively, to reaffirm the ravisher's identity (*ibid.*). When a person is ravished, however, that person's core selfhood remains unviolated even when their body is abused. Rather than disrupt one's identity, ravishment solidifies it or even transforms it into a new identity in relation to the other party—for example, if a ravished person is able to overcome the one who has ravished them, then their new identity is articulated in this way.

Returning to the study conducted Bivona, Critelli and Clark (2012), a ravishment scenario would accommodate some of the most popular explanations behind submission fantasies. A ravished person is rendered deeply desirable; they are coveted by a ravisher who experiences an overwhelming desire towards them. Due to some form of coercion, they are unable to refuse, and thus encounter or participate in different types of sexual experiences (pleasurable or otherwise)—such as physical restraints, unusual sex acts or the use of toys or objects. Given that they were ravished by a domineering party, the ravished person is perceived to have retained their moral purity; they are able to employ blame avoidance frameworks to either protect their identity or transform it as a result of the ravishment. This is particularly prominent in Gothic literature where the swooning of parties faced with an overwhelming (and often supernatural) force of desire, such as the thrall of a vampire, can be read as a form of active defense, providing a political separation of the enraptured body from the moral will and identity. Barring some inevitable exceptions, many dub-con narratives operate under similar frameworks.

Given that popular fiction is both a product of and a response to constantly evolving social imperatives and concerns, it is both surprising and unsurprising that this trope has persisted despite major cultural shifts—particularly in the last fifty years. An example of the successful revival of the ravishment trope can best be seen in the form of the Bodice Ripper romances of the 1970s and 1980s, so named for the stereotypical cover art depicting heroes so consumed with passion that they are using their bare hands to rip open the bodices of their swooning heroines in their urgency to disrobe them. Evidently, though, there is a significant amount of troubling discourse within this inherently problematic genre. Where is the line to be drawn in this hypothetical framework of acceptable coercion? If the application of one partner's coercive behavior inflicts lasting damage on another (such as injury, psychological harm or economic downfall), does this change the seemingly arbitrary benchmark at which coercion is then perceived as unacceptable? The concept of forceful persuasion is a dangerous one, but I would argue that what makes it dangerous is not the existence (and popularity) of the enforced submission trope itself, but how it is positioned within the structure of the heteronormative paradigm and construed as a normal, natural result of a clash between sexualities from either side of the binary.

In stories of sublimated desire, opportunities arise to reframe very real scenarios of a loss of control in a way that becomes pleasurable rather than harrowing. In her rapturous negotiation of the tumultuous thoughts and feelings bursting inside her the morning after, Scarlett O'Hara has identified that which makes ravishments so enticing to the erotic imaginary; the conflict that occurs between your fiercely asserted autonomy, the societal expectations of your behavior, your involuntary wild emotional and physical responses and your subsequent navigation and reframing of your behavior in light of these other elements. The conflict, bewilderment and visceral excitement *is* the thrill. In fantasies like these, we create and exercise a safe, exciting space for our erotic imaginations which allows us to retain our agency and our personal control in the face of a frightening possibility—and to take pleasure how and where we want to despite the unpleasant realities which may oppose and constrain us.

Discussing Dub-Con

Dub-con, at the very least, is not an easy genre to deal with, and there are many compelling arguments to be made both for and against the presence and popularity of the enforced submission trope in literature. Dub-con scenarios are ultimately nothing new; they are constantly reframed in popular literature, operating in the murky haze of the erotic imaginary where pleasure and power intersect—and furthermore, coexist. In dub-con narratives, characters are regularly positioned with a ravishment scenario in order for them to experience pleasure (and less commonly, pain) with the intention that such an encounter might not fundamentally shatter their identities as much as the brutality of a rape. In both slash and femslash, this experience then provides an opportunity for characters (and in turn, readers and authors) to reassert or reconsider notions of identity and autonomy within the heteronormative binary, posing questions that problematize "natural" and "normal" modes of behavior.

Dub-con is not totally innocent of one of the faults of romance fiction: attempting to present contradictory and complex scenarios in a nice, dreamy way intended to avoid antagonizing modern sensibilities. However, while operating as a deeply pleasurable submission fantasy in which we remain in control at all times, dub-con makes no attempt to hide the contradiction between what we find erotic and what we believe is acceptable. The depicted relationship is usually unequal and deeply problematic, and while the scenario may be presented as culturally normal within the context of the story, a dub-con narrative does not allow a reader to believe that this is fair or correct. Additionally, dub-con is more than just one set of formulaic conventions wherein one character is ravished by another. Every dub-con narrative explores not only the murky waters of consent in fan fiction identified by Klink (2016), but the very nature of consent itself and the myriad ways in which it is obtained, ignored or abused.

There are dub-con stories where partners who once consented enthusiastically and who trust each other implicitly must now negotiate new situations where they are uncertain of whether they wish to continue. When one party consents in order to keep their partner happy and blissfully unaware of how they feel, painful conversations inevitably occur when the truth is revealed, providing readers with an opportunity to discuss the difficult themes involved in this scenario where both parties feel betrayed. In some, traditionally "weaker" characters are given all the power and seduce, coerce or ravish their allegedly higher ranking counterparts, while in others characters overcome their ravishers and publicly hold them to account to force a discussion about their actions. There are also stories in which one party is both the ravisher *and* the ravished, which explore how these conflicting identities shape that character's identity and behavior and their interaction with wider society. Additionally, there are stories where all parties involved have no choice but to engage sexually with each other, either because of an external force (such as magic or sex pollen), an irresistible sexual imperative, or a threat to the safety of themselves or others.

The common theme within all of these stories is therefore not who performs what action, how strongly or how often—it is a preoccupation with where and how control operates. What makes dub-con stories different is that in dub-con stories, control can be implied or explicit, concrete or malleable; it is shifted, reformed, invoked and interpreted through actions, words and/or external situations. Rape narratives are often unflinching explorations of the real consequences of the heteronormative paradigm, where violence often *is* the control; you either consume or are consumed, and those who do not behave in accordance with the contradictory rules that are presented as "good" and "natural" invite violence. Dub-con offers a range of flexibility and a space to explore the same violent nature of power and desire without the requisite presence of destruction and death, which can be deeply triggering. It is not inaccurate to suggest that this may make dub-con euphemistic, but it is still a powerful medium for those who want to explore these elements and better understand how their identities and desires operate within social frameworks in a pleasurable way.

Furthermore, dub-con is not without other issues, particularly when scenarios which appear non-consensual are labeled as dubiously consensual. It is a common understanding that the ways in which someone perceives a text are based on their personal reading positions—the social, cultural and ideological background from which any individual comes. What one person tags as a dubiously consensual encounter is likely to differ from another person's perception of the same scene. A writer who depicts a classic early modern erotic scenario in which Character A agrees to have sex with Character B, but who unknowingly has pleasurable sex with Character C (whom they may or may not have an equal or greater sexual interest in) may not feel that this deserves the label of rape with all of its connotations of pain, violence and aggression. They may instead elect to use the dub-con tag, while a reader may vehemently disagree and propose that someone who is deceived at any point in a sexual encounter cannot freely give their consent, no matter how much they may have enjoyed it. It is important to actively consider the significance of the ways in which problematic elements in fan works are tagged, the expectations, resonances and politics generated by the use of some tags over others, and the necessity of detailed content notes to negotiate these elements and contexts.

If popular literature is produced in a particular historic moment as a result of ongoing conversations, what is different now is the massively open global digital network of interpretation that dub-con narratives exist within. A process of interpretive exchange happens every time we encounter any text and it is a crucial part of our own personal meaning-making strategies; no two people will ever have the exact same response to a text and it is normal and necessary for opinions to clash and for ideas to be articulated and developed as a result. Discussions around sexuality, consent and violence remain rightfully passionate and are often deeply personal. It is vital to support the initiatives aimed at challenging the kinds of damaging understandings of these issues which lead to the silencing of abuse victims and the perpetuation of violence. However, at least within the open interpretive communities that generations of fans have fought hard to establish and defend, as fans and as academics we should strive to engage with and encourage conflicting ideas. Discussions about these complexities which simultaneously trouble and thrill us, and the ways in which we label, perceive and negotiate them, are necessary for both the genre and understandings of it to develop.

Dub-con simultaneously does and does not sit neatly with ideals of how slash fiction operates as a utopian, egalitarian genre, but ignoring the impacts and resonances of dub-con as a genre in its own right is regressive in and of itself. Doing so only serves to close off yet another avenue where people, particularly marginalized groups, are able to exercise their erotic imaginations to explore modes of being and systems of power. As explored Bivona, Critelli and Clark (2012), some survivors of sexual assaults have submission fantasies, for any number of personal reasons. It would be highly irresponsible and inappropriate to attempt to speculate about these personal reasons, but refusing to acknowledge how dub-con in slash fiction—as another broad and nuanced literary portrayal of the complexities of consent—encourages us to engage with wider issues and asks us to explore these elements just perpetuates another form of oppression. Ravishment as a trope has survived in various forms for centuries, but only now are we really in a position to try to understand how the complexity of dub-con in its newly evolved genre form might act in our benefit, and explore what its controversial popularity might say about current cultural climates and collective erotic imaginations.

Instances where violence and sexual domination are presented erotically in problematic fan works rarely represent an actual intention to hold these up as ideal scenarios. Building on the argument that reading romances allows readers to explore the meanings and consequences of modes of behavior, Janice Radway argued that we should understand romances as "the experimental projection of the consequences of masculine behavior and patriarchal control" (pp. 168–169). It is much more likely, then, that because these scenarios are so ingrained as being a natural, permanent and unchangeable facet of existence under the heteronormative paradigm, they cannot be easily imagined away and thus repeat in fan works and other forms of popular literature.

Dub-con narratives operate as sites where readers seek opportunities to experience these scenarios in pleasurable ways, rather than in the form of fantasies which depict the painful effects and aftermaths of these frightening threats which must be negotiated in order to survive. Works featuring dub-con in an eroticized setting may simply represent a need for producers and audiences to find ways to imagine that exaggerated displays of heteronormativity might not be harmful—even when they are told by the same behavioral frameworks that active sensuality and desire is dangerous to both those who have it and to those who may become so ensnared by it that they respond aggressively.

From a modern day reading position, it is often difficult for us to reconcile seemingly regressive fantasies with our individual subjectivities. Such fantasies conflict with our understandings of identity politics and go against what we would like to experience in a real life situation. This can cause misplaced guilt and a sense of unease about indulging these pleasurable fantasies—let alone sharing them with anyone else, lest we invoke further judgment or disapproval, or upset others who have experienced such brutal realities firsthand. We know that these are problematic fantasies and we understand that such a scenario of pleasurable submission against our will cannot (and should not) exist outside of a fantasy or fan fiction setting where we remain in full control of the scene and have intimate access to the perspectives of all parties involved. However, that does not make them any less fulfilling than other kinds of sexual fantasy, or any less effective in helping us to consciously or unconsciously navigate complex power structures. In scenarios like those we see appearing in dub-con again and again—where even in the absence of a concrete "yes," characters still often experience vivid pleasure in the heat of the moment despite whatever circumstances are constraining them—characters, readers and writers are all able to explore the complex relationship between power, desire and control. Perhaps what entices us most to dub-con and what makes it so subversive is not the depiction of violence, force or sex; it is how conflict, uncertainty and pleasure facilitate a temporary resolution of the contradictions between our social and sexual selves—if only for one thrilling, deeply private moment.

Wilkins (2016) notes that modern feminism can at times be accused of operating a censure of representations of sexuality and fantasies of domination and submission in an attempt to challenge potentially damaging representations of the forms of power which enact oppression and subjugation. Dub-con fantasies have been accused of being postfeminist—a term which refers to something or someone which has benefited from the movement towards gender equality, but which does not attempt to further the cause—and guilty of euphemistically eroticizing and perpetuating the same harmful behavioral ideologies of heteronormativity as other forms of popular literature. While there is credibility behind these suggestions that dub-con is antifeminist or postfeminist, this fails to acknowledge the spectacular range of nuance inherent within dub-con and the thriving discussions and communities which emerge around it.

Dub-con does not ask its readers to accept it as an ideal sexual paradigm. Where classic fiction throughout history has often presented ravishment scenarios as a natural, inevitable (and even desirable) product of heteronormativity, one which must somehow be simultaneously sought out *and* avoided, dub-con openly concerns itself with the representation of inequality and the means through which characters attempt to negotiate this. It asks its audiences to question its content and it asks its producers to consider the real life structures of power in which we operate. It makes explicit the understanding that consent, when it is not given freely, is dubious *only* within a fantasy scenario where we are able to represent, control, and intimately share the inner thoughts and feelings of the characters. When consent is not given in reality, where we cannot purport to know what someone is thinking or feeling, dubiously obtained consent is no consent at all.

Conclusion

I cannot speak of dub-con's audiences like some collective entity which approaches and accesses the genre in the same way for the same reasons. However, I argue that dub-con represents as much of a move as the wider genre of slash fiction towards an erotic and active feminist awareness of, and response to, the global impacts which contradictory and restrictive behavioral paradigms have on every person. I propose that in order to better understand dub-con, we should recognize its core as a fantasy of a pleasurable sublimation or exertion of control more than a fantasy about an attack on a person's agency or a loss of identity.

I concur with Constance Penley's iconic assertion that anyone reading, writing and discussing slash fiction "participates in and restages a scenario in which crucial questions about desire, knowledge, and identity can be posed, and in which the subject can hold a number of different identificatory positions" (1997, p. 480). Dub-con is a politically engaged genre; from the moment you search for it, from the moment you tag it as being dubious, you have already entered into a debate about the ways in which we articulate ourselves and our identities, the ways in which consent paradigms operate, and your own position within wider societal expectations and power systems. Writing and reading dub-con provides scope to explore very real concerns within the confines of an erotic fantasy; a fantasy in which we remain constantly in control, even as we reframe and re-imagine our relationship to power—including our own. Unlike the historical literary legacy from which it has developed, dub-con in slash fiction does not present its complex, contradictory and thrilling fantasies as an ideal paradigm. It does not allow us to forget that our concerns are fundamentally grounded in the real, unfair, unequal paradigms under which we all operate. Just like any trope within slash fiction, it facilitates an interpretive space in which are able to use our erotic imaginations to reframe our concerns, and provides an interpretive community in which we are able to engage in meaningful discussions. It is both progressive and regressive, both feminist and postfeminist—and it is constantly evolving.

While this essay has explored some of the basic effective and affective functions of the trope, there is so much space for wider study. There is a need for literary analysis of how latent textual elements in canon texts are extrapolated or subverted into dub-con scenarios in particular, the narrative function of these scenes within fan works, and explorations of which fandoms or pairings this trope particularly features in. There is clear scope for investigation into the ways in which premodern and modern cultural ideologies are addressed in dub-con and its surrounding communities. Additionally, given that dub-con is the product of an ongoing discussion and a thriving cultural dialogue, it would be difficult to theorize any further about the popularity of dub-con without working with readers and writers through ethical ethnographic studies. It is now time for fandom and academia to acknowledge this fascinating genre and to explore it with the passion, dedication and critical rigor it deserves.

Notes

1. Particularly the theories of MacKinnon (1991), Dworkin (1974) and Modleski (1999).
2. An abbreviation of the terms Bondage & Discipline (BD), Dominance & Submission (DS), and Sadism & Masochism (SM).
3. SCC, commonly cited as a phrase coined by David Stein in 1984, refers to a system of play in which attempts should be made to identify and prevent risks to health; activities should be undertaken in a sane and sensible state of mind; and all activities must involve the full and informed consent of all parties. Stein intended this to be put forward as a minimum standard for ethically defensible BDSM encounters in order to distinguish these from the perception of S&M as abusive. In contrast, RACK—a term credited to Gary Switch in 2001—acknowledges that nothing is ever 100 percent safe and what may be considered "safe and sane" by one person may not be by another. RACK places more emphasis on individual commitment to understanding and adhering to someone's personal limitations and kinks with regard to risky activities. Within RACK, there is no "safe" or "unsafe," only "safe" and "less safe." Additionally, other terms exist in the BDSM community—such as PRICK (Personal Responsibility, Informed Consensual Kink) and CCC (Committed, Compassionate, Consensual).
4. Also see Baumeister & Twenge (2002).
5. This is not to imply that there are not people who genuinely do have erotic fantasies about witnessing, committing or being a victim of an actual rape. This is also not to imply that these fantasies are any more or less legitimate than submission fantasies. However, given the focus and scope of this essay I am unable to explore this in any greater detail with the degree of academic rigor and sensitivity it requires.

6. Particularly Woledge (2006), Driscoll (2006), Kaplan (2006) and Kustritz (2003 & 2008).

References

Bataille, G. (2001). *Eroticism* (Trans: Colin McCabe). London: Penguin. (Original work published 1962).

Baumeister, R.F., and Twenge, J.M. (2002). Cultural Suppression of Female Sexuality. *Review of General Psychology, 6*(2), 166–203. doi: 10.1037//1089–2680.6.2.166.

Bivona, J.M., Critelli, J.W., and Clark, M.J. (2012). Women's Rape Fantasies: An Empirical Evaluation of the Major Explanations. *Archives of Sexual Behavior, 41*(5), 1107–1119. doi: 10.1007/s10508–012–9934–6.

Black, K. (2011, September 20). Safe, Sane and Consensual: Understand What It's All About. *Keeping it Kinky*. Retrieved from http://www.keepingitkinky.net/bdsm/kink-basics/consent/safe-sane-consensual/.

Castleman, M. (2015, August 1). Why Do Women Have Rape Fantasies? *Psychology Today*. Retrieved from https://www.psychologytoday.com/blog/all-about-sex/201508/why-do-women-have-rape-fantasies.

Critelli, J.W., and Bivona, J.M. (2008). Women's Erotic Rape Fantasies: An Evaluation of Theory and Research. *The Journal of Sex Research, 45*(1), 57–70. http://dx.doi.org/10.1080/00224490701808191.

Driscoll, C. (2006). One True Pairing: The Romance of Pornography and the Pornography of Romance. In K. Hellekson and K. Busse (Eds.), *Fan Fiction and Fan Communities in the Age of the Internet* (pp. 79–96). Jefferson, NC: McFarland.

Dub-Con. (2016). In *Fanlore*. Retrieved from https://fanlore.org/wiki/Dub-con.

Dworkin, A. (1974). *Woman Hating*. New York: Dutton.

Egbert, C.K. (2014, June 25). Why Consent Is Not Enough. *Feminist Current*. Retrieved from http://www.feministcurrent.com/2014/06/25/why-consent-is-not-enough/.

Felski, R. (2005). Redescriptions of Female Masochism. *The Minnesota Review* (63–64). doi:10.1215/00265667-2005-63-64-127.

Foucault, M. (1978). *The History of Sexuality, Volume 1: An Introduction* (R. Hurley, Trans.). New York: Vintage. (Original work published 1976).

Greenstadt, A. (2009). *Rape and the Rise of the Author: Gendering Intention in Early Modern England*. Farnham: Ashgate.

Jenkins, H. (2006). *Fans, Bloggers and Gamers: Exploring Participatory Culture*. New York: New York University Press.

Klink, F. (2016, October 27). Five Tropes Fanfic Readers Love (And One They Hate). *Fansplaining*. Retrieved from https://medium.com/fansplaining/five-tropes-fanfic-readers-love-and-one-they-hate-73843372408c.

Kustritz, A. (2003). Slashing the Romance Narrative. *The Journal of American Culture, 26*(3), 371–384. doi:10.1111/1542-734X.00098.

Kustritz, A. (2008). Painful Pleasures: Sacrifice, Consent, and the Resignification of BDSM Symbolism in *The Story of O* and *The Story of Obi*. *Transformative Works and Cultures, 1*. doi:10.3983/twc.2008.0031.

MacKinnon, C.A. (1991). Reflections on Sex Equality Under Law. *Yale Law Journal, 100*(5), 1281–1328.

Mr. Michael. (2010, March 22). SCC and RACK. *Louisville Munch*. Retrieved from http://www.louisvillemunch.com/article/ssc-and-rack.html.

Mitchell, M. (1936). *Gone with the Wind* [PDF]. Project Gutenberg Australia. Retrieved from http://campbellmgold.com/archive_ebooks/gone_with_the_wind_mitchell.pdf.

Modleski, T. (1999). *Old Wives' Tales: Feminist Re-Visions of Film and Other Fictions*. London: I.B. Tauris.

Morber, J. (2013, May 30). What Science Says About Arousal During Rape. *Popular Science*. Retrieved from http://www.popsci.com/science/article/2013-05/science-arousal-during-rape.

Pascoe, C.J. (2007). *Dude, You're a Fag: Masculinity and Sexuality in High School*. Berkley: University of California Press.
Penley, C. (1997). *NASA/Trek: Popular Science and Sex in America*. London: Verso.
Radxway, J. (1991). *Reading the Romance: Women, Patriarchy, and Popular Literature*. Chapel Hill: University of North Carolina Press. (Original work published 1984).
Rubin, G. (2006). The Traffic in Women: Notes on the "Political Economy" of Sex. In E. Lewin (Ed.), *Feminist Anthropology: A Reader* (pp. 87–106). Oxford: Blackwell.
Rubin, G.S. (2011). *Deviations: A Gayle Rubin Reader*. Durham: Duke University Press.
Toscano, A. (2012). A Parody of Love: The Narrative Uses of Rape in Popular Romance. *Journal of Popular Romance Studies, 2*(2), 1–17.
Wilkins, K. (2016). "Ravished by Vikings": The Pre-Modern and the Paranormal in Viking Romance Fiction. *Journal of Popular Romance Studies, 5*(2), 1–13.
Woledge, P. (2006). Intimatopia: Genre Intersections Between Slash and the Mainstream. In K. Hellekson and K. Busse (Eds.), *Fan Fiction and Fan Communities in the Age of the Internet* (pp. 97–114). Jefferson, NC: McFarland.

"Happy Consensual Gangbangs"

Deconstructions of Sports Cultures and Hegemonic Masculinity in Football RPF

MILENA POPOVA

Introduction

This essay uses a close reading of two stories within the gangbang/team sex subgenre of Football Real Person Fiction to investigate how marginalized sports fans can use fan fiction to negotiate the challenges posed to them by hegemonic masculinity within sports culture. These stories engage with themes of safety and vulnerability, hierarchies of masculinity, and issues of sexual consent through common fan fiction reading and writing practices. These practices allow readers and writers to make meanings from the similarities and differences between the fictionalized representations they create and their knowledge and experience of marginalization within sports culture. In this way, they are able to issue their own challenge to structures of patriarchy and hegemonic masculinity in their fan object—albeit one which is limited in scope.

Slashing Hegemonic Masculinity

On October 14, 2016, Welsh football player Ched Evans was found not guilty of rape at retrial at Cardiff crown court, having already served a two-and-a-half-year prison sentence for the crime (Morris & Topping, 2016). Male professional athletes from a range of team sports across Western cultures are accused of sexual assault with some regularity (see Nurka, 2013; Toffoletti, 2007), though convictions—such as Evans' original conviction—are much rarer (Burke, 2015). Writing about sexual assault in Australian professional team sports, Nurka (2013) characterizes the Australian football leagues and other "masculine sporting codes" as "privileged sites of the cultural construction of heterosexual masculinity in a homosocial setting" (p. 43). This exclusive and often hostile environment presents a number of challenges for women, both as participants and as fans of sport.

Reports of rape allegedly committed by professional athletes gain attention from media (Toffoletti, 2007) and sports fans (Nurka, 2013), but the discourses in both cases seek to silence and blame victims while exonerating the alleged attackers. As Nurka indicates, such challenges are rooted in the highly masculine construction of sports culture, a construction congruent with ideas of hegemonic masculinity. Connell (1995) defines hegemonic masculinity as "the configuration of gender practice which embodies the currently accepted answer to the problem of the legitimacy of patriarchy" (p. 77): it is a historically and socially contingent construction legitimizing gendered power relations.

Women, as spectators and fans of sport, struggle with the challenges posed by this frequently outright hostile, highly homosocial environment, where sexual violence is only the extreme end of a range of negative, discriminatory, and marginalizing experiences rooted in enactments of hegemonic masculinity. Gosling (2007) provides a comprehensive overview of the marginalization of women sports fans. Esmonde, Cooky & Andrews (2015) examine the complex ways in which women negotiate this marginalization. They find that women fans frequently police their own and other women's expressions of fandom, and even use gendered language in their definition of fandom, devaluing women's involvement as sports fans. One key strategy used to de-legitimize women's sports fandom is the allegation that they are sexually attracted to the players rather than genuinely interested in the sport, which in turn can be used to invalidate allegations of sexual violence on behalf of players. Women sports fans consequently developed strategies which let them challenge these stereotypes and other discourses used to marginalize them. These strategies include redrawing the lines around what it meant to be a sports fan to either be more inclusive of some women and femininities while still excluding others or, alternatively, to disclaim a fandom identity, thereby lowering their own personal stakes in the culture; denying or minimizing the exclusion they faced; and negotiating their relationship to common stereotypes of women sports fans. These strategies, however, frequently still built on dominant discourses of masculinity and the associated devaluing of femininity in sports and sports fandom. In this way, women's legitimacy as sports fans remained contingent on being able to construct themselves as an exception to the negative stereotypes associated with women sports fans. Yet as Esmonde, Cooky and Andrews argue, "it is possible to both love the game *and* Aaron Rodgers' eyes" (2015, p. 43), and for some women fans an aesthetic appreciation of, or even sexual attraction to, the players is indeed a key part of their sports fandom.

Waysdorf (2015a) traces the different forms women's sports fandom takes in different spaces. Football Real Person(a) Fiction (or RPF) is one such expression of (predominantly) women's love of the game and their attraction to the players. Football RPF is fan fiction centered predominantly around high-level European football (soccer) teams and players, and generally featuring sexual or romantic relationships between fictionalized versions of the real-life players. Some writers and readers of Football RPF start out as football fans first and come to fan fiction later. Others find it through other types of fan fiction (for instance by following a favorite author from the fandom of another media product), though many go on to develop an interest in football as a sport as a result (Waysdorf, 2015b). Waysdorf (2015a) argues that Football RPF is a space where certain kinds of fannish behaviors are normalized, which elsewhere are typically associated with women fans and used to police and undermine their identities as fans—and that participation in Football RPF is just as much an expression and performance of women's football fandom as attending matches and discussing trivia in other online forums. Given the hypermasculine culture of team sports and the frequency and regularity with which professional athletes across a variety of team sports are accused of rape and other kinds of violence against women, the appeal of football players to the slash community—consisting predominantly of women and non-binary people, many of whom identify as members of gender, sexual or romantic minorities (centrumlumina, 2013b, 2013c)[1]—is striking.

Waysdorf (2015b) identifies key features of football as a sport and media spectacle which make it an attractive site for RPF. The media narrative surrounding the sport—official promotional material, outsider perspectives such as journalistic reporting and, increasingly, social media interactions—creates a set of paratexts around the sport itself. Teams promote individual players as a way of fostering fans' personal investment in the sport. This in turn has the effect of turning star players into celebrities highly attractive to RPF communities. Seasons and tournaments provide an overarching narrative framework, so that individual games acquire meaning beyond the ninety minutes of play time. It is these individual and team narratives and the interplays between them, as players emerge as stars, are traded, or retire, which provide the starting point for sports-based fan fiction. Writers and readers of football RPF pay attention to the real-life physicality of both the sport itself and the players in their interactions with each other. Casual touches, goal celebrations and even the occasional joking or celebratory kiss between players are taken out of their homosocial context and imbued with emotional and sexual meaning. Yet these highly "slashable" elements of football do not erase, and are indeed often in conflict with, the homosocial, hypermasculine facets of sports culture.

There is a tension, therefore, in Football RPF between the popular, and homosocial, reading of sport and sports culture, and RPF writers' and readers' against-the-grain readings of homosexual desire. Investigating sports teams in a higher education setting, Dempster (2009) finds a strong link between sports and lad cultures at a UK university and identifies three key components present in both: sexualized behaviors (including the indictment of homosexuality), aggression and violence (especially in the sports context when there is a perceived threat to the player's position and standing within the hierarchy), and heavy drinking. Propositioning women is seen as a key "laddish" behavior that players of team sports engage in to position their own masculinity "as both different from, and superior to, women and femininities" (p. 488). In Football RPF, on the other hand, women—even players' real-life partners—play small and marginal roles if any (Waysdorf, 2015b), and the players' sexual and romantic desire is redirected at each other. This stands in stark contrast to Dempster's (2009) finding that "indictments of homosexuality was a key means through which male Westchester students policed masculinities" (p. 488). This reflects the conflicted relationship of women sports fans with their fan objects, who are steeped in a culture that is deeply misogynistic and homophobic, and which frequently marginalizes women and queer players and fans. It also raises the question of how such conflicts are resolved—or at least negotiated—in the community's fiction output.

In this essay, I explore how groups who are typically marginalized and even threatened by sports cultures rooted in hegemonic masculinity—women, non-binary people, gay and bisexual men—create spaces for the expression and critical exploration of their own relationships with these cultures, and thereby with hegemonic masculinity, particularly as fans. My focus is therefore on how stories circulated within the Football RPF community both reproduce but also challenge and deconstruct the trappings of lad and sports cultures. I use as my case study the subgenre of gangbang and team sex stories. These are the stories which not only crystallize the homosocial bonds between individual players into fictional homosexual relationships but also most clearly set these relationships within the wider context of the hypermasculine sports team culture. I perform a close reading of two such gangbang/team sex stories: a story published by Anonymous (2011) which I shall refer to as *Story A* and *firework boy* by meretricula (2011). The two stories are complementary, in that they both contain elements both typical and atypical of the gangbang/team sex subgenre. I relate these elements to wider theories on lad and sports cultures, meaning-making in fan fiction, and sexual consent, in order to show how Football RPF stories engage with and deconstruct the challenges and threats which sports culture and hegemonic masculinity present to the groups they subordinate or marginalize.

Team Orgies and Gangbangs: Two Stories

Intertextuality plays a key role in meaning-making in fan fiction based on other fiction. Derecho (2006) argues that fan fiction works add to an "archive" around the originary work and is particularly interested in the way fan fiction repeats and alters certain elements from the original. Such "repetition with a difference" (p. 73), she argues, allows for both works to be read at the same time, side by side, creating new meanings from the similarities and differences. In this way, each addition to the archive alters the entire archive, shedding new light on both originary work and other "archontic" works. As Waysdorf (2015b) argues, European football can be read as a media text in similar ways to TV series, books, or films, and so RPF too can be seen as characterized by intertextuality in similar ways. Willis (2006) also emphasizes the intertextual nature of fan fiction reading and writing, but provides a mechanism for resources beyond the immediately obvious texts to enter into a relationship with the fan fiction work. She argues that fan fiction readers and writers bring their own knowledge of the world to their readings of media, and this is a key mechanism by which the "gaps" which fan fiction fills are created. So, in the case of Football RPF a fan fiction reader or writer would not just refer to "canon" events and the media narratives around their favorite player or team, but also use extratextual resources such as their understanding of sports cultures in their engagement with fan fiction stories. This intertextuality and use of extratextual resources in readings is key to understanding how Football RPF may provide fans who are marginalized by sports culture and mainstream masculine fan communities with ways to engage with and challenge the culture.

Such intertextual readings are evident across Football RPF stories. A common thread in such stories is the sense of belonging to a team with a shared goal and the accompanying joint celebrations of successes or commiseration over losses. In this context, the team orgy or team gangbang is a popular subgenre within Football RPF. Typical ways to position this are the team bonding experience, the celebration of a major win, consolation after a big loss, or the team rewarding or "taking care" of a key player. *Story A* by Anonymous (2011) and *firework boy* (2011) by meretricula fall under the category of the "reward" story. A clue to this theme in Football RPF can often be found in the titles of fan works, which convey appreciation and celebration of someone's accomplishments. Both of these works were also originally written in response to requests posted on online Football RPF communities. *Story A* originated on a Football RPF kinkmeme—an online forum matching anonymous requests for particular types of stories with equally anonymous writers—and *firework boy* originated in a community where prompts may, but do not have to, be anonymous.

While both stories have elements typical of the Football RPF team sex/gangbang subgenre, both also play with variations on the generic conventions—a key fan fiction technique for creating meanings (Derecho, 2006). Stylistically, both stories are written in very close third person from a single point of view—the character at the center of attention in the orgy or gangbang. This allows the reader an insight into the character's intimate thoughts and emotions without fully immersing them in that character as a first-person narrative might. This is common in recent fan fiction, and particularly in RPF where a first-person narrative can often be experienced as too jarring and invasive, given that characters are based on real-life celebrities. Like a significant proportion of fan fiction and the vast majority of the gangbang/team sex subgenre, both stories are sexually explicit. Overtly erotic and sexual scenes in slash have an effect of "physicalising emotion" (Pugh, 2005, p. 102), and fan fiction writers often use such content to provide further intimate insight into characters. Gangbang stories also often feature some commentary alongside the text, for instance in tags and author's notes, with regards to the consensual—or otherwise—nature of the gangbang. The phrasing of such notes and tags varies, but some examples are "HAPPY CONSENSUAL GANGBANGS," "emotional resolution through gangbang," "consensual gangbang," or "comfort gangbang." Neither of the stories in this investigation comes with such accompanying material in any of their published versions, but themes of consent and overt consent negotiation are present throughout.

Fan writer meretricula's *firework boy* (2011) is set after the Champions' League semifinal game between archrivals Real Madrid and Barcelona on April 26, 2011. The point of view character is Sergi Roberto, a relatively junior player for whom the match was his Champions' League debut and therefore an important milestone in his career; a fact which singles him out for celebration and reward by his teammates. The other participants in the orgy are Lionel Messi (the team's star, who is is widely acknowledged as one of the best players in the world), Thiago Alcântara, Ibrahim Afellay, Gerard Piqué, and David Villa, while a number of other team members—notably Xavi Hernández—are shown to watch from the sidelines or decline to participate. The premise of *Story A* (Anonymous, 2011) is that the Spanish national team offer to reward midfielder David Silva after a particularly good performance in a friendly match against the U.S. After initial reluctance, Silva agrees to the proposal, as being gangbanged has been a long-standing fantasy for him, and eight other players take part in the gangbang: Carlos Marchena, Raúl Albiol, Álvaro Arbeloa, David Villa, Pepe Reina, Fernando Torres, Fernando Llorente, and Santi Cazorla. To aid clarity, from this point on I will use the full name to refer to the real-life football players and either the first or last name only, depending on predominant usage within the story, to refer to the fictional characters.

The various relationships and histories these players have with each other both within and outside the Spanish national team provide several emotional focal points. Many Football RPF gangbang stories feature more romantic or emotionally involved relationships between couples of players within the wider team environment. In reward stories it is often the player's longer-term romantic partner who will arrange the gangbang with the team and direct the action. *Story A* works both within and outside this template. Instead of a central pairing, the story focuses on the relationships between three players: Silva, Villa, and Carlos. Silva and Villa's past sexual relationship provides a counterpoint for Silva's long-standing and, as he believes, unrequited romantic feelings for Carlos. Similarly, *firework boy* (meretricula, 2011) also differs from the central romantic couple template: there are several established pairings, but as a player relatively new to the team Sergi isn't part of any of them.

The reward for a good performance scenario is a fairly common trope in setting up gangbang stories, but a key contrast between the two stories is that whereas *firework boy* is set within the regular league team setting, *Story A* takes place at the national team level. Relationships between players on national teams are often portrayed in Football RPF stories as more diverse and ambiguous, as well as less established than those on league teams. Stories are more commonly set in league teams, so the contrast here is a crucial resource for meaning-making and an important driver behind some of the stories' key themes: the interplay between safety and vulnerability; the exploration of hierarchies of masculinity; and masculinity, power, and sexual consent.

Safety and Vulnerability

The team environment in Football RPF stories is often presented as a safe space where long-standing homosocial bonds mean that everyone on the team can automatically be trusted. This is a contrast to, for instance, Dempster's (2009) findings of the importance of hierarchy and position within the lad cultures of university sports teams. This view of the team as a safe environment is particularly true of stories set in league teams, where players spend most of their time and effort and are often shown to have the greatest emotional investment in, and this is reflected to an extent in *firework boy* (meretricula, 2011).

As Sergi, the point of view character in the story, is relatively new to the team, he himself does not have the longstanding relationships and bonds with his teammates that they do with each other. Yet those bonds among the other characters are clearly shown in the story, through Sergi's point of view. The banter he observes among his teammates is clearly long-established, as are their post-game rituals. While one group of players engages in sexual acts in the dressing room, another goes about the business of post-match cooldown, both groups still interacting casually with each other. Initially, this serves to highlight Sergi's status as a newcomer and outsider, underscoring his sense of vulnerability in the new environment. Both groups of teammates, however, quickly move to include Sergi in their activities, congratulating him on his Champions' League debut and making him feel like a welcome and legitimate part of the team. By the end of the story, Sergi feels confident enough to take part in the banter and interact with his teammates on an equal footing, even though only ten minutes have passed. The new team environment has been made safe for him.

The setting of *Story A* (Anonymous, 2011) in the national team environment is an interesting counterpoint to the more usual league team story. National teams are often composed of players who during the regular league season are bitter rivals, players who may have once been on the same league team but have since transferred to other teams, or players who have little contact with each other because they play in different leagues. Football RPF writers often use their knowledge of the players' backgrounds and the real-life events in their sporting careers as a backdrop to the plot of stories (Waysdorf, 2015a). Therefore, this national team dynamic is one key factor in creating a sense of vulnerability for Silva, the point of view character in *Story A*. Another element of vulnerability is introduced through references to a past sexual relationship between the fictional versions of Silva and Villa, who in real life played together for Valencia between 2006 and 2010, and indications of long-standing romantic feelings Silva harbors for Carlos—another real-life former Valencia teammate. This triangle forms the emotional core of the story, with Villa constantly challenging and pushing at boundaries while Carlos is depicted as caring and protective.

This sense of vulnerability, however, is partially offset early on in *Story A* by a sense of homecoming. The story is set shortly after the real-life events of David Silva's transfer from Valencia to Manchester City in June 2010, where he was initially seen to be struggling with adjusting to a new country, team, and language. The fictional Silva in the story is surrounded by Spanish-speaking teammates, and he draws comfort from this familiarity and sense of belonging again. However, this bubble of safety is broken as soon as Villa extends his offer to give Silva something Villa claims Silva has always wanted. Silva remembers his past relationship with Villa, including an incident where he attempted to withdraw consent during a sexual encounter. He becomes aware of the other people present in the room, nervous of their looks and their judgment.

The tension between the safety of the team environment and the vulnerable position Villa's suggestion of a gangbang puts Silva in takes the form of ambivalence on Silva's part. The close third person style further highlights this by giving the reader insight into Silva's emotions. He is almost paralyzed with indecision, simultaneously aroused and embarrassed. Silva's indecision is resolved by Carlos. The two have a private conversation in which Carlos is shown as being protective of Silva, which is what finally gives Silva enough of a sense of safety to agree to Villa's proposal. Yet Silva's ambivalence reappears as soon as he is faced with his teammates again, and he is described as feeling simultaneously thrilled and horrified, and this ambivalence only fades gradually over the course of the story.

As the story progresses, various teammates' actions contribute to settling Silva's ambivalence. Raúl's smile and wave brings back a sense of normality and the training ground. Villa's acknowledgment and acceptance of Silva's vulnerability provides reassurance. Carlos makes Silva focus only on him when the attention of his assembled teammates makes him balk. This progressive shedding of vulnerability culminates when, after three or four of his teammates have fucked him, Silva experiences even his audience as pure thrill, no longer afraid of judgmental stares. This thrill then fades back into a feeling of safety at the end of the story, as Carlos is shown to provide physical and emotional aftercare for Silva.

Read side by side with fans' extratextual knowledge of sports culture, the interplay between safety and vulnerability in both *firework boy* and *Story A* becomes a sophisticated commentary on that culture. Where in an actual sports team a new player might expect to have to engage in prolonged jostling for position in the team hierarchy (Dempster, 2009), in *firework boy* the initially unfamiliar and threatening new team environment is rapidly made safe for Sergi by his teammates. This recreation or repetition of sports culture with a difference (Derecho, 2006) highlights the problematic elements of sports culture and at the same time opens up new possibilities for it. In *Story A*, the long passages where the point of view character is ambivalent towards his experiences are particularly significant. When it comes to the real-life counterparts of the fictional characters depicted in stories like this, allegations of harassment, sexual assault and rape surface in the media with some regularity, with many of the high-profile cases involving allegations of gang rape or involvement of multiple players in the assault (e.g., Burke, 2015; Nurka,

2013; Toffoletti, 2007). Fictionalizing this scenario in Football RPF opens up the potential of undermining the sexually aggressive culture of sports teams. The sexualized behaviors of sports culture are no longer directed outwards at women, but inwards at teammates who can be seen as equals.

Reading homosexual desire into homosocial environments is typical of slash fiction, and doing so in the context of the sports team as a dominant expression of homosocial sports culture challenges its claim to a privileged position within heterosexual hegemonic masculinity. Having Sergi's new teammates in *firework boy* (meretricula, 2011) acknowledge his vulnerable position and actively work towards including him immediately counters expectations of how such cultures operate. Similarly, for all the ambivalence and vulnerability Silva feels in *Story A* (Anonymous, 2011), there is a certain kind of safety implied in being able to show that vulnerability, to have it acknowledged by his teammates, and to be ultimately able to derive sexual and emotional pleasure from it. Positioning the team environment as a safe space for homosexual desire in this way opens up the possibility of inverting sports culture, mellowing its aggression and retargeting it inwards towards the players themselves rather than outwards towards marginalized fans. This in turn makes exploration of these themes safer for those outsiders, such as women, non-binary people, and gay and bisexual men, who are normally threatened by it. This opens up a space for expressions of sports fandom which include a sexual attraction to the athletes in an environment where such desires are otherwise not only stigmatized but also fraught with anxieties around real-life sexual assaults and other dangers sports culture poses to marginalized fans. Yet, both stories retain key elements of sports culture, particularly the fear of the judgment of one's peers and the emphasis on hierarchies within the team. The repetition with a difference of these elements both serves to anchor the stories firmly within sports culture and to challenge the version of masculinity that culture is built on.

Hierarchy

Elements of lad and sports cultures are used as extratextual resources in reading and writing Football RPF. Both the similarities and differences between sports culture as fans experience and know it on the one hand, and as they depict it in their fiction on the other, feed into the meanings which readers and writers of Football RPF create through their stories. Dempster (2009) notes the importance of hierarchy in lad cultures, noting that university sports teams often have elaborate initiation rituals, many of which involve heavy drinking. Undergoing such initiation affords access to the privileges of being part of the team and therefore at the top of the hierarchy. Yet once achieved, this position then needs to be maintained, and Dempster identifies a number of ways of doing this: banter within the in-group and aggressive behavior towards any outsiders perceived as a challenge; "regular sessions of heavy drinking" (p. 490); and sexualized behaviors towards women as well as "indictments of homosexuality" (p. 488).

Story A (Anonymous, 2011) explores the shape such hierarchies take within the team. Key ways in which the team hierarchy is established within the story include banter, and the demonstration of sexual competence or lack thereof. Notably, however, the banter never quite spills over into overt aggression, even in the sometimes borderline hostile interactions between Villa and Carlos, and alcohol is entirely absent from the story. These differences and similarities between sports culture as fans know it and sports culture as it is presented in the story are a key part of fans' meaning-making activities. There is, however, another more complex layer of simultaneous reading available here: there are two possible and quite different readings of the hierarchies depicted in *Story A*, available at the same time, in the same text, to those readers who have access to the extratextual resources and knowledge of sports culture to make sense of them. These alternative readings are a key way in which the trappings of sports culture are challenged in Football RPF fan fiction.

The first possible reading, within the dominant hegemonic grain of sports culture, would position Villa and Pepe at the top of the team hierarchy. Villa's dominance is clear from early on as he is the one to propose the gangbang and clearly holds enough sway within the team to organize it. He is portrayed as sexually confident and competent, both in Silva's memories of their past relationship and during the gangbang. His skill as a football player and experience also play a role here, as indicated by Silva's reaction to praise from Villa. Silva is reminded of his early days playing on the same team as Villa, and how much Villa's approval had meant to him then, reflecting that he still craves that praise and approval.

Pepe's position is similarly demonstrated by his sexual competence and his banter. Moreover, he positions himself as a mentor of Torres. In real life, Pepe Reina and Fernando Torres played together in Liverpool between 2007 and 2011. Pepe refers to Torres as "my Fernando," and while this may be partly to distinguish him from the character of Fernando Llorente, it nonetheless also expresses a certain possessiveness—and by extension a hierarchical relationship. He also refers to Torres as "Niño" (Spanish for "kid"), which is Torres's real-life nickname due to the young age at which he became a star, but which further serves to underline the inequality between them. Finally, Pepe positions himself as having the power to grant Torres a reward in the form of a blowjob from Silva.

Other players then slot into the hierarchy based on their relationships with Villa and Pepe, their relative sexual inexperience and portrayed lack of confidence, and to an extent the sexual acts they are willing to engage in, which puts Silva at the bottom of this hierarchy. This raises interesting issues for sexual consent in the gangbang scenario, where a player higher up in the hierarchy can be seen as having control over others' bodies and consent. Pepe's "reward" for Torres is a good illustration of this, as Pepe assumes he can make consent decisions for both Torres and Silva. In a reading with the grain of sports culture, this serves to underscore the hierarchical relationships within the team. Notably in this interpretation, Carlos and Santi can be read as refusing to participate in the hierarchy. Carlos engages in a struggle with Villa for dominance over Silva throughout the story, and this set of relationships forms the emotional core of *Story A*. Yet he does not engage in banter with the rest of the group and openly shows not only tenderness but also affection towards Silva. Santi's potential position outside the hierarchy is primarily determined by his open and sincere offer to perform oral sex on Silva, regardless of any loss in status this may cause, and his skill at this.

The alternative reading of the team hierarchy in *Story A*, however, goes against the grain of real-life sports culture. In this interpretation, all the players can be read as equal and refusing to engage with the hierarchical culture, with the exception of Villa and Pepe whose banter and jostling for position marks *them* as outsiders to this group of equals. Both Villa and Pepe are portrayed as reluctant to show emotion or empathy in their interactions with others. Villa only does so twice; once when he smiles at Silva in a way Silva thinks is meant to reassure him and once, briefly, after his orgasm. The vast majority of Pepe's dialogue in the story consists of banter which leaves little to no room for genuine emotion. By contrast, most of the other characters express a range of emotions throughout the story: surprise, curiosity, shyness, a sense of being overwhelmed, and perhaps most notably tenderness on multiple occasions. Álvaro, for instance, tenderly ruffles Silva's hair and checks that he is indeed enjoying himself. It is this refusal to engage in banter, as well as the characters' relatively unselfconscious engagement in sexual activities they don't necessarily feel confident or competent at, that are the strongest indicators that these characters may not be taking sports culture hierarchies at face value. Raúl, while not being skillful in his lovemaking is enthusiastic—an enthusiasm not curbed by Pepe and Villa's banter. Álvaro is mostly lost in his romantic attraction to Raúl and surprised when Silva offers him a blowjob, and Llorente's technique is described as a mix of some of the other characters' hard thrusts and enthusiasm.

While one of these readings goes with, and the other against, the grain of sports culture, neither reading particularly goes with or against the grain of the writing in *Story A*. It is the fact that both of these readings are equally plausible—the fact that, in Derecho's (2006) terms they can be read side by side, not only with sports culture as an extratextual resource but also with each other, within a single story—that makes the story such a powerful challenge to the norms of sports culture. Notably, both readings have the potential to be deconstructive, as ultimately the story focuses on homosexual relationships and acts within the team, something completely taboo within sports culture. With either reading, homophobia is not an element of the setting. Yet because the reader brings with them a knowledge of real-life sports cultures as an extratextual resource for their reading (Willis, 2006), this absence has the effect of highlighting the discontinuity between fan fiction and real life. The repetition with a difference of sports culture in the fan fiction text makes visible the contradictions and arbitrariness inherent sports culture's privileging of certain types of masculinities and homosocial relationships over others, and opens them up to questioning and critique.

In meretricula's *firework boy* (2011), a slightly different approach to both establishing and deconstructing the team hierarchy is taken. Here, the key factors which can be read as determining a player's position in the hierarchy are all related to their skill and experience on the team. Sergi, being a relatively new addition to the team, is shown to be overwhelmed and slightly intimidated by the proximity to older, more experienced, and in some cases extremely skilled and famous players. However, it is his own expectations of the team culture more than anything else that construct this hierarchy, and this is shown in the way his teammates treat him as an equal; as someone worthy of celebration and inclusion within the team.

Observing his new team's exuberant post-match banter, Sergi is comforted to find that "it wasn't that different from the B-team, after all" (2011, p. 1). As part of the team's celebration of Sergi's Champions' League debut, it is Messi—the star player, arguably the man at the top of the team hierarchy—who offers to perform oral sex for Sergi. Dialogue between other characters also serves to level any remaining sense of hierarchy as Piqué declares, "There are no children in a Barcelona locker room! Tonight they all are men!" (p. 2). Sergi's initial expectations of a strict team hierarchy determined by players' experience and skill can be read as reflecting fans' own experiences and expectations of a hypermasculine, strictly hierarchical sports culture. The team's efforts to make Sergi feel welcome as an equal then work to subvert these expectations and open up the possibility of different, less aggressive masculinities within the team and within sports culture in general.

Wellard (2002) demonstrates how attempts to make sport more inclusive can result in the reproduction of ideas of hegemonic masculinity. Such attempts, he argues, do not result in a dismantling of the hierarchies of hypermasculine sports cultures. Rather, they lead to the establishment of new such hierarchies modeled on the ideas of masculinity prevalent in mainstream sports culture, or a redefinition of who is in and outside those hierarchies.

This in turn leads to further struggle for position, expressed yet again through appeals to traditional hegemonic masculinity and the denigration of women and non-straight sexualities, reflecting the complicity of these efforts in sustaining hegemonic masculinity and patriarchy, as identified and explored by Connell (1995). In a more recent study of a rugby team at another UK university, Anderson and McGuire (2010) find less evidence for the prevalence of misogynistic and homophobic discourses in this environment. They argue that their participants are performing a more "inclusive masculinity" than that found in previous studies and link this to an overall reduction in homophobia in English culture. They do, however, also acknowledge that these findings cannot be universalized, and that sporting culture continues to have a public reputation linked with misogyny and homophobia.

In many ways, the masculinities presented in both *Story A* and *firework boy* better reflect and even extend Anderson and McGuire's reported inclusive masculinity than the traditional hegemonic or complicit masculinity associated with sports culture. This is not to say that fan fiction readers and writers believe that these different masculinities reflect reality—it is precisely the fact that they don't which makes them valuable as a vision of new possibilities. The multiple, simultaneous, contradictory possible readings of how the internal team hierarchy functions in *Story A*—available side by side, at the same time, in the same text—and the very clear and direct subversion of hierarchy in *firework boy* allow for precisely the kind of undermining and dismantling of masculine sports culture that Wellard (2002) does not find in other attempts to make sports more accessible.

Masculinity, Power and Sexual Consent

The examination of hierarchies in *Story A* and *firework boy*, and particularly the role sexual confidence and competence play in it, also has an impact on how sexual consent is depicted within the stories. As lad and sports cultures have been linked to sexual violence, and as both stories overtly deal with issues of sexual consent, it is worth understanding key feminist thought around consent in order to explore how it may apply to depictions of sex in Football RPF stories.

Two broad schools of thought have emerged in the feminist academic space around consent. Radical second-wave feminism asks key questions about structures of power and oppression which limit particularly women's ability to meaningfully consent to sexual activity with men. MacKinnon (1991), for instance, argues that the dominant discourses around gender and sexuality form an oppressive structure by socializing women to view their own bodies as "for sexual use by men" (p. 1212). A key issue with this school of thought is its foundation in essentialist notions of gender, which limit its analytical use for more complex and intersecting modes of oppression. The second strand of work on consent focuses on agency, and particularly the practicalities of consent communication from both a legal and a psychological perspective. Pineau (1989) identifies a dominant "contractual" model of consent, where unrelated actions such as accepting a drink or wearing a short skirt are read as consent for penile-vaginal intercourse. She goes on to propose an alternative model of "communicative sexuality," where both partners engage in verbal and nonverbal communication throughout the sexual encounter, driven by the desire and moral obligation to "promote the sexual ends of one's partner" (p. 235) as well as one's own. Anderson (2005) proposes a model of negotiating sex where both partners have an exchange of views and reach a mutual, generally verbal, agreement to penetrative sex. Moving beyond theoretical models, Kristen Jozkowski and collaborators have produced extensive work on the types of behaviors college students use to communicate consent (e.g., Jozkowski & Peterson, 2013; Jozkowski et al., 2014; Jozkowski & Wiersma, 2015). Their findings include gender differences in both how consent is communicated and how consent communication is interpreted. Specifically, they find that such communication is shaped by traditional conceptions of gender roles, where men are seen as the initiators of sex and women as gatekeepers. Thus, men tend score higher on "initiating behaviors" while women tend to express consent through passive acceptance and nonverbal signals of interest.

There are elements in both *Story A* and *firework boy* which examine consent negotiation at the interpersonal level. However, the potentially unequal relationships depicted also create a space for the exploration of socially constructed inequalities and their impact on individuals' ability to meaningfully consent to sexual acts. The fact that within the context of Football RPF all participants in the sexual acts depicted are men also allows for different approaches to issues of power, gender, and consent than those available from most academic research. Early studies of slash fan fiction have often emphasized the more equal relationship dynamic which can be enabled by both characters being the same gender (e.g., Lamb & Veith, 1986; Russ, 1985; Kustritz, 2003), so the fact that within the context of Football RPF all participants in the sexual acts depicted are men also allows for different approaches to issues of power, gender, and consent than those available from most traditional academic research. However, while some slash stories clearly do use same-gender relationships to successfully explore the effects of the leveling of socially constructed inequalities in sexual and romantic relationships, stories in the Football RPF gangbang subgenre more often than not explicitly examine the hierarchies and inequalities still possible within same-gender relationships. *Story A* (Anonymous, 2011) is ultimately just one such case.

As explored in the previous section, hierarchies operate on multiple different levels within *Story A*. Banter, sexual confidence and competence, as well as characters' skill as football players can all be read as being used to negotiate position within the team. Age is another key element, particularly within the Silva—Villa—Carlos relationship triangle. Silva is the youngest of the three, aged 25 at the time the story is set; Villa is 30 and Carlos 32. Both Silva and Carlos are portrayed as at least partially aware of these age gaps and the issues they raise in terms of power differentials. Silva's past hero worship of Villa is evident in his reaction to praise from him, whilst Carlos' reluctance to engage in a sexual or romantic relationship with Silva is clearly motivated by the age gap and concerns over the power he wields over Silva as a mentor. Carlos' reluctance extends to participating in the gangbang, although it is also made clear that this is not for lack of desire. He does agree to take part upon Silva's specific request, and remains very protective of Silva throughout the story. The two have a private and very clear conversation about consent, in line with Anderson's (2005) negotiation model, in which Carlos promises to ensure Silva's boundaries are respected and that consent withdrawal will always be an option available to him. In contrast, both Villa and Pepe use their self-appointed positions in the hierarchy to put pressure on others for their own sexual and social ends. Villa consistently pushes against Silva's boundaries, shutting down opportunities for consent to be denied or withdrawn. Pepe uses his sexual competence and Silva's arousal to put pressure on him to give Torres a "reward." This serves to establish his position in the hierarchy, relative to both Torres and Silva.

It is the characters who are portrayed as less sexually confident and competent, and who are either at the bottom of the hierarchy or not engaging with it at all (depending on which reading one chooses) that are particularly interesting when it comes to interpersonal interactions and consent negotiation. Torres, having witnessed Pepe put pressure on Silva, makes it clear that Silva is under no obligation to give him a blowjob if he does not want to. Llorente and Raúl either ask or wait for explicit verbal consent. These are also the characters who show the most tenderness and care for their partner. The two different possible readings of the hierarchy within the team then clearly correspond to different approaches to consent. Pepe and Villa, at the top of the hierarchy when the story is read with the grain of sports culture, represent the power relationships of hegemonic masculinity: the characters embodying that masculinity are willing to use their power for their sexual ends regardless of their partner's consent. Other characters whose behavior is more in line with "inclusive masculinity" (Anderson & McGuire, 2010), on the other hand, seek to dismantle power structures and ensure that Silva's autonomy and consent decisions are respected. In this way, the story offers clear challenges to hegemonic masculinity and shows how other kinds of masculinity may be able to counteract it. This inclusive masculinity, however, also has its limitations. Most notably, women are entirely absent from the story and thus there is no engagement with gendered power relations.

The multiple available readings of the team hierarchy and how they interact with issues of sexual consent in *Story A* clearly contradict views of slash as a genre of equality. While gender is not a factor in the power relationships in slash, other sources of inequality and power differentials are introduced. In the case of Football RPF team sex and gangbang stories these inequalities are frequently embedded in the team hierarchy and the hierarchy of masculinities that represents. What stories like this do, then, is explore ways of negotiating power differentials in intimate relationships and the ways in which consent in these situations can be made truly meaningful—as well as the limits to this.

It is also worth noting the absence of a key element of lad and sports culture from *Story A*: alcohol. Drunkenness and alcohol feature prominently in a significant proportion of Football RPF and especially gangbang stories, partly because so many gangbang stories tend to be set during the celebrations after major victories. The setting of this story after a low-key friendly match rather than a major international tournament makes the complete absence of alcohol more plausible and allows for focus on other elements of sports culture. Dempster (2009) finds that heavy drinking is a key part of sporting culture and alcohol consumption is often a point of contention when rape and sexual assault allegations are made against professional athletes. A rape victim's drunkenness is often interpreted as consent, which in turn allows for public discourse to silence, shame and blame them (Burke, 2015; Nurka, 2013; Toffoletti, 2007). While pressure is exerted on Silva and other characters in various ways throughout the story, alcohol is not one of them. When reading *Story A* as one story within the collective archive of the gangbang/team sex subgenre, one potential effect of this omission is to further foreground and crystallize the other factors which affect characters' behaviors and decisions with regards to consent, including the complex effects of the interpersonal relationships and social hierarchies at play within the team in the narrative.

In meretricula's *firework boy* (2011) there is a different, in some ways more direct, approach to issues of power and consent. As Sergi is relatively new to the team and has no pre-existing relationships with his new teammates, he automatically assumes himself to be at the bottom of the team hierarchy. When presented with the overtly homoerotic and homosexual behavior of his teammates—particularly Messi, whom Sergi looks up to as a player and a leader—he is initially shocked. Once he is invited to join them, there is a clear sense of uncertainty and ambivalence on Sergi's part. This can be read as linked to Sergi's own perception of his place in the team hierarchy in several ways. On the one hand, the players inviting him to join them—Messi, Piqué, Villa—are all senior to him, and there is a sense of Sergi, as the new player on the team, questioning his own worth in comparison to them. On the other hand, these players' seniority and therefore relative power over Sergi raises the question of whether Sergi could meaningfully refuse their offer and not suffer any negative consequences to his position on the team or his career. Sergi's indecision is resolved through the intervention of other senior players, particularly Xavi, who make it clear to him that he does have a genuine, free choice in the matter:

> "Kid, you don't have to," Xavi said quietly. Sergi jumped; he hadn't heard Xavi come up beside him, and also Xavi was naked, which under normal circumstances he wouldn't have thought twice about but now seemed extremely relevant. "Seriously, if you're not interested, just ignore them. You don't have to participate. Most of us aren't going to" [meretricula, 2011, p. 2].

On the surface level, this conversation is an overt and verbal consent negotiation, in line to some extent with Pineau's (1989) communicative sexuality or Anderson's (2005) negotiation model. What is, however, interesting about it is that in the context of the story, and of Sergi's at least potentially hierarchical and unequal relationship with the other players on the team, the conversation clearly acknowledges the power imbalances and validates any concern Sergi may have over how much agency and choice he has in this situation. At the same time, he is given a clear message that the choice is genuinely his, and he is shown senior, successful role models to follow if he does not wish to take Messi up on his offer. In *firework boy*, then, interpersonal negotiation and issues of hierarchy and power are very clearly shown to be inseparable, as Sergi's negotiating position is shaped by the power structures he is embedded in.

Both *Story A* and *firework boy* therefore explore consent issues both at the interpersonal communication level and the level of socially constructed power differentials, and intertwine the two in complex ways. *Story A* is less explicit in its linking of negotiation and power, but the way consent issues are depicted in the story is also very specific to its sports culture setting. The characters who have the greatest investment in the team hierarchy and who exhibit the greatest adherence to hegemonic masculinity are also the characters shown to have the least respect for their partner's boundaries and consent decisions. Conversely, characters with less investment in the hierarchy and hegemonic masculinity also show tenderness, care, and a genuine concern for Silva's wishes and wellbeing. In this way, the story presents different kinds of masculinity and explores their effect on issues of consent. On the other hand, *firework boy* explicitly depicts power and negotiation as inseparable. While the power structures depicted in the story are not the gendered structures the readers and writers of fan fiction frequently negotiate in their own lives, they are still made explicit in the story, allowing audiences and authors to explore their effects and providing the opportunity for fans to attempt to find effective ways of negotiating them.

Conclusion

Professional team sports and sports cultures rooted in hegemonic masculinity present significant challenges for fans who are oppressed, excluded and marginalized by structures of patriarchy and masculinity. Women, nonbinary people, and gay and bisexual men in particular frequently struggle to access sport both as participants and fans. Professional athletes at all levels and across many team sports are frequently associated with sexualized behaviors towards women, the denigration of homosexuality, and in extreme cases rape and sexual violence. Against this backdrop, marginalized fans employ a range of tactics to negotiate the challenges of their involvement with professional sports culture and the fandoms surrounding it. The production and consumption of Football RPF is one such tactic, where the expressions of fandom which are denigrated in mainstream spaces (such as sexual attraction to the players) are legitimized and celebrated. Football RPF, however—particularly as reflected in the team sex/gangbang RPF subgenre—also allows readers and writers to engage in a highly sophisticated exploration of, and challenge to, sports cultures and hegemonic masculinity.

By reading homosexual desire into the homosocial environment of the football team, Football RPF stories challenge dominant constructions of sporting masculinity, and create spaces for the expression of vulnerability, care, and tenderness in these environments. These stories stand in stark contrast to the often hostile realities of sports culture which readers and writers of fan fiction are familiar with, and it is this contrast which serves as a challenge to the sports team's claim to a privileged position within heterosexual hegemonic masculinity. Through their treatment of the concept of hierarchies within sports teams, both stories examined in this essay construct different, more inclusive versions of masculinity, challenging outright the hierarchical structures of patriarchy. Through their engagement with issues of sexual consent, both stories also directly address the challenges which the frequent sexual violence allegations against professional athletes present to an expression of fandom which incorporates a sexual attraction to the players. Moreover, both stories problematize issues of sexual consent beyond mere interpersonal negotiation and show how power relationships are inextricably linked with such negotiation. In these ways, Football RPF team sex/gangbang stories allow readers and writers to negotiate the complex challenges posed to them by their engagement with a fan object which is highly problematic in its enactment of hegemonic masculinity and patriarchy. Alternative, fictionalized, non-threatening versions of masculinity which are read side by side with readers and writers' knowledge of the realities of sports culture allow the Football RPF community to issue their own, albeit limited, challenge to the cultural structures which marginalize them as fans.

Within the wider context of slash—frequently seen as a genre of equality—stories like *Story A* and *firework boy* clearly explore issues of inequality in intimate relationships and sexual situations beyond gender relations. The emphasis on hierarchy within the professional team sports environment allows for a re-introduction of power relations into an environment supposedly devoid of them since gender is removed from the equation. Thus the focus in both stories on sexual consent then serves to further highlight and problematize inherent inequalities. What is, however, truly transformative about these works is that they explore ways of negotiating around power relations, challenging hierarchies, and making consent meaningful within the constraints of patriarchal structures. Viewing slash as a literature not of equality but of *negotiated inequality* opens up new avenues of research around the kinds of inequalities presented and explored in slash stories, and particularly their intersections (or lack thereof) with issues of gender and sexuality.

Note

1. The "AO3 census" was a fan-run effort conducted by metastatistician centrumlumina to gather demographic data on the community of fan fiction readers and writers who use the Archive of Our Own (AO3), one of the current primary sites of fan fiction activity. Due to the way the survey was promoted, there are some limitations (centrumlumina, 2013a) to the findings and it is likely that rather than representing the demographics of AO3 users it represent a more selective (and self-selected) sample consisting predominantly of AO3 users who also use the social networking site Tumblr. Nonetheless, much of the data corroborates and expands existing small-scale ethnographic work, and despite the known limitations provides useful insight into the demographics of some parts of the fan fiction community.

References

Anderson, E., and McGuire, R. (2010). Inclusive Masculinity and the Gendered Politics of Men's Rugby. *Journal of Gender Studies, 19*(3), 37–41. http://dx.doi.org/10.1080/09589236.2010.494341.

Anderson, M. (2005). Negotiating Sex. *Southern California Law Review, 41*, 1401–1438.

Anonymous. (2011). *Story A*. Footballkink2. LiveJournal.

Burke, L. (2015). The Right to Rehabilitation After Punishment? *Probation Journal, 62*(1), 3–6. doi:10.1177/0264550515573103.

centrumlumina. (2013a, September 30). Limitations and Uses of the Data [Blog post]. Retrieved from http://centrumlumina.tumblr.com/post/62748999135/limitations-and-uses-of-the-data.

centrumlumina. (2013b, October 1). Gender [Blog post]. Retrieved from http://centrum lumina.tumblr.com/post/62816996032/gender.

centrumlumina. (2013c, October 2). Gender, Sexual or Romantic Minority [Blog post]. Retrieved from http://centrumlumina.tumblr.com/post/62890602051/gender-sexual-or-romantic-minority.

Connell, R.W. (1995). *Masculinities*. Berkeley: University of California Press.
Dempster, S. (2009). Having the Balls, Having It All? Sport and Constructions of Undergraduate Laddishness. *Gender and Education, 21*(5), 481–500. http://dx.doi.org/10.1080/09540250802392299.
Derecho, A. (2006). Archontic Literature: A Definition, a History, and Several Theories of Fan Fiction. In K. Hellekson and K. Busse (Eds.), *Fan Fiction and Fan Communities in the Age of the Internet: New Essays* (pp. 61–78). Jefferson, NC: McFarland.
Esmonde, K., Cooky, C., and Andrews, D.L. (2015). "It's Supposed to Be About the Love of the Game, Not the Love of Aaron Rodgers' Eyes": Challenging the Exclusions of Women's Sports Fans. *Sociology of Sport Journal, 32*(1), 22–48. https://doi.org/10.1123/ssj.2014-0072.
Gosling, V.K. (2007). Girls Allowed? The Marginalization of Female Sport Fans. In J. Gray, C. Sandvoss, and C.L. Harrington (Eds.), *Fandom: Identities and Communities in a Mediated World* (pp. 250–260). New York: New York University Press.
Jozkowski, K.N., and Peterson, Z.D. (2013). College Students and Sexual Consent: Unique Insights. *Journal of Sex Research, 50*(6), 517–523. doi:10.1080/00224499.2012.700739.
Jozkowski, K.N., Sanders, S., Peterson, Z.D., Dennis, B., and Reece, M. (2014). Consenting to Sexual Activity: The Development and Psychometric Assessment of Dual Measures of Consent. *Archives of Sexual Behavior, 43*, 437–450. doi:10.1007/s10508-013-0225-7.
Jozkowski, K.N., and Wiersma, J.D. (2015). Does Drinking Alcohol Prior to Sexual Activity Influence College Students' Consent? *International Journal of Sexual Health, 27*(2), 156–174. http://dx.doi.org/10.1080/19317611.2014.951505.
Kustritz, A. (2003). Slashing the Romance Narrative. *The Journal of American Culture, 26*(3), 371–384. doi:10.1111/1542-734X.00098.
Lamb, P.F., and Veith, D.L. (1986). Romantic Myth, Transcendence, and Star Trek Zines. In D. Palumbo (Ed.), *Erotic Universe: Sexuality and Fantastic Literature* (pp. 235–256). Westport, CT: Greenwood Press.
MacKinnon, C.A. (1991). Reflections on Sex Equality Under Law. *Yale Law Journal, 100*(5), 1281–1328.
meretricula. (2011). *Firework Boy*. Archive of Our Own.
Morris, S., and Topping, A. (2016, October 14). Ched Evans: Footballer Found Not Guilty of Rape in Retrial. *The Guardian*. Retrieved from https://www.theguardian.com/football/2016/oct/14/footballer-ched-evans-cleared-of-in-retrial.
Nurka, C. (2013). Shame and Disgrace in Australian Football Culture: Rape Claims and Public Affect. *Women's Studies International Forum, 38*, 43–51.
Pineau, L. (1989). Date Rape: A Feminist Analysis. *Law and Philosophy, 8*(2), 217–243.
Pugh, S. (2005). *The Democratic Genre: Fan Fiction in a Literary Context*. Bridgend, Wales: Seren Books.
Russ, J. (1985). Pornography by Women, for Women, with Love. In *Magic Mommas, Trembling Sisters, Puritans and Perverts: Essays on Sex and Pornography* (pp. 79–99). Trumansburg, NY: The Crossing Press.
Toffoletti, K. (2007). How Is Gender-Based Violence Covered in the Sporting News? An Account of the Australian Football League Sex Scandal. *Women's Studies International Forum, 30*(5), 427–438. doi:10.1016/j.wsif.2007.07.004.
Waysdorf, A. (2015a). My Football Fandoms, Performance, and Place. *Transformative Works and Cultures, 18*. http://dx.doi.org/10.3983/twc.2015.0636.
Waysdorf, A. (2015b). The Creation of Football Slash Fan Fiction. *Transformative Works and Cultures, 19*. http://dx.doi.org/10.3983/twc.2015.0588.
Wellard, I. (2002). Men, Sport, Body Performance and the Maintenance of "Exclusive Masculinity." *Leisure Studies, 21*(3–4), 235–247. http://dx.doi.org/10.1080/0261436022000030641.
Willis, I. (2006). Keeping Promises to Queer Children: Making Space (for Mary Sue) at Hogwarts. In K. Hellekson and K. Busse (Eds.), *Fan Fiction and Fan Communities in the Age of the Internet: New Essays* (pp. 153–170). Jefferson, NC: McFarland.

About the Contributors

Laura Campillo **Arnaiz** is a lecturer in English literature at the University of Murcia, Spain. She holds an MA in translation and interpretation and a Ph.D. in English philology. Her research focuses on Shakespearian topics and characters in popular culture. She is working on a Spanish translation of John Fletcher's *The Tamer Tamed* and is the author of *Echoes of The Tempest in Tron: Legacy*.

Jesse **Ashman** earned a degree in English literature from Queen Mary, University of London, and a distinction master's degree in sexual dissidence from the University of Sussex. He is transgender, a reader of slash fiction, a youth worker and mental health support worker.

Samantha **Close** is a Ph.D. candidate in communications at the University of Southern California. Her research focuses on creative work, particularly as it occurs over and through networked technology. Her scholarly work has appeared in *Transformative Works and Cultures* and *Feminist Media Studies*.

Cait **Coker** is an associate editor for *Foundation*. Her research focuses on depictions of women and sexuality in science fiction and fantasy and the history of women in non-traditional publishing. Her reviews and essays have appeared in *The Journal of Fan Studies* and *The SFRA Review*, among others. She is working on a literary history of fandom and finishing her doctorate.

Zsolt **Demetrovics** is a clinical psychologist and cultural anthropologist and he has a doctorate in addiction science. He is a professor of psychology and director of the Institute of Psychology at the Eötvös Loránd University, Budapest. His research focuses on the epidemiology and psychological background of legal and illegal substance use and behavioral addictions.

Charity A. **Fowler** is an assistant professor teaching writing and popular culture in the English Department at the University of Virginia. She received her Ph.D. in media, art and text at Virginia Commonwealth University. Her research interests include feminist and queer media studies, transmedia storytelling and media and law.

Divya **Garg** earned her BA in English from Lady Shri Ram College, University of Delhi, and her MA in English from Jawaharlal Nehru University. She has written various articles on popular culture and continues to develop her deep interest in fan fiction.

Rukmini **Pande** completed her Ph.D. on intersections of identity in media fandom communities at the University of Western Australia. She is part of the editorial board of the *Journal of Fandom Studies* and has been published in multiple edited collections on race in media fandom.

Milena **Popova** is a fan, researcher, and activist. Their research focuses on representations of power and sexual consent in erotic fan fiction as a form of cultural activism, and this spills over into some of their own activism.

Ashton **Spacey** earned her BA from the University of Portsmouth and her MA in sexual dissidence in literature and culture from the University of Sussex. Her research focuses on consent discourses within fan fiction, the operations of power, taboo and shame within the erotic imaginary, and fan fiction's evolution as a form of popular literature.

Cynthia **Wang** is a Ph.D. candidate in the Annenberg School of Communication at the University of Southern California. She uses critical/cultural perspectives to understand the impact new technologies and social media have on social relations and cultural practices, particularly around the creation and sharing of cultural artifacts and media.

Lýsa **Westberg Gabriel** earned a BA in English and Japanese studies and an MA in English, studying at the University of Southern Denmark and Kwansai Gakuin University, Japan. She chaired *Patronus 2006*, an international scholarly Harry Potter conference at the University of Copenhagen. Her research focuses on intercultural fandom cooperation and the use of fandom platforms, among others.

Ágnes **Zsila** is a Ph.D. student in clinical psychology and addictions at Eötvös Loránd University, Budapest. She holds an MA in psychology from the University of Debrecen. Her doctoral research focuses on the psychological aspects of contemporary fan studies and the behavioral dynamics of online communities. She is the author of three books and the editor of an anthology.

Index

www.ingramcontent.com/pod-product-compliance
Lightning Source LLC
Chambersburg PA
CBHW021649110726
47902CB00007B/1894

* 9 7 8 1 4 7 6 6 7 1 2 1 5 *